EDUCATION UNDER MAO

Studies of the East Asian Institute
Columbia University

Education Under Mao

CLASS AND COMPETITION
IN CANTON SCHOOLS,
1960–1980

JONATHAN UNGER

New York
Columbia University Press
1982

Library of Congress Cataloging in Publication Data

Unger, Jonathan.
  Education under Mao.

  (Studies of the East Asian Institute)
  Bibliography: p.
  Includes index.
  1. Education—China—Canton—History.
  I. Title. II. Series.
  LA1134.C35U53   370'.951'27   81-15470
  ISBN 0-231-05298-7   AACR2

Columbia University Press
New York   Guildford, Surrey

Copyright © 1982 Columbia University Press
All rights reserved
Printed in the United States of America

Clothbound editions of Columbia University Press books are Smyth-sewn
and printed on permanent and durable acid-free paper.

For my parents,
Sidney and Naomi Unger

The East Asian Institute of Columbia University

The East Asian Institute is Columbia University's center for research, education, and publication on modern East Asia.

The Studies of the East Asian Institute were inaugurated in 1962 to bring to a wider public the results of significant new research on modern and contemporary East Asia.

Contents

List of Tables
and Figures

Acknowledgments

Special appreciation is owed to Ronald Dore and John Oxenham. Professor Dore's encouragement and insights helped at each stage of the writing. Dr. Oxenham's determination that this type of research should be carried out helped conjure up the financial wherewithal, and he subsequently provided valuable suggestions on the manuscript's first draft.

Debts of a different sort are owed to my interviewees, whose willingness to share their experiences made this study possible. Unfortunately, their present circumstances do not permit me here to identify their names and individual contributions.

A debt is owed, too, to fellow scholars who generously made available interview notes to supplement my own: in particular, Stanley Rosen's voluminous transcripts on high school Red Guard factions in Canton; Edwin Lee's transcripts on the Communist Youth League; and Ezra Vogel's extensive interview notes on Canton schools dating back to his research in Hong Kong during 1962–64. Appreciation is owed also to Ng Chung-yin, who helped unearth relevant news articles and data in the Chinese-language files at the Union Research Institute. The greatest research debt of all goes to my wife, Anita Chan; the interviews which she conducted for her own book on the political socialization of Cantonese young people provided well over a thousand pages of rich interview material, which has educated me in areas that my own interviews covered less fully and less sensitively.

Gratitude also goes to several colleagues and friends who read and made instructive comments on various manuscript chapters: in particular,

Tom Bernstein, Deborah Davis-Friedmann, John Gardner, Angela Little, William Parish, Gordon White, and Martin K. Whyte.

I want to thank Henry Lucas for helping to transform the questionnaire data into coherent tables, and Maureen Dickson, Nancy Kaul, Ann Manley, Fiona Pearson, and Ethel Royston for their patient good will in deciphering and typing successive drafts.

The Institute of Development Studies at Sussex University, England, supported the project from its inception; and the Universities Service Center in Hong Kong graciously provided office space for the research.

Material from some of the chapters has appeared in papers written for *China Quarterly* (Autumn 1980), *Comparative Education Review* (Summer 1980), *Contemporary China* (Summer 1979), and *Pacific Affairs* (Spring 1980).

Introduction

THE ORIGINS of this study lie in a project sponsored by Great Britain's Institute of Development Studies. The project sought solutions to the "diploma disease" that has beset the educational systems of many of the Third World countries.[1] The thesis which our project was exploring in the Third World goes somewhat as follows:

The school systems of most of the late-developing nations are in a state of crisis. In the eyes of their students, the education system's primary function is to provide the paper credentials necessary for a job in the modern economic sector. For this very reason, hoping for a decent job, a great many young people have flooded into the schools. But a vicious circle has ensued—for as the numbers of students crowding the schools have expanded, the numbers of their graduates have inevitably expanded in similar fashion. In a great many countries this rate of student growth has been faster than the expansion of jobs in the urban economy. In consequence, career posts that primary school graduates had been able to secure a decade earlier begin to be besieged by secondary school graduates.[2]

In such circumstances, many a young person's solution has been to strive for a yet higher education, to get above the crowds of competing job applicants. As this occurs, the reputation of a school and often the careers of its teachers become more dependent upon obtaining a respectable pass rate of students on the examinations for the *next* higher level of schooling. With the school increasingly geared toward "prepping" its students in the subjects that are most important for such examinations, other school subjects receive short shrift.[3]

Each high school realizes that it will be able to get more of its graduates into universities if it enrolls only those primary school graduates who show themselves likely to be "university material." The schools' own selection examinations become geared to discovering such pupils. Both rural and urban primary schools prepare their students with these secondary school entrance examinations in mind. A mad situation appears, where the curriculum of even a rural primary school is influenced more by the manner of questions posed ultimately on university (and hence secondary school) entrance examinations than by the more practical need to prepare the village's sons and daughters for more modern roles within the village economy.

The results of such a misorientation of education can be crippling. The great majority of pupils can never "make the grade," and find themselves deemed "failures" of a system skewed dysfunctionally toward the narrow upper reaches of the educational ladder. They are the products of schools that had spent years drilling them for examinations most of them would never succeed in passing, schools that had trained them in rote "skills" that would have little relation to their own later lives, schools that had influenced students to regard the most common occupations of their society with disdain and then consigned most of them to those very occupations.

Such problems may await even those pupils from the cities who successfully climb up through the secondary schools. Many frustratedly end up among the swelling ranks of the educated unemployed, having been provided with 'credentials' that did not in the end 'qualify' them for anything and having been instilled with attitudes and yearnings that incline them neither toward independent entrepreneurial pursuits nor gainful manual employment.

These were the problems of Third World schooling against which I wanted to counterpose China's experiences in education. I was expecting to trace the differences between pre- and post-Cultural Revolution schools. Before the Cultural Revolution, a young person's life chances and career had been determined largely through success on the educational ladder. I hoped to compare this system with China's schools after the Cultural Revolution, when postgraduation careers were entirely divorced from academic achievement. My plan was not just to examine how curricula and teaching methods were altered in China by cutting education loose from the "credentials" competition. More than this—and of the greatest personal interest to me—I wanted to explore how these two different time periods in Chinese education had differently influenced students' attitudes and values.

Finally, I wanted also to examine the politically sensitive issue of educational opportunity. Mass public education claims to promote a greater equality of opportunities. But study after study around the world has shown that the children of the educated urban elites, coming from literate homes and with access to better schools, consistently are among the principal beneficiaries of the all-important examinations to determine who will climb the educational ladder into modern-sector jobs. As one comparative study has observed, "Even when an educational system can stay justly selective from generation to generation, it will be governed by the children of the well-to-do, who persistently score better on examinations even when such examinations are not intentionally skewed in their favor."[4] The great expansions in educational systems thus do not necessarily promote a genuine equality of opportunity. The political leaderships of most countries are content with this state of affairs; but in China it was the subject of repeated debate among the highest leaders in the 1960s and 1970s, and also a matter of great concern to the populace at large.

As we will observe in the first chapters of this book, China had become caught in the early and mid-1960s in an educational crisis somewhat similar to those of other late-developing countries. Education had developed more rapidly than job opportunities, the competition to enter higher education had become increasingly tight, and the students increasingly competitive. In most of the Third World this competitiveness would have centered on an increased prepping for exams. But in China the tightening educational contest brought the second of our themes to the political forefront—the question of whether students from one or another type of family background should be favored for higher education. As shall be seen in chapters 5 and 6, it was this issue more than any other which sparked the infighting between urban high school Red Guard groups in the Cultural Revolution.

After the Cultural Revolution of 1966–68 the "proletarian class line" (in the phraseology of Chinese newspapers) triumphed. The examination system was abolished. It was done more for "class line" than for "diploma disease" reasons, but both played a part in the decision. Students from advantaged households would no longer be allowed to climb into a high-status job through success in their studies; and education as a whole no longer would suffer from a "diploma disease." But the net results were shatteringly disappointing to the new system's supporters. Extensive interviewing in 1975 and 1976 with students and teachers from China reveals that Chinese students in the 1970s generally paid scant attention to their coursework. Educational standards plummeted, and the behavior and attitudes of the young people worsened. In chapters 7 through 10 we shall observe why and how this occurred. By examining these difficulties readers will, I hope, gain a better understanding of the sociological complexities of an educational system—and the corresponding complexities of any efforts to move away from the competitive examination ladder.

ON METHODOLOGY AND INFORMANTS

Because China is vast, its government judiciously has not tried to administer all educational affairs from Peking (Beijing). Only China's major universities have fallen under direct central control. The hundreds of thousands of other schools in China instead have come under the jurisdiction variously of provinces, cities, counties, communes, or even villages. Any scholar who tried to follow concretely the debates, experiments, failures, and successes in all of China's diverse regions would very likely end with a welter of indistinct and confusing images.

I therefore found it helpful to concentrate on the education system of one province—Guangdong—and in particular its capital city Canton (Guangzhou). Through this I was able to examine in an integrated fashion the different facets of a single school system. For example, I was able to examine the relationship between Canton's job market and the educational ladder, and to observe how the competition for jobs influenced specific local schools. More generally, by collecting sequential data from within the same region, I was able to make more precise sense of statistics than would have been possible had I compiled only the vast and loosely defined national figures. Yet at the same time, by keeping an eye on China's two national news dailies, it was always possible to relate the local debates and practices to trends in the national Party's policies on education.

Guangdong itself is of substantial size. Its population of some 56 million is about as large as Great Britain's. The capital, Canton, contains more than 3 million people (including the several rural counties that are inside the metropolitan administrative perimeter). Both Guangdong and Canton have their own peculiarities that distinguish them from other Chinese provinces and cities, and I had to take these carefully into account. But in many respects it was still possible to consider Guangdong as a China writ small. Almost the entire spectrum of issues and debates that were to be found in the pages of the national press were pertinent to at least some schools in urban or rural Guangdong, and almost all the educational experiments and youth campaigns that were announced in the Peking press had their counterparts in the southern province and city.

For the researcher outside of China, Guangdong and Canton hold a particular advantage. They are adjacent to the British colony of Hong Kong. Thus the documentary evidence is far more complete than for all the rest of China. Before the Cultural Revolution brought the flow of materials from China to a near halt, one or the other of Canton's three newspapers reached Hong Kong almost daily, and substantial numbers of the province's magazines and school texts crossed the border with travellers. Canton's proximity also allowed a large quantity of relevant Cultural Revolution-era Red Guard writings to reach Hong Kong—in fact, most of the Red Guard materials that are available outside China came from Canton and Peking.

Of special importance to me was the availability of interviewees. Interviews would provide the only effective means to examine the impact of both pre- and post-Cultural Revolution schooling upon the attitudes of students toward their studies and toward career prospects. Tens of thousands of former residents of Canton now make Hong Kong their home, and among these a large number had been either students or teachers. In all, 43 former residents of China were interviewed during 1975–76 for a total of 191 interview sessions. About two-thirds of the time we met at my office at Hong Kong's Universities Service Center; the other third of the interviews were conducted in coffee houses, neighborhood restaurants, or respondents' homes. Each of these interviews ranged from one to three hours.

The respondents normally were friends or the friends of friends. Their individual motives for talking to me varied: in some cases friendship, in others curiosity or a simple desire to discuss themselves and China with a foreigner who was of the same generation as most of them and who spoke their own language. Sometimes I taught an interviewee English in exchange. Other times I tried to persuade interviewees short of regular incomes to accept remuneration. Most refused. In all, only 8 of my 43 respondents received any monetary compensation whatsoever for their time.

In many cases, I was able to elicit personal information from an interviewee on more than one type of educational experience. For example, several respondents who were primary school and/or high school

Reports of Personal Experiences

Before the Cultural Revolution		After the Cultural Revolution
Primary school		
as students	7	0
as teachers	2	6
High school		
as students	17	9
as teachers	3	4
University		
as students	7	0
as teachers	1	2

teachers during the seventies also related to me their experiences in the sixties as high school or university students. Some of my 43 respondents are thus listed more than once in the adjacent table.

On the whole, my interviewees who went to high school before the Cultural Revolution and those who went after the Cultural Revolution had arrived in Hong Kong by very different means. Most of my respondents from that older group of students had been assigned to the countryside at the end of the Cultural Revolution and eventually had illegally left the difficulties of rural life by swimming across the bay to Hong Kong. Contrarily, 6 of the 9 interviewees who had been students after the Cultural Revolution were legal emigrants. A couple of them were overseas Chinese who had returned to China with their families in the 1950s and early 1960s and were now in Hong Kong in transit back to their home countries. Others were Hong Kong residents whose parents had sent them to socialist China for their educations and who had recently returned to Hong Kong to rejoin their families. Still other interviewees (from both pre- and post-Cultural Revolution schools) had elderly relatives in Hong Kong or the neighboring Portuguese colony of Macau, and the Chinese government had permitted them to leave China to take care of these relatives. Similarly, all six of the post-Cultural Revolution high school and university teachers who are cited in this study fit one of these three categories of legal emigrants.

My impression was that the legal and illegal emigrants were about equally objective in their responses. This is not to imply that each of the respondents did not have his or her own biases. Nor, of course, were most of them recollecting incidents and attitudes that were still entirely fresh in their memories. But I came away from the great majority of my interviews convinced that the respondents had tried to answer my questions as precisely and honestly as they could. To lessen the potential for subjectivity in their responses, whenever possible I asked them about individual classmates and the discrete details of particular classroom practices. I tried not to pose broad questions of the type which might have elicited opinionated answers. In most cases I tried to place on myself rather than upon the interviewees the task of interpreting and generalizing from their experiences.

By the time that Mao died in September 1976 the research in Hong Kong had been completed and the book's basic arguments already formulated. At points in the following text I refer to the more recent accusations from China about educational excesses under the "Gang of Four." But these later accusations did not provide the bases for what I have written. My essential sources have remained the interview transcripts collected in 1975–76 and the documentary materials from Canton of the decade and a half before Mao's death.

For obvious reasons, an exception is the last chapter dealing with education after Mao's death. For it I surveyed the more recent literature and conducted a modest number of additional interviews in Hong Kong in 1978, and further interviews in 1980 with several students and professors from China who were studying at American universities.

PART I

The Sixties:
Impending Crisis

CHAPTER ONE

Up the School Ladder

SCHOOL SYSTEMS obviously provide more than just book knowledge. They provide also the means by which any modern society's official values are transmitted to its younger generations. In addition—and just as important—schools provide modern societies with the mechanisms for determining which of their young people will "qualify" to enter the prestigious and well-paid occupations. Before the Cultural Revolution, China's urban schools emphasized all three of these functions: as places of learning; as socializing agents; and as selectors of the next generation's professional strata.

Each of these three facets of the school experience was imbued with a certain degree of competitiveness, precisely because the schools were responsible for selecting the youths best "qualified" to succeed. This is not peculiar to China, but the Chinese case differed in one important respect. In China the schools as competitive "selectors" and the schools as socializing agents—teaching children that they should be self-abnegating "new socialist people"—were simultaneously encouraging contrary modes of behavior. In the first five chapters of this book, we will be witnessing how, in Canton's school system of the 1960s, this conflict between the values taught and the students' own pragmatic career interests was partially resolved, and how in certain crucial respects it was left dangerously unresolved.

THE QUESTION OF SELECTION PRIORITIES

Let us examine first the students' contest. Their strategies were strongly influenced by the shape and the particular pressures of China's academic ladder. China had inherited from the Guomindang a 12-year system of schooling based on the American model. This was retained up to the Cultural Revolution. Students worked their way up a ladder of six years of primary school, three years of junior high school, three years of senior high school and, for most academic disciplines, four years of university study. What interests us here is that at each higher rung of this ladder there were selective admissions procedures; and much more than just exam results were taken into account.

The Party leaders were determined to play an active role in deciding the composition of the next generation's technical, industrial, and scientific elites. They laid down in the guidelines for educational admissions that three of the Party's fundamental beliefs and goals had to be reconciled. Not just academic performance would count, but also class origins and political behavior.

Academic performance. The government had a firm commitment to develop and modernize the nation, which demanded that the high-skill posts be filled by the most competently educated people. Thus it was the policy from the founding of the People's Republic in 1949 up to the Cultural Revolution in 1966 to weigh academic accomplishment (*chengji*) heavily in school admissions policies. For admissions to junior and senior high school, entrance examinations were devised by the city or province, while for university admissions the examinations were composed in Peking and used uniformly throughout the nation. (Course grades were not taken into consideration, on the grounds that the grading standards at different schools varied widely.)

Family class-origins. The Party also interpreted the revolution as a triumph of the formerly exploited classes over their exploiters. As one crucial aspect of this triumph the Party wanted to give educational priority to the children of workers and peasants, classes which in earlier times largely had been denied schooling. There was a special edge to this commitment, since in China, much more than in most other states, educational attainments traditionally had served as important symbols and legitimizers of elite status. A second motive for drawing upon the laboring classes was the strong feeling, central to the Party's "class line," that such children had greater devotion to the Party and revolution. It was believed that if the reins of authority and expertise were placed in their hands, they would be less prone to conservatism and opportunism than the children of the former exploitative classes or petty bourgeoisie. These combined arguments—that the revolution had been fought for and would be protected by the proletarian classes—urged that consideration in school admissions always be given to a youth's family class-origins (*chengfen*).

It was relatively easy to determine exactly where a student ranked in terms of class background. In the early 1950s the Party had conducted methodical investigations into each man's employment and sources of income for the three years prior to Canton's Liberation. A permanent "class" label, inheritable in the male line, became affixed to each and every family as a result of these investigations.[1] These class designations went into every student's dossier. They were rather exactly ranked. The "good" (or "red") classes included the pre-Liberation workers and the former "poor and lower middle peasants." Some other class labels were based upon political criteria rather than economic origins; for example, family heads who had participated in the revolution before Liberation as army officers or Party officials had been granted the special "good class" (*chengfen hao*) label of "revolutionary cadres." Such a title ranked highest socially, higher than the "proletariat." The families of the pre-Liberation professionals, white-collar workers, peddlars and middle peasants were now ranked as "middling class," neither entirely trusted nor discriminated against. Among the "bad classes" the former capitalist families (as "national bourgeoisie" whom Lenin believed were opposed to imperialism) fared better on the scale than the families, say, of landlords or of persons labelled officially as "counter-revolutionary." This hierarchy of classes was essentially congruent with Mao Zedong's original dichotomization of Chinese society into the "reliable" classes, the enemy classes, and the wavering classes that could be "allied with."[2]

The standing of each student's "class origins" could be weighed fairly precisely by the higher-school admissions officers, in approximately the following rank order:

Good-class origins (jieji chengfen haode), also referred to in China as the "five red kinds" (hongwulei). These five are in two broad categories:

(a) Politically red inheritances (the families headed by pre-Liberation Party members, plus the orphans of men who died in the revolutionary wars);
   (1) Revolutionary cadres
   (2) Revolutionary armymen and

    (3) Revolutionary martyrs
  (b) Working-class:
    (4) Pre-liberation industrial workers and their families
    (5) Former poor and lower-middle peasant families

Middle-class origins (yiban chengfen):
  (a) Non-intelligentsia middle class:
    Families of pre-Liberation peddlars and store clerks, etc.
    Former middle-peasant families
  (b) Intelligentsia middle class:
    Families of pre-Liberation clerks, teachers, professionals, etc.

Bad-class origins (jieji chengfen buhaode):
    Families of former capitalists
    *Families of "Rightists" (the label denoting those who were too out-
    spoken in the Hundred Flowers campaign of 1957)
    Pre-Liberation rich-peasant families
    *Families of "bad elements" (a label denoting "criminal" offenders)
    Pre-Liberation landlord families
    *Families of counter-revolutionaries

Political performance. In addition to the entrance-examination scores and these inherited "class" labels, there was also always a third criterion for admissions. Attention was to be given to the student's personal commitment to the revolutionary cause. The young people with "good class" labels held an advantage here, since they were presumed to have inherited their parents' "feeling of gratitude" (*ganen*) toward the Party. But it also was official doctrine that children of petty-bourgeois or even exploiting-class background, having been brought up under socialism, could successfully reshape their own attitudes and behavior. It was always considered possible, moreover, for a youth of "red" class background to succumb to retrogressive attitudes. Since attitudes only could be judged through a student's behavior, a brief dossier on "political performance" (*zhengzhi biaoxian*) accompanied each application for higher education; and a key measure here of a student's political standing was whether he or she had been able to get into the Communist Youth League.
    Enrollment policies rested simultaneously on all three of these pil-

---

* Since these particular "class" labels were not derived from prior economic standing but from the family head's political or criminal errors, such students' "class label" had a special complexity. E.g., the son of a "rightist" of proletarian origins was of a better "bad-class" status than the son of a "rightist" of bourgeois origins.

lars—class background, activist performance, and academic accomplishment. But which of these three should be given the heaviest weighting? It became a ticklish question to which there was no fixed answer. For one thing, schools of different types and of different qualities were supposed to tilt their admissions decisions differently. A technical university, for example, was to place greater emphasis on academic excellence, while a rural junior high school laid greater stress on class origins. For another thing, even at any given school the relative importance of the three admissions criteria fluctuated over time, as different constellations within the leadership gained influence over policy. Sometimes proponents of a stronger "class line" (*jieji luxian*) in educational policy gained a louder voice, as in the Great Leap Forward of 1958–59; sometimes advocates of "modernization" (*xiandaihua*) and of high academic standards regained the initiative, as in 1962.

China has moved through several such cycles in the short history of the People's Republic, from periods of "moderation" toward periods of "radicalism" and then back again, and each time the debate had been replayed—where should the relative stress in admissions lie? The question could arouse passions among the families concerned. This was partly because the futures of all of the students were directly affected, and partly also because the issue involved high-sounding ideological principles.

From 1963 onward, the weighting in admissions priorities gradually had shifted leftward once again, and there was a special impetus to this new swing. Whereas there were too few educated good-class children immediately after the Liberation of 1949 to provide a major recruiting ground for the senior high schools and universities, the rapid expansion of the urban elementary school systems during the 1950s had brought large numbers of good-class youths into the secondary schools by the late 1950s and early 1960s. The children of the former middle classes retained their hold on academic excellence. But as the numbers of students swelling the school systems continued to mount in the years leading up to the Cultural Revolution, the pressures increased within the Party for the senior-high and university admissions criteria to be tilted more in favor of the good classes. There was, furthermore, an increased constituency of interested good class households to support those pressures.

In the pages which follow, we shall be tracing Canton's educational ladder during the set of years when the earlier numerical pressures on the primary schools began moving upward into the secondary schools. Those competing for places were no longer children but adolescents. Consequently, we shall be examining not just the structure of the school ladder in the sixties but also the ways in which the tensions in the system grew as the ages of the contestants changed.

ONTO THE LADDER'S LOWEST RUNG:
ENTRY TO CANTON'S PRIMARY SCHOOLS

Throughout the 1950s, Canton's authorities had rapidly expanded primary schooling, and never more so than during the Great Leap Forward. By 1959, at the height of the Great Leap Forward, 94 percent of the city's children were entering elementary school of one sort or another.[3] But the tone of newspaper reports from the later 1950s suggests that the demands for education more than kept up with the expansions. Most parents in the cities apparently had soon begun to feel that an elementary school education was the absolute and minimal necessity for a child.

The Canton authorities soon discovered, though, that maintaining the near-universalized school system would be a very costly proposition. Canton had experienced a baby boom in the 1950s. This generation was just coming of age, and to place all of them in school was going to require a rapid continued expansion in the city's school facilities. In 1960–61, when economic depression followed closely on the heels of the Great Leap Forward's collapse, the city suddenly found itself caught embarrassedly between the expectations for primary schooling and the painful realities of shrinking urban finances. Many Canton primary schools went into double shifts of classes so as to accommodate the crush of new pupils. But with no funds available for new school facilities, such a strategy did not meet the needs of all the city's expectant 7-year-olds. In 1961–62, there simply were not enough school places to go around.

In the pattern familiar to China, the children's opportunities to enter would be determined by the standards of class background and academic potential. A child's class origins took priority here, since the issue was one of *mass* education, not the training of higher level expertise.[4] But it was not just bad-class children who lost out. Eligibility for enrollments was determined by neighborhood boundaries, and children were turned away mainly in those city districts which were the most overcrowded and had expanded in population most rapidly in recent years. These included several of the working-class neighborhoods. In such neighborhoods even a portion of the children of pre-Liberation blue-collar families had to be turned away—and tests were given by their local school to determine who they would be.[5]

The most impoverished working class families had already been eliminated from the contest by the depression. While both parents sought work, their children were needed at home to mind the youngest siblings, to undertake domestic chores, and to engage in contracted-out piece-work.[6]

The Canton government had become committed along with most of the populace to the notion that primary schooling for every child was a necessity, and it proceeded to organize a jerry-built solution. The city enacted regulations in 1962 letting neighborhood groups establish make-shift schools called *minbans* (literally, "people-managed" schools).[7] It was stipulated that these could be set up in abandoned factories, in store fronts, in private homes or during the evenings in primary school build-ings. But the depression's depletion of the city's budget meant these "irregular" schools would have to be self-financed through pupils' fees.[8] This was, indeed, the key element behind the establishment of the *minban* system. Yet it ironically foreclosed entry to some of the poorest children, whose interests the schools ostensibly had been established to serve.

Those who ultimately benefited were those who had the financial means to do so. Many of these families apparently hoped that their children would proceed even beyond primary school. To accommodate these parents, the city decreed that all of the *minban* schools would grant regular diplomas which "their graduates could use to take part in the entrance examinations for the regular junior high schools."[9] They could feel their children were still on the ladder upward.

Such desires were not unrealistic. As the depression lifted, the urban government had sufficient political influence to secure funding for a substantial expansion at both the primary school and secondary school levels. As a result, half the *minban* elementary schools were able to close down; Canton had had more than 200 *minbans* in 1962–63, but only 108 had to open their doors for the 1964–65 school year.[10] The expansion in the junior-high system was similarly rapid, so much so that by 1964–65 fully 45 percent more children got into a junior high school than in 1960–61.[11] Had the Cultural Revolution not intervened in 1966, most of the depression-year *minban* pupils probably *would* have entered a regular junior high.

PRIMARY SCHOOLS:
POOR, GOOD, AND BEST

Canton could not afford to provide most of its new crowd of elementary school pupils with a pleasant or sometimes even an adequate physical plant. Any passably suitable buildings which could be found were converted and renovated: pre-Liberation commercial premises, former ancestral halls and the like. A substitute teacher from the 1960s describes a primary school typical of those at which he taught:

> Each of the halls of this former temple was divided off into classrooms by plywood partitioning. You could practically see through from one class to another, and you could hear everything that was going on in the classes next door. The classroom had one blackboard and practically no other teaching aids. There was no playground either. Buildings especially erected to be schools weren't that many.

This description holds true up to the present day.

Such schools were and are especially prevalent in the inner city districts. Before the Communists came to power, Canton had been more a center of commerce and government than of industrial activity, and the truly "proletarian" population had not been very large. Many of the downtown districts even today contain very substantial numbers of families whose heads had earlier been retailers and wholesalers, shop clerks, peddlers, professionals, and petty administrators of the former regime. In the 1960s, when determining where the new school facilities should be built, the Education Department employed the Party's political criterion, the "class line," and discriminated against these downtown districts. As a Canton newspaper observed in 1964, "when it arranges to construct or expand primary and secondary school facilities, the municipal committee gives priority to looking after the overcrowded *working-class* districts and the new industrial districts."[12] In its expenditures the education department was pursuing a bifurcated policy: when it came to primary education, the red-class children were to benefit most; but when it came to the higher levels of urban education, as shall be seen, the children of the former middle classes, by dint of their superior school performance, held the greater chances of entering the better equipped schools.

At least *some* of the primary schools in the non-working-class central city were housed in reasonably good facilities. These schools had a special status. Canton had been divided into five administrative districts, and each of the five district education bureaus had divided their domains of several dozens of primary schools into subdistricts called "study districts" (*xuexi qu*). These "study districts" contained several schools apiece,[13] and the best of these several schools—usually an older and more established school in better premises—had been designated that small study district's "central school." As such, it received slightly greater funding and the allocation of comparatively better teachers.

These "central schools" were to provide the other local schools with a literal *model* of how to provide better education. Teachers from the local schools would come here to sit in on well-taught classes, or to learn about and see new educational methods. It was for this reason that the teaching staffs which were assigned to the central schools tended to be better and the funds greater: they were to provide a demonstration effect.[14]

Just as a "central school" served as an example for a small "study district," a "key-point" (*zhongdian*) school provided the model for almost an entire district.[15] These "key-point" primary schools, as of the 1960s, took only children from the immediate neighborhood. But these schools were the best of the best, favored in facilities, teaching staffs, and funding. New campaigns and innovative methods often were first tried out here— and if successful, the streams of visiting principals and teachers increased. Key-point schools sometimes even found themselves put to the services of particular groups within the Party, who sought out key-point units that could stage-manage a "proof" of their own proposals' viability. Sometimes different Party factions provided laudatory media exposure to different key-point schools.

All of these various functions were performed even more prominently by key-point high schools. And for ambitious students, getting into a key-point school at the junior-high level was seen as a leg up, because of the better preparation these schools provided for the senior-high and university entrance examinations.

INTO JUNIOR HIGH SCHOOL

All primary school graduates were permitted to list four schools in order of preference on a unified application form. On the day of the citywide examinations they traveled to their first-choice school to take two exam sections: one in arithmetic and the other in reading and composition.[16] These were graded centrally by the city's Education Department and were then passed back to the child's preferred school, which would examine the results, peruse the primary-school class mistress's comments on the child and glance at the "class" category listed for the child's father. If the applicant were not up to the school's admissions standards, the materials would be passed on to the child's second-preference school, and so on down the line to the child's fourth and final listed choice.

One former pupil recalls that in the 1950s and early 1960s, when many of the primary-school graduates could not get into a junior high school, "our teachers in the final year of primary school constantly had nagged at us to study, regarding the exams as very important." But these pressures from schools and teachers had almost entirely ceased in the 1960s, once the schools' reputations were no longer at stake. As a former primary school teacher remarks, "It had become near impossible to use the percentage admitted to junior high schools as the way of telling whether a primary school was good or not, because just about everyone got into a junior high school." Except for those students who were striving to enter a key-point junior high, there was no longer any reason for students to be nervous or any pressures on them to spend much time cramming for the selection examinations.

Why had Canton and other city governments been able to universalize junior high school education while tens of millions of children in China's countryside had not yet had the chance even to enter *primary* school?[17] Beyond the fact that the metropolitan areas were politically influential in a way the countryside was not, a major reason was that the formal urban job market could no longer absorb youths under the age of 16. Without additional schooling most urban primary school graduates would have been left at loose ends for several years. In this sense, junior high schools in Canton were now to serve as a sort of baby-sitting service, keeping teenagers off the streets, out of trouble, and accessible to some additional knowledge and adult influence until they were ready to enter the regular labor market.

By 1964–65, once the junior high school system had become large enough to play this role, factory work began going almost solely to applicants of at least junior-high attainment. Any primary school graduates who did not continue into junior high school but instead sought immediate employment were likely to find themselves trapped permanently among the young urban unemployed or semiemployed (what the Chinese euphemistically call "social youths"). Almost every parent whose immediate economic plight was not desperate accordingly chose after 1963 to delay their child's hunt for a job until the youngster had gotten into and through the three years of junior high school.

Yet only a minority of families had expectations of regular schooling beyond junior high school. Every interview with former teachers and students has provided independent evidence that the great majority of working-class parents wanted their children to become industrial workers rather than compete to enter the professions through higher education. For one thing, to be an industrial worker of good-class background in Mao's China was a social standing of at least some dignity. More important, a skilled worker in a state-managed factory obtained a relatively decent income and was nearly assured of life tenure, whereas the career road upward through the educational system was slippery and fraught with the possibility that no urban job would at the end be available.

As much to the point, the youth who wanted *only* a factory job had no need to fight further for it through the school system. In this, China differed radically from many other developing countries, where young people desiring a manual post in the modern sector must compete in a race to obtain ever higher diplomas. The Chinese government, probably for "class line" reasons, established job recruitment policies that avoided this type of credentials competition. Interviews reveal that the factories in Canton, though already preferring applicants to possess at least a junior-high-school degree, did not begin to look for credentials beyond this. In the ordinary junior high schools this fact was reflected in lessened academic competition.

Many working-class parents, to be sure, still had high admiration for education—probably more so than in most other countries, since education traditionally has been so highly esteemed in China. Yet they usually recognized that their child's schoolwork was inadequate to sustain grand hopes.[18] Coming from semiliterate homes, their children had received no preschool training, and once they entered school could not receive much parental supervision in their schoolwork. From early on, working-class youngsters tended to find their studies difficult.[19] Whatever their parents might desire, without the reinforcements which came from academic success they usually did not want to continue their studies at the end of junior high, especially if they already held chances of securing regular work.

Even those who did well at school and wanted to go on found obstacles in their way. Among other things, there normally were considerable costs to bear (see table 1-1).[20] For junior high school the tuition fees, book fees, and ancillary expenses amounted to about 5 percent of the father's factory salary; and senior high school, with slightly higher tuition fees, would require about 6 percent. With four or five children to see through their schooling, the cumulative expenses cut markedly into a worker's household budget. To send a child on to one of the better schools would impose an even greater sacrifice. Most of Canton's good

Table 1-1. Secondary School Fees

Necessary School Expenses	
Junior high school tuition	Y5 per term (2 terms = schoolyear)
Senior high school tuition	Y7 per term
Notebook and stationary fees	Y4 per term
Book fees	Y4 per term
Activities fee	about Y.50 per term
Additional Boarding School Expenses	
Dormitory fees	about Y3-10 per term
3 meals a day	Y9-10 per month
Wages	
The average middle-aged male factory worker earned about 40–50 *yuan* a month.	

schools drew upon a city-wide student body and so had boarding facilities. A working-class family living in industrial suburbs beyond daily commuting distance usually could not afford the extra boarding costs. In recognition of these problems, at every secondary school a student in financial straits could apply for a remission of fees and for monthly financial assistance (including 3 *yuan* of pocket money). But such aid was not considered until the student had already enrolled; the grants were hard to come by; and a needy entrant always ran the risk that the necessary assistance would not be forthcoming.

The former middle classes tended to have rather higher salaries than the blue-collar households, and they were very willing to put these incomes into schooling. From early childhood onward, almost all of my interviewees from educated homes (the teachers, professionals, former businessmen, and technicians) had been exposed to strong parental aspirations for them to achieve high levels of education. They had absorbed from their parents a set of sentiments which they hold to this day: the traditional notion that learning was intrinsically ennobling; the feeling that to be educated was prestigious; the corrolary belief that the occupations which required high-level training were the most to be admired; and the conviction that knowledge and professional skills provided the most efficacious way of "serving" China.

A certain pragmatism reinforced their strivings to advance educationally. The former middle classes were not markedly discriminated against (unlike the bad classes), but their non-red status made some parents at least modestly insecure. They saw education as a protection for their children. As the daughter of a doctor observes, "The intelligentsia in Canton felt that if their kids could obtain skills the country needed, the state wouldn't dare to look down on the children." Bad-class families in particular seem to have held such hopes—though they had to recognize at the same time that their changes of success would be rather less than those of the middle classes.

Yet with most of these families, both middle and bad class, pragmatism ended up taking the back seat. As shall be seen, even when the chances dimmed of their child gaining a satisfactory position through the regular education system, many of these households stubbornly persisted in attempts to climb the ladder into the universities. The pull of traditions and attitudes held them to this single route.

Many of the children of the "revolutionary cadres" (the pre-Liberation Party officials) were also aiming for the universities. Most seem to have felt from early childhood that it was both their duty and their right to tread in the footsteps of their parents and become "revolutionary successors" (the Chinese phrase which denotes ascension to a position of decision-making by a member of the new generation). They and their parents recognized that the path to posts of responsibility lay most readily through acquisition of at least a certain expertise, whether it be through the university-level military academies or through regular university coursework. As the offspring of the reddest of the "red" homes, if they could secure a specialized education they would be entrusted with more sensitive posts than would personnel of non-red heritage. They would be able to move readily into supervisory jobs in the technical or administrative or military spheres. As the first leg up, they too sought admission to the key-point high schools. There they found themselves in competition primarily with the brightest of the middle-class youths.

SCHOOL STATEGIES
FOR WINNING REPUTATIONS

The key-point high schools were not just perceived by the educational authorities as places for testing out and demonstrating educational programs. Early in the 1950s the authorities had also come to see the key-points as providing a solid secondary-school training for those teenagers who were most likely in the next generation to fill the leadership posts in the scientific, technical, and academic fields. The authorities judged the success of such a school by noting how the school fared in getting its students admitted to universities. This provided an administratively convenient index; a school which got 64 percent of its senior high school graduating class into universities was considered to be more effective than a school which sent only 42 percent.

Applicants to high schools were looking from the bottom up at the same figures in deciding which of the city's schools to apply to. The most highly esteemed schools in Canton tended to be long established schools. Several in fact had been the best of the missionary schools. Good initial reputations had enabled them to attract student bodies of sufficiently high quality to assure continued high rates of university acceptances. But if a school miscalculated in its admissions strategy or educational programs and its university acceptance percentages dropped off relative to other schools, new applicants of high potential would begin shying away. If so, the educational authorities might no longer even want to retain the school's role as a "key-point" model, and the school's privileged access to funding might be withdrawn.

Such schools accordingly paid close attention to the annual university enrollment trends. The universities for their part were independently selecting their own student bodies. But the relative weight they placed each year on each of the three criteria—entrance examination scores, political record, and class background—was influenced heavily by the Party's political line of the moment. As this shifted, the universities followed suit, using guidelines devised by a provincial University Enrollments Committee. From the top down, through these university enrollment biases, the Party indirectly influenced the enrollment programs of the high schools.

The senior high schools also tried, however, to evolve more long-term admissions strategies of their own. This gave rise in the years before the Cultural Revolution to complex tactics on the part of different schools. We can observe this by way of two examples—Canton High School No. 21 and Girls' High.

No. 21 had been established in 1955. As with most new schools in Canton, it had had little reputation during its initial years. Located in the suburbs of Canton near a village of Overseas Chinese (people who had returned to China from abroad), the school at first made do with a student body composed largely of these families' sons and daughters. But in 1959 a teacher-training institute was errected nearby, and No. 21 established formal links with the institute. Under this aegis the school was quickly able to improve its teaching staff. But how could it attract students of university caliber? To elevate the school's status to the very first rank it would need to attract students who had both high academic achievement and a respectable class background. Any student who possessed both of these advantages was all but assured subsequent admission to a university. But as an alumnus of No. 21 explains,

> such students were already getting accepted by the very best high schools. So our school's leaders adopted a compromise program. They accepted principally two types of students: those of insubstantial academic achievement who therefore could not get into the top schools but who were of "aristocratic" (Party-official) class background; and as the second group, those of high academic achievement who had not dared to apply to the top schools. Many of these latter students were from non-good-class intellectual family backgrounds.[21]

The composition of No. 21's student body soon gravitated toward a noticeably high percentage of children from Canton's Party elite. The school was convenient to some of the suburban housing estates of the officialdom, and No. 21 had been particularly careful, more than most schools, to cultivate a reputation of doing well by Party cadre children. The school's enrollment officers had apparently calculated that the universities would have to take the class line increasingly seriously; and if so, no household could be of "redder" class background than that of a veteran of the Long March.

Girls High faced the same initial problem as No. 21. But as the "class line" began to gain modestly in importance it took a tack quite different from No. 21. Explains one of Girls High's alumna:

> Canton's two best schools had adopted admissions policies of giving greater preference to cadre kids in admissions than previously. So there was a batch of youths from middle-class "professional" families who would have been accepted if the places hadn't been taken by those cadre kids. My own school recruited these girls of "intellectual" (zhishifenzi) middle-class backgrounds. The school wanted to increase the percentage of its graduates who made it into university and therefore went for these very bright students.

These two schools, though ending up with student bodies of rather different composition, came to hold about equal standing among Canton's schools. Both were rated among the top dozen schools in the city.

As the "class line" strengthened after 1963, the good schools generally also began taking larger quotas of "proletarian" youths. But these students still were very much a minority. In general, a worker/peasant class origin was not quite "red" enough to make up for an average or poor showing on the selection examinations. Working-class youths who continued into senior high school did so predominantly at the third-rate schools. The student composition of these lesser schools generally reflected the populations of the districts in which they were located. Several of the neighborhood high schools in the traditional blue-collar districts contained almost only children of the pre-Liberation laboring classes. Similarly, a few on the west end of the city, where prior to Liberation the city's most exclusive neighborhoods were located, held large numbers of the other major category of losers in the educational competition, the children of Canton's former capitalists.

Different "classes" of youths, in short, were concentrated at secondary schools of different qualities. This can be observed in table 1-2. This table was compiled in collaboration with Stanley Rosen and Anita Chan, using questionnaires filled out in Hong Kong in 1975–76 by 74 former Canton students. These respondents have supplied us with information about each of the students in their own high school classrooms— a second-hand survey of 3,524 students. They were very familiar with the circumstances of their classmates, because they had been kept to-

Table 1-2. The "Class Composition" of Canton Secondary Schools, 1962–66

Official Pre-Liberation Backgrounds of Fathers	(N = 74 classrooms) "Key-Point" Schools		18 ordinary schools[d]	28 neighborhood jr. highs
	"Best" 4 schools	Next-best 8 schools		
SENIOR HIGH SCHOOL				
"revolutionary cadre"	27%	16%	7%	
good-class worker and peasant	12%	16%	16%	
non-"intelligentsia" middle-class[a]	16%	11%	17%	
"intelligentsia" middle-class[b]	34%	43%	27%	
overseas merchants[c]	2%	3%	6%	
bad class	9%	11%	27%	
	100%	100%	100%	

Table 1-2. (Cont.)

Official Pre-Liberation Backgrounds of Fathers	(N = 74 classrooms) "Key-Point" Schools		18 ordinary schools[d]	28 neighborhood jr. highs
	"Best" 4 schools	Next-best 8 schools		
No. of classrooms surveyed	5	8	18	
No. of students in sample	223	351	813	
JUNIOR HIGH SCHOOL				
"revolutionary cadre"	48%	17%	9%	8%
good-class worker and peasant	11%	24%	34%	42%
non-"intelligentsia" middle-class[a]	3%	14%	19%	16%
"intelligentsia" middle-class[b]	32%	30%	19%	20%
overseas merchants[c]	2%	4%	8%	3%
bad class	4%	11%	11%	11%
	100%	100%	100%	100%
No. of classrooms surveyed	5	12	12	14
No. of students in sample	234	603	578	722

NOTE: The table excludes the couple of Experimental Schools in Canton, since these used different criteria in recruiting students.

The strengthening of the class line in the mid-1960s can be observed most clearly in the junior high school enrollments of the better schools. In their senior-high enrollments the schools tended to look kindly upon their own school's junior-high graduates, and therefore the senior-high figures partially reflected the higher mix of middle- and bad-class students who had gotten into the better junior highs in the early 1960s.

[a] The children of pre-Liberation peddlars, store clerks, craftsmen, middle peasants, etc.

[b] The children of pre-Liberation white-collar staff, professionals, teachers, etc.

[c] Children sent to be educated in Canton by parents living abroad.

[d] A number of our respondents from the neighborhood senior high schools were, by chance, clustered at the several schools in Canton which are located in the traditional neighborhoods of bad-class households. Accordingly, a disproportionately high number of bad-class students appear in this column, and a disproportionately low number of working-class students.

gether in the same classroom units throughout the several years they were enrolled at their high school. Moreover, as we shall later observe, when the Cultural Revolution erupted the students generally had not dispersed. They had remained at school during the two years of combat, with some of their classmates as comrades-in-arms and others as antagonists. And the factor of signal importance when they split into these opposing factions was a student's "class origins." It is not surprising that many of these students can remember faces and details that had had such central relevance to their own lives.

To err if need be on the side of caution, any respondents whose recollections seemed incomplete or internally inconsistent were culled from the sample.[22] Furthermore, a careful double check was made of many of the remaining respondents' memories several weeks after they first filled in the questionnaires. Those whose recollections appeared erratic were also deleted. The remaining body of data, from 74 respondents, should be treated as inexact, but the survey does provide strong suggestive evidence on how students were distributed in Canton's high school system.

These statistics back up our discussion of the previous pages. The table shows, for example, that the working-class youths still tended in the mid-1960s to be concentrated in the poorer junior high schools. They tended also to be better represented at the junior-high level than in the equivalent senior high schools.

It is also evident that young people from the white-collar middle-class homes were still disproportionately winning entry to the better schools at both junior and senior-high levels; generally, the better the category of school in this table, the higher the percentages of these youths. The four elite schools continued to accept the very brightest of the middle-class youths, but satisfied the class line by turning almost exclusively toward the "reddest" of the "red" background children—those of the Party elite. At these best schools, as table 1-2 shows, the classmates of white-collar middle-class and revolutionary-cadre background together comprised a very substantial majority of the student body.

These children of the Party officialdom and of the middle-class intelligentsia would be very differently affected by the weighting given to "class" as against "academic achievement." The structure of the high school system, in short, was channeling students of different backgrounds into schools of different qualities, and was doing so in ways that promoted frictions among them. It was precisely at these good schools and between these two groups of achievement-oriented youths that the Cultural Revolution would be most fiercely contested.

Some of the more ambitious working-class youths, moreover, had good cause to feel that the recruitment strategies of the key-point schools were not at all ideologically justified. When the Cultural Revolution exploded in 1966, the class composition of the best schools would come under attack from below. A broadside against the principal of Attached High (Canton's most prestigious high school) charged,

> Not only would he not admit the children of workers and peasants but he even yelled, 'Attached High is a key-point school where studying comes first, so we do not enroll worker-peasant children who have poor grades. We have a lot of professors' children with good grades whom it wouldn't do to reject.' Later, so as to be in accord with the (illegible) necessities, he slowly changed his policy, opening wide the door of convenience to the high-level cadres' children of the black Provincial Party Committee. . . . Worker-peasant children were squeezed out at admissions time and those who did get in had to taste the bitterness of being held back a grade and being dropped from the school.[23]

LEAVING JUNIOR HIGH SCHOOL

An urban secondary school education in most countries is supposed to serve at least three funtions: to prepare most youths directly for their adult career-lives; to prepare some students for university; and to sift out those qualified to enter universities from those less qualified. In the 1960s Canton's junior high schools served the former purpose for most students—their final academic training before they began their occupations. The much smaller senior high system tried to serve almost exclusively the latter two functions.

The authorities had already, *de facto*, bifurcated the secondary school system at the junior high school level to take these factors into account—dividing off some students from the others and providing this minority at the key-point schools with a better preparation for the universities. But this bifurcation of the junior high school system did not mean establishment of a vocationally oriented junior-high education at the ordinary neighborhood schools. The curricula of all the schools (key-point and neighborhood schools alike) were exactly the same; *all of* the schools prepared the students for senior-high coursework. The authorities were not willing to completely block off educational advancement to the pupils of the inferior quality junior highs[24]—especially since so many of these students were from the good-background working classes. Nonetheless, leaders who had backed the bifurcated school structure were later to come under attack during the Cultural Revolution. It was to be charged in the official press that the school system had consigned the children of the laboring classes to manual occupations which were "ruled" by those who had climbed the ladder through the key-points into the mental occupations.[25]

The atmosphere in the various schools differed as graduation from junior high school approached. As expected, interviews suggest that the students at the "better" schools prepared more for the examinations and with greater nervousness.[26] But the key-point schools themselves were not putting pressure on the students over the examinations. The reputations of these schools, which were almost always combined junior/senior high schools, depended only on their graduating senior-high classes' university entrance ratings. And the neighborhood junior highs, though not attached usually to any senior high school, had neither reputations to defend nor any need to compete to attract new students through better exam showings.[27]

The senior high schools' admissions personnel gave preference to their own junior high's graduates. But they also did take the opportunity to drop from their rolls students of inferior academic quality and those whose chances for university entry had been damaged by the changing political environment. As one example of the latter, an interviewee who was of bad class background had won admittance to one of Canton's better schools in 1961, a conservative year. He stood academically at the top of his classroom, but when he graduated from junior high school in 1964 he found himself rejected by his own school and by the other three schools of his choice.

Such disappointments inevitably bred a certain degree of bitterness—feelings that the criteria used were unfair. This was true not only among many of the youths who suffered such experiences but also some of those who felt threatened. Several interviewees of middle-class origins had fixed on discrimination as the *excuse* for their failures. One such interviewee, a Communist Youth League member, had overestimated her academic and political achievements and applied unsuccessfully to four of the half-dozen best senior high schools in Canton, without bothering to put down a mediocre school as her "safety" fourth choice. More than a decade later she remains convinced that she had been the victim of her father's middle-class standing. A second interviewee, dropped during the depression of the early sixties from a white-collar job in an office where he was the newest member, today rationalizes bitterly that his middle-class status had done him in. The government's use of the "class line" during the 1960s was creating a climate of grievances which sometimes went beyond what the class-line policies actually entailed.

Students who were turned down by the senior high schools or universities still had opportunities to pursue their dreams of higher education. So long as their parents were willing and able to support them financially, they had the choice, for one, to remain at home rather than seek a job, preparing on their own to retake the annual examinations a second or third time. It was state policy to consider such applicants as showing poor political attitudes, since they were supposed to have accepted the state's appeals to volunteer to settle in the countryside. Their chances the second time around were accordingly damaged. But such young people had hopes that by lowering their sights considerably in the quality of schools to which they applied, they might be able to squeeze through. A third-rate school might well calculate that the applicant's examination scores were so much higher than their normal enrollees as to outweigh the candidate's "political" defects.

There was also a second and safer way to continue on the upward ladder. If their parents had sufficient income, disappointed junior-high graduates could apply to a *minban* high school. Like the *minban* primary schools, these were self-financing. They provided a means to assuage the frustrations of upwardly aspiring households at no cost to state coffers.[28] A teacher from such a school recalls that his classes held predominantly two types of students: children of lower-ranking Party cadres and military officers who had been too bad academically to get into a regular senior high school; and academically excellent bad-class students who refused to accept the "verdicts" of the regular senior high schools. They still held to the slim hopes that their academic performance at the *minban* high school could somehow win them a place at a university.

THE ALTERNATIVE EDUCATIONAL ROUTE: VOCATIONAL SCHOOLING

Junior high school graduates, however, had more than just the plain choice of continuing up the general-education ladder or seeking a job at 16. Branching off from the general-education ladder were several forms of vocational schooling for students of lesser ambitions, providing terminal training for specific careers.

In some of the Third World nations, unlike China, vocational programs have become little more than a refuge for students unable to climb onto the next higher rung of the regular ladder. Knowing that their country's modern-sector employers prefer to hire young people who had been "good" enough to graduate with an academic-track diploma, these Third World vocational students, as in the "business schools" of Ghana, try to rejoin the regular track at the next higher level by prepping for the entrance exams. The curricula of Third World vocational schools often get badly distorted in the process. The real role such Third World vocational schools play for many of their students becomes similar to the function the *minban* senior highs fulfilled in China.

But China's own vocational schools were rather different. These *did* provide a practical means for obtaining modern sector employment. Such schools had the singular advantage of direct links to industrial bureaus and factories. Unlike China's academic-track senior high schools, whose graduates normally had to scramble on their own to find jobs, the vocational system in the 1950s and 1960s was able to *assign* its graduates to be the new accountants for government offices and factories, new locomotive engineers, lathe operators, etc. These vocational schools' annual enrollments were geared to the projected manpower needs of the various industries and government units, to ensure that there would not be any shortages of new skilled personnel.

Hence most vocational students were purposely made ineligible to take the university entrance examinations, to prevent them from turning their studies back toward "examination prepping." The vocational school administrators very likely supported this regulation, since their schools were partially funded by the various industrial bureaus and were under pressure to supply these government organs with adequately trained personnel.

Canton's vocational school program accordingly was linked to the job market in ways that both encouraged the learning of actual vocational skills and attracted students. In 1965–66 Canton's vocational system *in toto* contained about 80 percent as many students as Canton's academic track senior high program;[29] and at many of the vocational schools the competition to get admitted was fairly tight.

These vocational schools were of three broad types:

(a) teacher training schools (*shifan xuexiao*), for prospective elementary school teachers (mostly young women);[30]

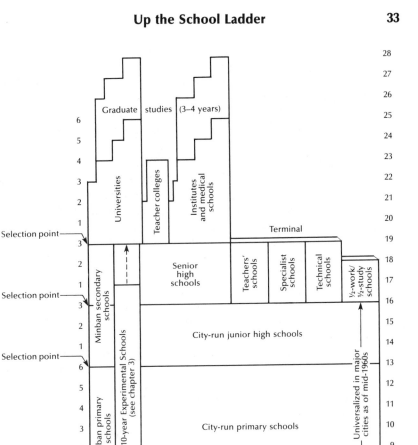

Note: At the start of the 1963–64 schoolyear, Canton contained approximately fifty-five municipally run junior high school programs, as well as ten junior highs in suburban peasant villages which were run by village primary schools. These various junior highs emptied graduates into: 30 academic-track senior high programs; 3 teacher-training schools; 15 technical and specialist schools; and 4 full-day technical workers schools (including one for training agricultural mechanics). Each of the junior high programs normally had many more students than the average senior high. In the entire secondary school system — including both the junior and senior high schools — Canton enrolled 83,000 students in 1963–64, the great majority of whom were in the junior high sections. (Source: *Yangcheng Wanbao*, July 12, 1963, p. 1; February 2, 1964, p. 1; May 5, 1964, p. 1.)

Figure 1-1 Canton's Ladder of Education Until 1966

(b) technical/technical-worker (*zhongji*) schools, which trained young people for skilled manual careers;[31] and

(c) specialist (*zhongzhuan*) schools, which prepared students for white-collar staff positions.

As an alternative to going to a technical high school, young people who had the proper family connections (*guanxi*) could try to get themselves hired by a factory directly upon graduating from junior high school. This had the advantage of providing immediate wages as an apprentice (for three years at half the minimal pay for regular workers). Since Chinese factories (like those in Japan) laid stress on job seniority, youths who entered the industrial work force at a young age would benefit also from higher salaries in later years. But attendance at a technical high school counted equally toward job seniority; and the practical coursework at the technical school would help them later in life to get a higher skill ranking, the second major determinant of a blue-collar worker's wages. Thus, even taking into account the three years of apprentice-level wages that a technical student sacrificed, he or she ended up with slightly greater longterm earnings and status. These schools were consequently very popular with working-class youths.

Contrary to most other developing countries, in China it was the high prestige academic track which provided a considerably *reduced* opportunity for obtaining work. As we earlier noted, whatever the psychic gratification and status of holding a senior high school degree, the senior-high graduates who took their diplomas with them in their search for jobs soon discovered their papers were barely of greater use than a junior high school certificate. Moreover, even if they did secure a job, they had incurred financial losses by pursuing the higher degree. They received no credit in their wage packets for their diplomas, received no seniority credit, and had to undertake the obligatory three-year stint as apprentices.

When the type of students who contemplated the senior-high-school/ university route decided to play it safe and go instead for vocational training, however, they did not usually opt for the technical schools. They normally applied to the most prestigious and the most difficult to enter of the vocational schools—the specialist schools. These were for training white-collar personnel, be it accountants, laboratory aides, draughtsmen, medical aides, etc.[32] These specialist schools, unlike the technical schools, took the academic calibre of candidates strongly into account, and made use of the same entrance examinations as the regular senior high schools.

But this specialist schooling all but precluded further education. The specialist schools very rarely granted permission to any of their students to take the university entrance examinations, since the schools had to provide the state with prearranged numbers of needed middle-level personnel. Specialist students who did well in their studies knew they could only benefit through assignment to a better initial job posting in their chosen profession, not upward mobility into a better occupation. The graduate of a medical specialist school was destined to be only a medical aide, not a physician.

Since the regular senior high schools were the only realistic means to reach higher, the ambitious teenager had to calculate whether to take the gamble. An interviewee of worker-class origins recalls his own family's debate:

> I discussed what I should do with my mother, with an uncle who was a factory blue-collar cadre, and with my teacher. My mom wanted me to go to a senior high school. She was hoping I'd be able to get to college, and was willing and wanted to support me through university, because I was the only son. My uncle and teacher advised a specialist school which trained white-collar industrial personnel. My uncle said that if I were [politically] active at my job I could rise into higher positions through that. [This was an avenue for upward mobility available pretty much only to youths of good-class backgrounds.] My uncle claimed that a university degree meant little in China. My teacher told me it was better to get an assurance of a good job: what if I went to a regular senior high and then didn't make it into a university?

This particular teenager heeded the advice of his uncle and teacher and enrolled in the specialist school. Most of the other achievement-oriented youths chose the academic-track senior high schools. As shall be seen in the next chapter, they were placing themselves on an increasingly precarious path. The tensions they would be facing in the senior high schools would be sufficient by 1966 to lend impetus to the Cultural Revolution uprisings.

CHAPTER TWO

The Senior High School Bulge and Dwindling Career Openings

THE "BETTER" senior high schools consistently remained more difficult to get into than the best of the specialist schools. Yet these young people were embarking upon a bet they were very likely to lose. The chances in senior high school of jumping the next hurdle into a university were shrinking steadily as the sixties progressed. A great many students would eventually be left stranded without marketable skills, and would have to settle as peasants in the countryside. That explains why it is relatively easy in Hong Kong today to find former students from Canton's most prestigious senior high schools but rather difficult to find former students from the specialist schools. The latter have had access to careers and presumably have little impulse to seek new lives abroad.

THE NARROWING OF UNIVERSITY OPPORTUNITIES

Until the early sixties any competent students who chose the regular senior high schools usually had been acting in their own best interests. Their chance of getting through the university gates had been good. In fact, during the First Five Year Plan, with its demands for a large number of new experts, the government's higher education program had called for *more* university entrants than there were senior high school graduates available.[1] The state was obliged to recruit out of government offices and from among primary school staffs to make up the difference. The government even offered such applicants a quarter year's paid leave to prepare for the university examinations. In 1957 the rapidly expanding output of the senior high schools had finally overtaken the intake needs of the universities.[2] But almost immediately, with the emergence of the Great Leap Forward, the estimates of China's future needs for skilled manpower soared, and renewed university expansions again outpaced what the senior high schools could provide. As late as 1960, *People's Daily* was fretting that it would be difficult to fill the university openings for the 1960–61 school year.[3] Up through 1960, in other words, students who got admitted to senior high schools had felt all but assured that they would be able to go on to a university.

The situation very quickly changed after 1960, however. Most of the crowds of 1960–61 enrollees had to be dismissed within a year of entering universities, as the Great Leap Forward collapsed into severe economic depression. The contracting economy could not even utilize all the expertise it was already turning out; an interviewee who graduated in 1962 from Peking University, the nation's foremost school, was sent to his dismay to labor in the countryside. Not surprisingly, in such straits the authorities let new university enrollments drop sharply in Canton. In 1959, during the euphoria of the Great Leap, the fulltime institutes of higher education in the Canton metropolitan area had accepted 9,500 new enrollees; in 1962 they accepted only 3,000.[4]

The rates of admissions were to rise again in succeeding years, but not by a great deal. The major expansions in university places had been brought to an end in Guangdong—and elsewhere in the country. Government organs had apparently come to the realization during the early sixties that most of their vacancies for highly trained personnel had been gradually filled since the early 1950s and that the time would soon arrive when they would require little more than replacements for retiring personnel. The province's fulltime university population was accordingly permitted to decline by perhaps 10 percent between 1964 and 1966,[5] despite the renewed prosperity in China.

In keeping with this decline, no additional academic-track senior high schools were established in Canton after 1961. But the high school program that had been inaugurated before that date assured a continued overproduction of senior high school graduates. From extensive interviewing it can be estimated that in 1965, the last year of enrollments before the Cultural Revolution, less than 30 percent (perhaps only 20 percent) of Canton's senior high school graduates were getting into a university—a far cry from the near certainty of success half a decade earlier. Young people had been faced within a short period with the painful option of either lowering their sights or stepping up their own competitive efforts to succeed.

A great many of the students chose the latter competitive course. One strong reason was that if they failed to climb into a university they would have to confront an increasingly serious crisis in Canton's job market.

JOB HUNTING

On the one side Canton was paying the price for the baby boom of the 1950s. In 1949, on the eve of Canton's Liberation, the city's birth rate had stood at 27 per thousand population.[6] But with peace and growing prosperity it had shot up to 44 per thousand by 1954.[7] Almost every one of my interviewees came from households of four, five, six, or more children; almost annually by the mid-1960s, a brother or sister from such a home was entering the job market.

On the other side of the supply-and-demand equation for labor, there had been a 12.6 percent annual growth in industrial employment in China during the First Five Year Plan of the 1950s.[8] That earlier rapid expansion in factory employment meant that in the 1960s the industrial workforce was still comparatively young. With relatively few workers retiring, there was little room for replacements from the new generation of school graduates. Making matters worse, during the "three years of hardship" of 1960–62 Canton's industry had needed practically no new personnel at all, and had in fact sacked a portion of its labor force. A backlog of unsuccessful young jobseekers had built up, and as industry and commerce revived in 1963 and 1964 these youths competed with the new and yet younger jobseekers. The near universalization of junior high school education left those still under 16 temporarily out of the informal job sectors and briefly staved off the day of reckoning; the job situation apparently improved in 1963. But within a year or so the search for jobs was worsening again.

Ever since the early 1960s the process of finding a position was catch-as-catch-can. The senior high schools began in 1964 to establish job links for some graduates—but only for a small minority.[9] Interviews reveal that most young people had to rely on relatives to find a job opening for them. Teenagers whose parents were either Party officials or industrial workers of good-class background held a decided advantage here: the children of officials because their parents were in a position to trade favors, and those of workers because it was customary for factories to give preference to their own blue-collar employees' children. This was so much the case that it had literally become a regulation at some factories that when a worker retired, one of his or her children was guaranteed a job (one reason being that the child could then help to financially support the retired parents).

Youths had a very hard time lining up work if their parents' factories were already overstaffed. If their parents were not liked at their places of employment or the father was not of adequate class background, their job problems were compounded. Such youths could resort to making the rounds of the small low-paying workshops which comprise the "informal sector" of China's urban economy. These are run by local administrative organs called Neighborhood Committees. But even here work was hard to find and "connections" helpful. Sometimes, if desperate, youths would curry favor with the Neighborhood Committee by laboring without pay at odd jobs in the community, in the hopes of being offered paid employment when a vacancy opened.

Several interviewees had found the scramble for odd jobs embarrassing, disheartening, and even humiliating. "Achievers" at school, their earlier successes had led them to look down upon the unskilled manual occupations—though perhaps less so in China than in most other countries. The problem was noticeable enough, however, that Liu Shaoqi sardonically quipped, "Generally, those who have graduated from a junior high school despise the peasants; those graduated from a senior high school despise the workers; those graduated from a university despise all of them."[10] Be that as it may, many of the graduates who could not find a job had to begin seeking out employment even in the despised service trades.

The government in the 1960s had tried to make a dent in the traditional Chinese prejudice against the service trades by running articles in the press extolling conscientious shop clerks, restaurant waiters, sanitation men et al. But almost every one of my interviewees (regardless of their social backgrounds and, significantly, including all of my interviewees from post-Cultural Revolution high schools) persisted in holding the service trades in considerable contempt.[11] Yet, from the time of the Great Leap's collapse up to the Cultural Revolution in 1966, even a youth willing to take a "face-losing" job in a restaurant or night-soil corps normally had difficulty locating an opening.

The authorities, looking ahead to the numbers of youths born after Liberation who were poised to start leaving junior high school after 1965, began to warn the public through the newspapers that the urban job situation would only continue to worsen. In March 1964, *People's Daily* stated bluntly that

> several million students graduate annually from secondary and primary schools in the urban areas. With the exception of the few students who will continue to study at higher level schools or be employed in urban areas, the majority will take part in agricultural tasks . . . in hilly and rural areas.[12]

Most of the better-than-average students ploughed on undeterred with their regular studies. But under the new circumstances increased numbers of graduating junior high school students began shifting away from the academic-track senior high school route and toward vocational training. A 1965 graduate of a key-point junior high school recalls that "because their academic grades weren't so good, and seeing their classmates studying their butts off, [some students] realized they'd lose out in the competition and have to become peasants. So they aimed for the technical schools."[13]

In earlier years, the less prestigious types of vocational training had appealed almost exclusively to youths of working-class background. But now, having sometimes spent months unsuccessfully seeking jobs, teenagers of all class backgrounds sought entry in 1964–65 even to the crude new half-work/half-study technical worker schools that were being opened in a new government campaign.[14] So eager were youths for jobs that even the despised trades such as the "sanitation" trade[15] found applicants for several work/study schools.

Canton's leadership came alive to the tightening competition to enter the work/study industrial schools and through them industrial careers, and in late 1964 the city leaders passed a directive expelling bad-class teenagers from the program so as to make room for additional workers' children. Six hundred students—10 percent of all the work/study enrollees in Canton—were weeded out on the basis of their class origins and pressured into "volunteering" to settle as peasants in the countryside.[16]

Work/study schools increasingly boasted in newspaper stories of their high percentages of students from worker/peasant class origins—much as the key-point schools took pride in high university acceptance rates. In short, as the prospects for jobs tightened in Canton a terminal-degree mass education program such as the work/study system came under a particularly special pressure to take the class line seriously. Accordingly, whereas the half-work/half-study schools initially had given entrance examinations, after 1964 these were no longer administered.

Shanxi province in 1965 turned to a new system of recruitment even at its full-time vocational schools. Applicants were to be selected only from among youths who were already employed. They would have to be recommended by officials at their place of work, based on the youths' good records at manual labor and their political activities.[17] Under this scheme, workers' and good-class peasants' children and Communist Youth League Members would receive priority regardless of their academic skills.

Precisely this same system of recruitment would be adopted after the Cultural Revolution for the selection of university students. The government would defend such a policy on the grounds that prior to the Cultural Revolution

> . . . university students were recruited directly from senior high schools, and the success of the applicants depended on the examination marks they obtained. Wasn't it due to the use of these methods that revisionist education excluded vast numbers of children of workers and peasants from schools?[18]

TO THE COUNTRYSIDE

The unemployed young people in Canton had begun coming under pressures to settle in the countryside. Many of them had been surviving in the city by seeking out low-paid casual work by the day or week: hauling goods, digging ditches, or reinforcing factory production lines during emergency peak periods. They had obtained such work either by applying through the city's Labor Office (Laodong ju) or by making the rounds of employers to offer their own services. But as high unemployment began to seem like a permanent urban fixture, the Canton city government in 1963 stepped in to cut off the informal means of obtaining casual jobs.

All casual labor henceforth was to be administered solely through the Labor Offices and a network of "service stations" (fuwu zhan). In 1965, in a move to oblige increased numbers of the youths to emigrate to the countryside, these service stations began to offer work only to specified categories of persons: those were already over 25; or whose family already had a member who had volunteered for the countryside; or who were the sole support of their family; or who had a sibling in the armed forces.[19]

Increasingly, coordinated mechanisms were urging the young people to put their signatures to applications to rusticate: intense political proselytization to graduating high-school classes; repeated editorials in the mass media; dwindling opportunities to climb further up the educational ladder; the restrictions both official and unofficial on urban employment; special political courses for unemployed youths;[20] and even promises that a willingness to settle in the countryside would improve one's chances for career and study opportunities in the future.[21]

All of these appeals, though, were broached in a strongly ideological/ moral language. The youths were to view their "voluntary" settlement in the countryside as a victory in a test of their own political convictions, not as their personal failure to climb into higher education or as a failure by the economy to provide the necessary jobs. The authorities thought that if the teenagers felt they were going to the countryside of their own free choice, they would be able to adjust equably and even with political enthusiasm to the difficulties of rural life.

In the schools, a fair number of students did in fact regard favorably the challenge and the hardship involved. An interviewee whose own dream was to be a writer and who had held most of the urban manual occupations in disdain recollects that "I was willing if need be to go to a village, because I felt then that the peasant villages were good and the countryside wide. Our school had told us so. I knew it would be a tough life but believed the experience would be meaningful." Adds a second former student:

> The way the kids looked at these volunteers of 1964 was that they weren't very bright because they couldn't get into higher education, but that they were good in their political thinking. So in our minds going to the countryside was a glorious thing, because it showed you were revolutionary. If a person refused to go and stayed on in the city [without work] we would think of him as comparatively "backward". . . . But of course, studying continued to be the first choice. This was even what they demanded from

above: to study hard in school. So if you went to the countryside you felt it a bit shameful but at the same time felt it revolutionary and glorious.[22]

When facing a final decision, however, most students and unemployed young people were not inclined to commit themselves to go. All urban dwellers held residence cards, which allowed them to live legally in the city. If they gave up the card for a rural one they ran a high risk of consigning themselves to a lifetime as a peasant. A Canton teenager, whatever his feelings of dedication and idealism, would not lightly take a possibly irreversible plunge.

In the light of this, Tao Zhu, the Party leader of south-central China, reportedly promised in the early Sixties that all of the urban youths who settled in the countryside would be able to retain their urban residence cards; in addition, a fair number during the depression years were informed by their Neighborhood Committees that they could return to definite jobs in Canton after a specified number of years.[23] But by 1965 it had become obvious to Canton officials that such urban jobs would remain permanently in short supply, and all rusticating youths henceforth were to go for life. As the years passed, in short, the ramifications of rustication became increasingly severe. In the Cultural Revolution, when the central government took further stock of the cities' future manpower needs, it made retroactive the new policy of lifetime rustication and withdrew the urban residence cards from those teenagers who had volunteered in the earlier part of the Sixties. (Zhou Enlai lamely told a Cultural Revolution audience of Guangdong youths that the now-fallen Tao Zhu had let them keep their registration cards so as to purposely mislead them into believing they were to be only temporarily rusticated.)[24]

In some of the smaller cities of Guangdong where unemployment was more severe than Canton, the local authorities before the Cultural Revolution were already applying directly coercive pressures on youths to force them out of town. Red Guard documents charged, for instance, that in the Pearl River delta city of Jiangmen the local education bureau had stipulated in 1964 that:

a school should be rated as first-class not only when its students gained the highest [examination pass rates] but also when the number of its students going to the countryside was the largest. As a result, the various schools left no stone unturned in "mobilizing" their students to go to the countryside. . . . In 1965, such schools as the No. 1 and No. 2 High Schools of Jiangmen invented a new "mobilization" method. After they had taken the senior high school entrance examination and before notices of the results were issued, all graduates had to surrender their residential cards. It was stated that if they refused to do so, no notices [on whether their school applications had been successful] would be issued to them, and that they would not be given jobs if they failed to pass the examination.[25]

This type of coercive manipulation was not, however, a path often taken. Canton, for example, never resorted to such blatant techniques. At least officially, rustication at almost all times up to the present day has required voluntary applications in Canton. But this "volunteeriza-tion" of the program was never entirely successful, since it remained obvious that most of the volunteers were compelled to go due to their own economic circumstances. The government acknowledged as much in the mid 1960s in a high-level Party directive to officials stating that "Youths with family [financial] difficulties and in urgent need of em-ployment should be the first to be mobilized to go to the countryside."[26] In 1965, as an increasing proportion of the bad-class youths found them-selves rejected by senior high schools, they too became prime candidates for persuasion. The argument implicitly was presented to them that by going they could prove their loyalty to socialism and chart out their own futures less encumbered by their family histories.

Despite the rustication campaign's overt rhetoric, the countryside by 1965 was coming to serve largely as a dumping grounds for the cities' failures: the impoverished unemployed and the bad-class youngsters. Overcrowded villages resented that the urban areas were unloading their surplus population onto the peasant communities, spreading even thinner the rural collectives' meager resources. A group of young settlers from Jiangmen, for example, were told bluntly by an angry peasant cadre that "Good people don't come to the countryside; even your family origins are bad. . . . 99 percent of you are beyond salvation! You came here because you couldn't make a living in Jiangmen!"[28]

This notion that rusticating youths were discarded "failures" of the cities was reinforced in many of the youths' own minds by the very structure of the educational system which they had so recently left. A group of them later were to complain in a Red Guard newspaper that the "movement of going to the rural areas is subordinate to the old educational system. Schools at a higher level selected and accepted students who were 'excellent in [political] conduct and [academic] study' and the to-the-countryside movement accepted the dregs."[29] Notably, as the numbers obliged to rusticate increased and as the program became less truly voluntary, the less did rustication seem a "glorious" ideological challenge and the more it took on the mirror-image of a purgatory for urban rejects.[30]

As yet, only a small minority of the graduating students and unemployed young people actually were going to the countryside. But it was apparent to Canton's residents that the numbers already far exceeded the exodus of the depression years. In 1962, during the depths of the bad times, no more than a thousand of Canton's graduating secondary school students had left for the villages, and more than half of these were actually peasants' children returning to their home villages.[31] By contrast, in 1964, the first year of Canton's return to normal economic conditions, 11,000 new emigrants were dispatched—and almost all of them were from urban homes.[33]

Ninety percent of the volunteers of 1964, however, were unemployed urban youths, not recently graduated students. And most of these unemployed teenagers were, at best, primary school graduates (and some not even that) whose chances for urban employment had been badly hurt once junior high school degrees had become commonplace. Secondary school students were not yet seriously affected. Only slightly more than 1,000 of the 11,000 rusticants had volunteered directly from school.[34] This was only about 6 percent of the students in 1964's graduating junior and senior high school classes.[35] Nevertheless, it was by far the highest absolute number in the city's history; and it looked like a record that would be annually surpassed. In 1965, the final year before the Cultural Revolution, 5,100 out of the 12,000 rusticants from Canton were going directly from graduating classes.[36] This was five times the 1964 record, and comprised about a quarter of the entire city's graduating high school students. The handwriting was clearly on the wall for their younger brothers and sisters still in school.

THE PROCLIVITY TO TAKE RISKS

In short, junior high school students in the mid-sixties increasingly faced the prospect that if they entered a regular senior high school they were likely to lose out in the competition to enter a university or even to stay in the city. With the class line strengthening, this was especially threatening for the middle-class and bad-class students. Alternatively, the graduating junior high school student could apply to a specialist school. Since in Guangdong such schools still took entrance examinations strongly into account, these schools were still accessible to middle-class and even bad-class students. Entry would assure them a reasonable career. Yet the great majority of the better students continued to compete to get into the academic-track senior high schools.

A prime reason was that many of them held onto unrealistic notions of their own personal chances for success. Most interviewees had expected that they would be among the lucky ones who got into a university (a belief found, too, among the students of other countries). As one young man recollects:

> I was confident I stood a chance of going to a university. I didn't think much about my career. I just let things happen. When and if problems came one day, I'd figure them out then. I was only thinking of going to a university.

But what of their parents? The urban white-collar classes more than any other groups should have been aware of the sharply increasing competition in both the educational system and the job market.

It may be helpful here to look back in history. In traditional China, this same type of all-too-hopeful academic risk-taking activity was commonplace. In the nineteenth century, as the historian Frederic Wakeman notes,

> each of the two million students waiting outside the prefectural examination halls of the empire in any given year knew that he had only one chance in six thousand of ever reaching the top rank where a bureaucratic post would be guaranteed him. [But] so honored was the title that the remotest chance of acquiring it spurred millions of scholars, year after year, to study for the examinations.[37]

Too much should not be made of this analogy. Certainly, Canton in the 1960s was far removed socially, politically, and economically from the days of the Manchu dynasty. But like some of their own great-grandfathers, the students of middle-class origins were bent on securing the high prestige and image of the well-educated man. In the modern era, this largely meant pursuing the technocratic professions of socialist China. I got the feeling from many of my interviewees that had they been consciously and realistically aware of the odds against themselves, they still would have made the attempt.

This is not necessarily a uniquely Chinese phenomenon, either. In many other nations, middle- or upper-class traditions grant high status to the titles and jobs associated with higher education. Nor are these simply cases of economic pragmatism. Even where it no longer pays to pursue higher degrees, the children of such classes persist in the effort, as in socialist Czechoslovakia.[38] Whereas some observers of Third World education argue that the "diploma disease" largely can be cured by reducing the importance of general-education diplomas in the urban job market, we suggest here that it might not be so easy to remedy the "disease" just through that. Reforms in hiring practices or in a school system's structure will not necessarily dampen the middle and upper classes' quest.

CHAPTER THREE

Flawed Reforms: Rural and Urban Alternatives to the Regular Ladder

THROUGHOUT THE 1950s, the Ministry of Education had been under pressure to satisfy two different demands: to produce contingents of highly trained experts for China's modernization; and to provide for a greatly broadened mass education. But the funds available for education were limited, and painful choices between these two demands constantly had to be made. During the more "radical" periods such as the Great Leap Forward (and later in the Cultural Revolution's aftermath) when economic development strategies were directed toward mass mobilization and grass-roots economic development, the government's decisions veered toward greater attention to mass education. During the more "conservative" periods, when the government shifted toward bureaucratic planning and drives for modernization, relatively greater attention in education was paid to the need for higher-level expertise.

The dilemma was ever-present, though, and it was always one of finances. Party officials were anxious to devise a system that would cut the costs of education to the point that they could have it both ways, providing adequately for both higher and lower schooling. Two such programs were attempted from the late 1950s through the mid-1960s. The first of these was a rural half-farming/half-study system, and the second was an urban 10-year experimental curriculum. Both were attempted in a major way. But it was evident by the eve of the Cultural

Revolution in 1966 that neither of them could succeed on their own terms. The programs were stymied by their need to compete at a comparative disadvantage against the 12-year primary/secondary school ladder. In tracing their failures we shall see something important about the difficulties any other developing nation will face if it tries to establish programs that ignore the pull of the regular educational ladder. We shall also observe how certain aspects of these attempted Chinese reforms became, in ways not quite envisioned by their original proponents, points of inspiration for the radicals within the Party. As such, these failed programs would become touchstones for Chinese educational policy ater the Cultural Revolution.

THE DILEMMA OF URBAN VERSUS RURAL: THE SOLUTION OF THE RURAL HALF-FARMING/HALF-STUDY SCHOOLS

The issue of whether to emphasize the universalization of education was, by the 1960s, largely a question of whether the cities or the countryside should receive the bulk of the education expenditures. On the one side, cities like Canton had already universalized not only primary education but junior high school education as well. The best senior high schools were concentrated in the cities; and the great majority of the students going on to the universities were from the cities. In the Chinese countryside, meanwhile, as of 1965 upward of thirty million school-aged children were still without any primary education whatsoever.[1]

The administrators in charge of national education policies were perhaps sympathetic to the educational needs of the countryside; at the very least they vociferously claimed to be. Yet even during periods when the government pursued rural-oriented policies, as in the Great Leap Forward, state funds did *not* pour into the countryside to expand the rural school systems. (This consistently has remained the case up to the present day.)

In the 1960s the reasons for this urban bias in educational funding were several:

(1) The cities already possessed a developed educational infrastructure. To put a similar infrastructure into the countryside would take extensive administrative resources. Funds continued to go more conveniently into the urban educational channels already erected.

(2) The government had inherited strongly urban-oriented policies from the 1950s. The state's five year development plans of 1951 and 1956 had indicated that large numbers of specialists would be required by the modernizing economy. These demands took precedence in budget decisions over the plans for rural mass education. Since rural primary schooling could claim less direct benefits to the economy, it could be "put off" until China could better afford it. Between 1949 and 1962, while both secondary school and university enrollments increased six-fold, primary school enrollments went up only four times.[2] This was the case even though the cost per student at these higher schools was far heavier than for elementary education, as can be seen in the table 3-1.[3] The result was that in 1963 fully 60 percent of China's education funds were going into secondary and university programs.[4] And it must have seemed cost-effective to the authorities to give the urban high school systems most of the funding for secondary education, since urban young people whose parents were literate tended academically to be considerably better than the rural teenagers.

(3) Even when it became clear in the 1960s that the supply of urban senior high school graduates was becoming overlarge, the program that was already in place proved resistant to cutbacks. Everywhere throughout the late-developing world the story has been the same. Urban constituencies generally have greater clout politically than peasant villages; and in China, as elsewhere, a lot of urban parents were still desperately intent upon getting their children into a senior high school. As a study of Third World education notes, moreover: "The city is the home of those who largely control educational policy." The end result is that "In Ghana . . . the population in cities of over 50,000 had fourteen times more chance of entering a fifth [year] of secondary education than did the people in villages of under 5,000."[5]

(4) A final reason why more of the Chinese government's funds were not put into rural education was that the rural areas could be made to support their own local school systems. The Chinese rural economy is based on peasant production cooperatives, called production teams, which control the proceeds from their own harvests.[6] The government could try to get the peasantry to tap these local proceeds to erect their own village schools. With the central government always hard pressed for funds, this solution has appealed strongly to all factions in the leadership.[7] Well before the Cultural Revolution, "self-reliance" became a government slogan for village education.

The question for a great many years was what shape such locally

Table 3-1. Costs of Educating, Per Year
(National Figures, 1963)

Primary school pupil	38 yuan
High school student	106 yuan
University student	784 yuan

financed education should take. Drawing upon the Yenan experience of the 1930s and 1940s, various forms of "irregular,"* inexpensive, locally sponsored schools for peasant children were established in the early 1950s outside the regular state-run school system.[8] When during the Great Leap Forward a massive drive was launched to expand rural education, much of the effort went into enlarging the boundaries of these "irregular" types of schooling. Especially prominent play was given to a system of newly devised half-farming/half-study schools.[9]

First appearing in March 1958, these half-and-half schools spread rapidly throughout the rural districts. By 1960, 2.9 million students were enrolled, fully 27 percent of the junior high school enrollments in China.[10] These were tiny, scattered, hastily improvised schools that averaged only three teachers apiece. But their patent advantage was that their student bodies, by laboring part-time on school-managed lands, could help finance their own schooling. Hence, even though this new half-and-half system initially was opposed by cautious ministry personnel, it subsequently won their acceptance as a means of achieving rural mass education with a minimum of financial problems. At the same time there was strong radical support for this new half-and-half program, in that it integrated labor into schooling, fulfilling the Leap's dream of melding "manual with mental."

Similar to the half-and-half agricultural secondary schools were the even greater numbers of new part-time primary schools. Often called "simplified primary schools," they offered just a couple of daily classes taught by locally recruited teachers, usually themselves only primary school graduates. As with the half-and-half secondary schools, their facilities were often crude: a hastily erected shack or the floor of a barn.

Most of these vast locally funded programs folded as the Great Leap Forward collapsed into the economic depression of 1960-62. With the

* "Irregular" is a chinese term (bu-zheng-gui) denoting, sometimes with disdain, that a school does not conform to the curricula or meet the standards established by the state's education bureaus.

villages straining their resources simply to prevent serious malnutrition, the new elementary schools must have looked to many village officials like unneeded luxuries. The half-and-half secondary schools, for their part, had owed their rapid expansion in the Great Leap partly to the fact that the necessities of life, such as food, had been temporarily distributed free of charge. Once the depression struck, the free food distributions stopped, and many of the students dropped out of school to take up full-time work in their production team's fields (at about 70 percent of a full adult wage). Unlike state-run schools, the half-and-half schools were financially dependent on this teenage labor, and the schools fell apart when enrollments declined. Only a small portion of them survived the depression. By 1964 the state-run primary and secondary schools accounted for the great majority of the rural schools that remained.[11]

These state-financed schools were often located in the commune market towns and county capitals rather than in peasant villages per se. They were similar to their urban counterparts, with their curricula oriented toward the entrance examinations of the next-higher levels of schooling. In the 1960s there seems to have been growing disquiet in official circles about this curriculum, especially at the secondary level. Only a small percentage of the rural secondary-school graduates were succeeding in getting into a university, and for all those who did not get admitted there were few jobs any longer available outside of farming. In the 1950s such students had normally been employed in the rural administrative infrastructure. But these county and commune staff positions had gradually been filled and overfilled. China's urban enterprises were simultaneously becoming overstaffed to such an extent that the state erected residence barriers in 1958 to prevent any further influxes of rural job seekers into the cities. Consequently, increasing numbers of the graduates of rural high schools in the 1960s were being forced back into the villages from which they had come.

Complaints began cropping up in the press over the discontent and maladjustment of such youths to rural life.[12] Complaints were heard even about the primary-school graduates who were returning from studying at their commune market towns.[13] In these circumstances the national educational authorities became increasingly alert to the attractions of an educational framework suited better to rural life. The failed half-and-half experiment seemed to provide a ready-made solution.

The ministries of education and agriculture saw the revival of such a program as resolving five major questions simultaneously:

(1) how to detach most of rural education from the university-ori-

ented educational ladder, since the countryside was the weak link in that system;

(2) how to reorient the rural students' expectations and attitudes;

(3) how to provide the manpower skills needed by the villages;

(4) how to spread mass education in the rural districts and, related to this,

(5) how to raise the numbers of good-class children in school.[14]

In August 1964, the Party Central Committee passed a directive sponsored by Liu Shaoqi calling for a resurgence of the half-farming/half-study schooling.[15] An upsurge in half-and-half rural education followed, inspiring the parallel expansion in "irregular" factory-run technical schools in China's cities that we observed in chapter 2.

As of 1964, the premises underlying the "irregular" rural schools seemed to have appealed to both moderates and radicals alike. All factions, after all, wanted to expand rural education without adding to the state's expenditures, and the statistics on financing the half-and-half schools spoke clearly to the issue. A nationally touted investigation of a dozen high schools in one rural Guangdong county (my figures come from a 1964 talk by Mao Zedong) revealed that it cost the state fifteen times more per year to support a student at a regular county senior high (and eleven times more at a junior high) than at this county's half-and-half agricultural secondary school.[16]

When a campaign is seriously mounted in China the speed with which results are achieved can be astounding. With the officials of each county, commune and village pressed by the Party to organize whatever schooling they could, and with an economically reviving countryside hungry for increased educational opportunities, there was a veritable explosion in the number of rural half-and-half schools in Guangdong. This can be seen in table 3-2. Within one and a half years, a fifth of all the primary school children in Guangdong and a third of all the secondary school students were enrolled in new "irregular" part-time rural schools.[17]

But a glance at the table reveals also that by May 1965 or even earlier, the expansion in the simplified primary school system had tapered off. Since young children would not be able to generate much revenue for their primary school through field labor, a new primary school still seemed too expensive a proposition to the officials of Guangdong's poorest villages. Moreover, since China's peasants raise livestock privately and can engage in private cottage industries, small children can earn much-needed money by staying home; in one village cited by the press, children earned half or more of an adult's income by minding their

Table 3-2. The Expansion in Guangdong's "Irregular" Rural School System

Date of Report	Simplified Primary Schools	½/½ Agricultural Secondary Schools	Agricultural Labor Universities*
End of 1959[a]		875 schools (70,000 students)	
1961–62[b]		140 schools (14,000 students)	4 labor universities
August 1963[c]		119 schools (15,000 students)	
August 1964		Central Committee's "Two Systems" directive	
September 1964[d]	16,000 schools		
October 1964[e]		774 schools (70,000 students)	57 universities (5,000 students)
February 1965[f]		1,000+ schools (80,000 students)	
May 1965[g]	36,000 schools		87 universities
August 1965[h]			
October 1965[i]	36,000+ schools (1,234,000 pupils)	1,350 schools	
November 1965[j]	37,900 schools (1,390,000 pupils)	2,629 schools (197,000 students)	
January 1966[k]			115 universities (20,000 students)

SOURCES: [a]*Shang You* (Canton), January 25, 1960; [b]*Zhongguo Xinwen* (Canton), January 19, 1966; [c]*Zhongguo Xinwen*, August 19, 1963; [d]*Yangcheng Wanbao* (Canton), October 19, 1965; [e]Canton Radio, October 6, 1964, in *NCPRS*; [f]Canton, Radio, February 21, 1965, in *NCPRS*; [g]Canton Radio, October 20, 1965, in *NCPRS*; [h]*Xing Dao Ribao* (Hong Kong), August 8, 1965, citing Peking's *Guangming Ribao*; [i]*Yangcheng Wanbao*, October 19, 1965; also *Wen Hui Bao* (Hong Kong), October 12, 1965; [j]*Zhongguo Xinwen*, January 19, 1966; also *Wen Hui Bao* (H.K.), November 21, 1965; [k]Canton Radio, January 5, 1966, in *NCPRS*.
NOTE: Guangdong's total rural population stood in early 1966 at 34 million (*NCNA*, February 19, 1966, in *SCMP* 3644).

 * These rural half-and-half labor universities were run by districts and counties. Modeled on the Jiangxi Province network to which Mao had given strong support during the prior years of depression, they received students nominated by the party branches of their local units and sent the graduates back to these same units—what was called the "from the commune, to the commune" policy. After the Cultural Revolution, this policy and its slogan were trumpeted as "newborn things of the Cultural Revolution." But like many Cultural Revolution innovations, it was, as seen here, already rooted in a pre-Cultural Revolution program.

families' pigs and geese.[18] In the poorer villages, many families could not afford to forego this income.

At least a quarter and probably considerably more than a quarter of the province's rural children remained outside any sort of primary classes.[19] The irony was that the best-off villages also tended to be the ones already possessing government-financed schools.[20] The new programs persuaded the middle range of villages to foot their own school programs and left the poorest villages unwilling to participate.

Even in the broad middle range of villages—according to several former rural schoolteachers interviewed in Hong Kong—the peasants did *not* view education as providing any real economic advantages for their children. But a respect for education has deep roots in China, and the peasantry of these somewhat better-off districts could afford to see schooling as a desired commodity in its own right: their sons (girls were enrolled much less frequently)[21] would be better men for being able to read and write. In the richer districts, this view seems to have created a "bandwagon" effect even in terms of enrollments at the half-and-half secondary schools.

In addition, in such districts there was a certain competition for local jobs at stake: for junior-cadre positions such as work-point recorder, team cashier, accountant, etc. Such posts brought in little or no extra family income, but they did bestow on their occupants a modest degree of prestige and individual authority. More than that, they provided a route by which young people could escape a lifetime of gruelling fulltime field labor.

In some cases the local authorities were actually deluged with more applicants than the new schooling could accommodate. The "class line" was then brought into effect; local rules sometimes literally forebade entry to the children of the former rich peasants and landlords. The news media wrote approvingly of such rules. From the educational administrators' perspective, the half-and-half system, being both terminal and geared to the provision of low-level rural office-holders, had better reason than most other parts of the educational system to give precedence to the Chinese revolution's "class" goals. It was proudly revealed in the news media that well over 90 percent of the youths in Guangdong's half-and-half agricultural secondary schools were from the homes of former poor and low-middle peasants.[22]

In other respects, the hopes expressed for the new half-and-half schooling in Chinese news editorials resembled the type of schooling that many educational reformers in the Third World have advocated.

Like them, the Chinese were concerned to redirect the students' coursework and expectations back toward their own villages. The schools' financial need to have the students do farm labor dovetailed nicely with this. To take advantage of this labor, the curricula of the schools were adapted to the agricultural cycles of the local district, with the students at their desks during slack seasons and in the fields when the peak agricultural seasons arrived. Additional work usually was interspersed with the schooling, with laboring and studying reserved for alternate days, or mornings against afternoons, or in weekly rotation.

The proposed school curriculum was supposed to contain some of the usual junior high school subjects, such as the regular Chinese language course. But the math was to be linked to surveying techniques and bookkeeping, and the chemistry and biology were to be geared to lessons in soil characteristics, fertilizer application, seed culture, and crop protection. Most of these school lessons were to be tied directly into the fieldwork. The teacher was supposed to interrupt the labor sessions to point out improved techniques and was supposed to bring classes out into the fields during class periods to conduct crop experiments. Those were, at least, the hopes.

The Party leadership was in agreement on the desirability of this type of curriculum and the fiscal benefits of half-and-half schooling. But the radical Party intellectuals, unlike some of their colleagues in the leadership, believed that labor within the schools would have an additional profound merit—an ethical import. Whereas in Marx it is the methodical rigor of industrial work which helps shape proletarian consciousness, with the Chinese leftists it is simply the sweat and tempering of hard labor. For this, the countryside is even more appropriate than the factory. A 1965 conference on the half-and-half schools in Guangdong hence instructed that even agricultural secondary schools in overcrowded districts which had no real need for extra labor "should seriously organize the students to participate in labor, for the purpose of achieving transformed men."[23] (As we shall later see, post-Cultural Revolution labor was to be structured around this same notion—and often had few educational or economic benefits attached.)

With the more "Maoist" wing of the Party throwing its weight behind such concepts, selected parts of the regular full-time educational structure began to be shifted toward the half-and-half program. In mid-1965 it was announced that all the full-time agricultural senior high schools, which had been devised in the image of the Russian model, would be converted into half-and-half schools,[24] and the university-level agricultural institutes began following suit.[25] By the close of 1965 nearly 10,000 students at other types of institutes in Peking had also adopted the half-and-half structure, with engineering students put to work in factories both on campus and off.[26]

In the rural half-and-half schools, however, this concept of intermingling labor with studies did not enjoy an entirely enthusiastic response from the peasants. The peasants' view of their children's education was, like the peasants' view of physical labor, rather more mundane than the Party philosophers'. The primary benefits of the half-and-half system to rural parents were the lower costs and the greater availability of school places. But the labor was *not* often seen by parents (if we may be permitted to read between the lines of media reports of that period) as either morally invigorating or as improving their children's agricultural skills. What they saw instead was that the children had less schooling than in the regular junior high schools. Worse yet, the students had to spend time doing free work for the school, which the parents could otherwise put profitably to use on the family's own private endeavors. Tussles between the peasant parents and the schools sometimes ensued, with the parents wanting the schools to pay at least something for the work and the schools (and the state behind them) wanting to reduce educational costs by securing the students' labor free.[27]

Some parents felt, too, that they were paying for second best, that what counted in education were the academic skills of increased literacy, math, and so forth—among other things, the skills legitimized by the regular schools—and that when it came to transmitting such academic knowledge and skills, the poor quality of teachers at the new schools and the reduced time appropriated to academic studies led to mediocre results.[28] If possible, they wanted more of a "regular" education for their children, as defined by the curricula and educational concerns of the regular schools.

The half-and-half schools, being locally initiated and financed and therefore swayed by local opinion, tended to respond somewhat to such parental complaints. This was particularly the case since, as the Chinese press itself kept admitting, these opinions were shared by many of the teachers at the new schools and by many administrators in the lower echelons of the educational bureaucracy. The teachers feared that their own status suffered because the status of their schools compared badly with the regular schools. The administrators were concerned with "standards" and were afraid that the education system in their districts was slipping away from "proper" educational control.[29] In keeping with the combined preferences of teachers, lower officials, and parents, many of the half-and-half schools began to edge toward (or tried to adopt from the start) the type of "regular" education that the full-day schools provided.

The provincial authorities found themselves trapped between their own initial hopes for a village-oriented schooling and their need to make the half-and-half schools more credible to parents as real centers of education. This had serious implications for the schools. As just one important example, had Guangdong Province officially denied the rural students access to the regular educational ladder, it would have been tantamount to verifying their inferior educational status; so even though very few of the rural half-and-half secondary-school students had either the financial resources or the hopes of going on to further education, Guangdong had had to provide from the very first that "graduates from [half-and-half] agricultural secondary schools may take the entrance examinations to go to senior high schools and universities."[30] But such a regulation had had the effect of throwing the half-and-half schools into direct comparison with the regular schools. And in terms of the standards of classroom teaching which the half-and-half schools actually ended up providing (very often the same core courses as the regular junior high schools, plus a course on "agricultural knowledge"), the half-and-half schools *were* inferior, as even the articles in the mass media implicitly acknowledged. The coursework in the half-and-half schools, trying simultaneously to accommodate two different goals, was falling short on both: it was neither sufficiently oriented toward the half-and-half programs' purported purpose of supplying only knowledge useful in rural life, nor able to provide a proper education as defined by the regular schools.

By the time of the Cultural Revolution the half-and-half structure had gained the opposition of the "Maoists," who attacked the program in their essays not because of any intrinsic drawbacks in the system but rather because the broader educational milieu in which it operated had led so many of these schools to move away from the hopes the Party's radicals had placed in them. They seem to have felt that the half-and-half system could only succeed if all the schools were converted to half-and-half—if the paradigm provided by the full-time schools disappeared. They believed it was this comparison which caused students and parents to see the half-and-half program's extensive schedule of labor as a "price" that they had to pay—a price that they could see the preferred full-day schools doing largely without. The issue, as the radicals came to see it, was the Liu Shaoqi and company were using the half-work/half-study program as an inexpensive sop to the laboring classes. (Such accusations were leveled even against Liu's advocacy of the urban half-and-half vocational schools.)[31] As a Cultural Revolution essay put it,

> his "two types of educational systems" was but a reprint of the "double-track system" of the capitalist countries of "education for the talented" and "education for the laborers."[32]

In short, Party radicals had concluded that the program had—purposely—been second best in a two-halved structure and had been poisoned as a result. Their attack was on the idea that Chinese education could "walk on two legs." The radicals in effect denied the possibility and, even before the Cultural Revolution, had demanded an end to China's full-day schools.[33] Reforms of education, they believed, could only take place in an environment dominated by those reforms. It was a notion which after the Cultural Revolution they were to pursue, along with the large doses of labor associated with the half-and-half schools, even in the cities of China.

EXPERIMENTAL SCHOOLS AND THE STRATEGY OF COMPRESSED CURRICULA

The second major form of new schooling in the 1960s was the 10-year Experimental School which, like the half-and-half system, had grown out of efforts to introduce a less expensive means of education. As we shall see, this 10-year structure, again similar to the half-and-half program, became bent through competition with the regular educational ladder. Once more like the half-and-half system, it was to be transformed by Party radicals and used as one of the bases for post-Cultural Revolution education.

During the Hundred Flowers of the spring of 1957 and again during the Great Leap, there had been debate as to whether the course of study in Chinese schools could be made shorter.[34] The People's Republic had inherited a system of 12-year schooling based on American practices, and the model that was pointed to as preferable was the socialist schooling of the Soviet Union. Russia had been using a 10-year primary/secondary school program since the 1930s, but in 1958 Chinese attention was caught anew by Khrushchev's well-publicized reforms of Soviet schools and the new talk in Soviet educational circles about the possibilities of teaching children at a more rapid rate and a higher level of difficulty.[35]

As we shall observe, different groupings in the Chinese Communist Party extracted from these Russian ideas quite different messages on what a compressed curriculum and faster learning entailed. But there was broad agreement that a primary/secondary-school curriculum shortened to 9 or 10 years might provide a solution to the same fiscal problem that the half-and-half schools had sought to resolve: how to provide a widened mass education without having to cut back on higher education. If the school curriculum could be shortened by 20 percent, that meant, after all, that 20 percent more students could be passed through the available classrooms and teachers with little extrà cost.

In keeping with this idea, the various Party leaders had convinced themselves, probably to an exaggerated degree, that China's 12-year educational curriculum contained a large quantity of "waste" which, if remedied, could cut years off the regular coursework without ill effect: that textbooks could be made somehow clearer, leaner, and simpler; that courses could be streamlined and their unimportant lessons deleted; that the more minor courses could be merged or cut out altogether.

Again akin to the half-and-half program, this proposed 10-year compressed system initially also was meant to provide a schooling that did not unduly interfere with the labor potential of teenagers. Vice-premier Lu Dingyi, who at the time was concurrently head of the Party's propanganda bureaus and chief Party spokesman on educational affairs,[36] was arguing enthusiastically that children possessed the innate intellectual capacity to begin their primary-school experiences at 6 rather than the customary age of 7, and through a nine or ten-year course could graduate from senior high school at the ages of 15 to 17.[37] Lu Dingyi seemed to be arguing that freeing all youths entirely from secondary school at the point when their labor value became mature could take the place of having youths working part-time and studying part-time for a few years extra.

In the Great Leap period, Lu Dingyi and his associates had thrown their support behind half-and-half schooling, but they had seen it as a temporary expedient.[38] They remained resolutely opposed to the radicals' notion of swinging wholesale toward half-and-half education. Their concern was to retain a quality education that could feed readily into high-level tertiary training, so as to be able to produce a new generation of high-quality technocrats. But at the same time, like the Party radicals, they were aiming greatly to enlarge the student population, so as to bring in more of the worker-peasant youths. The experimental 10-year schooling was an effort to combine what they considered to be a high-quality academic training *with* universalization, an expectation which was to prove quite at odds with the outlook of the Party's "Maoists."

For one thing, their views on the purposes of education diverged considerably. Lu Dingyi and the Education Minister, Yang Xiufeng, seem to have represented a strain of Party thinking which was entranced with science. They felt that the route to China's development lay largely through "modernization" and improved expertise, requiring more advanced manpower-training programs. Nowhere was this perspective propounded more clearly than in a brace of speeches the two men delivered to a session of the Second National People's Congress in 1960, in which they itemized their hopes for the newly devised 10-year experiments.[39] To read speeches such as that of Education Minister Yang is, at certain points, to hear echoes of the American dreams for education following Sputnik. Yang was proposing that the 10-year curriculum should so stress the hard sciences and math that it would be possible to "transfer downward" into the proposed 10-year secondary schools a number of university-level subjects: not only analytic geometry and differential and integral calculus, but also the study of transistorization, nuclear physics, rare elements, and heavy atomic particles! (In compensation, the social sciences were to be cut back sharply, with history and geography compressed into a couple of brief courses; the teaching of "politics" received barely a nod.)

This type of education was to be not just for a small group of elite students preparing for university but, rather, for an eventual dreamed-of production of 10 million senior-high graduates per year. Since science and technological know-how would, they believed, pave China's road to modernity, it would be useful for *all* of the younger generation of Chinese to be able to comprehend and apply sophisticated scientific concepts. They thought of it as a forward-looking vocational training, as it were.

At the other end of the spectrum of views within the Party stood Mao and a group of radical followers who were to become influential in education after the Cultural Revolution. They took an entirely skeptical view of the need for rigorous training in the sciences—and had, in fact, little appreciation for either science or technology. While Lu Dingyi and Education Minister Yang had wanted to transform mass education into the image of an expertise-oriented elite education, the Maoists conversely would later transform all education into the image of a mass, terminal, ethics-oriented education, with short shrift paid to the "bourgeois book-learning" of the experts. After the Cultural Revolution they would incorporate the idea of an abbreviated curriculum (Canton in the mid-1970s offered a total of only ten years of schooling), but fitted to their own ideals. Labor—purifying practice—was to take the place of honor rather than the high-level science and math theory beloved by Lu and Yang. Hence, instead of posing the 10-year system against the half-and-half system, as had Lu Dingyi at one point, the Maoists were to *combine* the concept of fewer years of schooling with the labor-heavy curriculum of the initial half-and-half concept, leaving little time at all for any academic study. Moreover, rather than trying to intensify the learning process, as Lu and Yang had proposed, the radicals were to attempt to simplify drastically what was learned, for the benefit of the working-class children from illiterate homes who had difficulties at school. Schoolwork after the Cultural Revolution was to become a means for leveling differences among youths, not so much a means for modernizing China. We shall return to these themes at a later juncture.

As of 1960, Lu Dingyi and Yang Xiufeng held sway as the Party's spokesmen on education, and the 10-year experimental schooling was a project under their own initial guidance. Cautious men, they proposed that 10 or 20 years of experimentation would be necessary before all of China's schools could convert to the new compressed model. To carry out these years of testing and refining, they turned as a first step to favorably contrived key-point schools, in keeping with the normal way of proceeding with innovations in China. Fifty special combined primary/secondary schools would pioneer their 10-year system.[40]

The education departments of both Guangdong Province and Canton each wanted a site under its own jurisdiction, and so in 1960-61 two such special elite experimental points were established in Canton. To bolster their own department's prestige through success in the experiment, each school took to recruiting only students of very high acedemic calibre. With fine students provided with experienced teachers and excellent equipment and buildings, the scene was well set to demonstrate the workability of Lu Dingyi's and Yang Xiufeng's ideas.

However, these two experimental schools did not end up abiding by the initial proposals for educational reform. Instead, the schools shortly accommodated themselves to the prevailing educational framework—just as many of the half-and-half schools had done.

The difficulty was that the experimental school system could neither ignore nor attempt to have its students bypass the university entrance examinations. After all, one of the principal goals set for the schools was to legitimize 10-year schools on the grounds of academic accomplishment—and success through this examination system was the criterion by which urban China was accustomed to judging a school's worth. Yet once committed to competing for high levels of passes, the experimental schools found themselves caught up on China's regular educational ladder. If an experimental school could not assure its students a likely chance of doing well in these examinations, it would find it more difficult to recruit a good student body: for what upwardly aspiring young people would enroll in a school that might hamper their opportunities for further schooling? With the all-crucial university entrance examinations based on the regular senior-high coursework, the experimental schools would have to adhere more closely to the regular school system's basic curriculum.

Various means can be imagined by which the experimental program could have been extracted from this trap—but it is perhaps a telling commentary on the early 1960s that the program became dominated by the ladder. Within the space of only a year or two of their founding, the experimental schools had become fairly much replicas of the best 12-year schools of Canton, following a curriculum rather the same as their competitors. The major remaining difference was that they used abbreviated textbooks of the 10-year system's own devising. These deleted the "frills" of the regular textbooks: that is, deleted the sections that would not turn up on the university entrance examinations. The need to sustain the schools' reputations and their abilities to attract good students had ended up reshaping the experiment itself.

The 10-year experimental schools subsequently tried to show merely that it was possible to compress the curriculum and yet bring students satisfactorily up to the university entrance examination standards. In this the schools did prove themselves in Canton. When the first 5-year high school class of the provincial school graduated in 1965, it secured what was reported to be the second highest rate of university admissions of all the high schools of Guangdong.

But the school had in no way shown that a 10-year curriculum was viable for *typical* senior high students. In point of fact, the provincial school had attained its high university entrance examination scores partly by weeding out and dumping the bottom quarter of its exceptionally bright student body. It had done so through formal tests halfway through the 5-year curriculum, on the grounds that they were not up to the pace demanded of them by the school's accelerated program.[41] The school ended up securing a prestigious name, but at the price of throwing into question the relevance of its results.

During the period of 1960-62, half a dozen of Canton's best 6-year high schools started equivalent 5-year programs in several of their classrooms, and here as much as in the special experimental schools the programs became shaped by the standards established by the regular educational ladder. These key-point schools had wanted to participate in the new innovations in order to boost their own reputations, and they took steps similar to the Provincial Experimental School. As a teacher from an excellent 6-year-track Shanghai school recalls:

> For our school's accelerated program they chose the *best* students in the school, since they wanted the school to be famous for having conducted such an experiment successfully.

However, such schools in Canton soon began dropping the program, one after another, beginning as early as 1963-64. Despite their precautions, it appears they had come to the opinion that their programs' results would not enable them to become more "famous"; sticking to the regular 12-year system would provide higher rates of university admissions and hence safer payoffs to their reputations.[42]

It had not taken long for the 10-year curriculum, as with the half-and-half program, to be defeated by the pull of the 12-year ladder. Curriculum reforms could not readily surmount the broader Chinese educational milieu, where a school's standing was measured by its success in conforming to the educational standards laid down by higher-school examinations. There was, in short, a large degree of justice to one of the charges leveled during the Cultural Revolution against the university entrance examinations:

> The failure to thoroughly carry through . . . educational reforms was due to the fact that these university selection examinations have provided the ultimate ends for the education system.[43]

The radicals among China's leaders would be acting on that notion—dramatically.

CONCLUSIONS

Of what relevance to Third World schooling are the findings of this chapter? We have just observed that the strong influence of China's higher-school exams on rural and urban education did not stem simply from the fact that diplomas were needed for modern-sector jobs. In fact, we have noted that in China's countryside secondary school diplomas were of scant use; even the full-day senior-high graduates had little chance of getting out of the villages permanently. Moreover, in the cities the government tried to favor working-class youths by making factory jobs as readily available to junior-high as to senior-high graduates. And though the contest for diplomas did directly concern the students at the elite experimental schools who were vying to enter a university and a *high*-level career, even here we have seen that the experimental schools were pushed into the entrance-exam arena in the first place because the education officials felt they had to demonstrate to the public that the new program could provide as good an education in 10 years as the old system had in 12 years.

In short, we have observed that both the rural half-and-half schools and the urban experimental schools were pulled back toward the standards set by the higher-school exams and toward the curriculum of the regular academic track because that curriculum and its exam system defined what the public and school staffs took to be the *legitimate* system of schooling. Neither of these failed reforms could buck that sense of where educational legitimacy and quality lay.

If this generally is the case, educational reforms in the Third World which try to eradicate the "diploma disease" will have to do more than weaken the linkage between academic-track diplomas and job-hiring practices, as a number of the more thoughtful educational reformers have proposed. Any serious reform efforts would *also* have to try to alter the entire way the general public is accustomed to judging a school system. It was this that defeated the Chinese government's reforms of the sixties.

CHAPTER FOUR

Memorization and Tests

A NUMBER of scholars have argued—correctly, I think—that a great deal of the current stress on memorization in Third World schools is induced by competition to climb the education ladder.[1] With the schools intent upon promoting as many pupils as possible into higher schools, students from their earliest years of study learn to consider education as the memorization of facts in order to pass classroom tests that are preparations for the all-important selection examinations for higher-level schools. Because this pattern is so commonly found around the world, some observers viewing a Third World school system would go so far as to presume that classroom *test*-oriented memorization and *ladder*-oriented (that is, selection-examination-oriented) memorization are practically one and the same thing. But the distinction is important.

China is a good example here. The pre-Cultural Revolution school system would at first blush seem to provide an obvious example of ladder-oriented learning. China had a competitive ladder and an elaborate structure of tests and grading. Its students engaged in what British or American students would consider an inordinate amount of memorization, especially in the lower levels of schooling. In fact, it would be difficult to find a primary school system in the Third World whose pupils put in as many hours in rote learning as China's urban children did in the 1960s. Even in the secondary schools a great many of Canton's students blindly memorized an unholy proportion of their course work, word by numbing word.

Yet this rote learning was *not* primarily encouraged by a concern with selection examinations or credentials. In fact, it becomes evident in examining Canton's primary schools that a very high degree of test orientation and a great deal of memorization and cramming was combined with a rather low degree of orientation toward either the graduation examinations or the junior high school selection examinations. We observed in chapter 1 that teachers were under few pressures regarding these examinations once the junior high school system had been near-universalized; and we observed also that most families did not pressure their children to prepare for the examinations, since only a minority of the parents were eager for their children to enter a key-point junior high school. Instead, the lower schools in China were *starting* with the premise that great amounts of memorization are good and necessary for children. Upon this basis they were consciously erecting an intricate test and grading system to spur the desired rote learning.

ROTE LEARNING IN PRIMARY SCHOOL

Why this extraordinary stress on memorization? There were at least three reasons specific to China:

(1) One was the nature of Chinese writing. A child learning to read and write is confronted not with 26 letters, but with almost endless streams of complicated characters. As of the mid-1960s, a child leaving primary school was expected to know at least 3,500 of the most frequently used of these.[2] All these characters had to be remembered on sight, and all their strokes had to be registered in the mind through laborious repetition in writing. (For the Cantonese child the chore was even greater. Though the Cantonese dialect was the language of instruction in the primary schools, the children had to learn how each character was pronounced in Mandarin—the very different dialect of north China that is officially promoted as China's common language.) The first several years of schooling depended largely upon the child's discipline in mastering these various difficult tasks. It is little wonder that even in secondary school the children and their teachers often continued to see learning as a similar project: the discipline to memorize words, phrases, and whole chapters.

(2) This practice of committing whole passages to memory has further origins specific to China. A good writing style in Chinese is much more of a stereotyped formula than is, say, written English. In China students learn through memorization the time-tested writing patterns and

learn also how to plug in appropriate ready-made phrases, such as the traditional four-character metaphors (*chengyu*) and the new political idioms. A pre-Cultural Revolution teacher explains this method:

> Sometimes in the four higher grades of primary school, we had the kids memorize whole chapters word for word. By this method the kids learned the sentence patterns and would later be able to use them flexibly. No, the entrance exam for junior high school *didn't* ask students to repeat any of the sentences or passages they had memorized. But some of the questions on the Chinese language (*yuwen*) part of the exam would require short essays or replies in sentence form, and I thought the memorization would help the children in writing good sentences.

Here we have a case where memorization was stressed even though it would have *no* direct application on the examination; indeed, a foreigner might assume that children who occupied their time learning more "creatively" might do better in such an examination. But the view of former Chinese teachers and students was that primary school memorization *led* to a more proper and more creative use of language: that it was, simply, a worthy teaching method and in *this* respect helped the children on the examinations.

This reasoning is observable most readily through descriptions of Chinese primary-school drawing classes, both before and after the Cultural Revolution. Very little improvisation in artwork is permitted—no Western-style striving to bring into play the "creativity" of children. Instead, the teacher draws the picture line by line for all the children to see, and then they try to copy what the teacher has drawn as closely as they can. Only very occasionally are pupils freely allowed to compose their own pictures. Chinese art traditionally has been taught in a similar manner, and it was only when an artist was already quite proficient that he stopped literally copying and began devising his own paintings. "Creativity" has a different connotation in China than it does in the modern West. There was and still is the belief that once the craft becomes mastered through precise practice using commendable models, creative freedom would emerge *within* the bounds of discipline—a freedom derived through familiarity with the usage. This idea quite obviously extends to the learning of a prose style and to other forms of learning throughout a person's life.

(3) Finally, the persistence of rote learning in the schools springs also from an explicitly political/moral cause: namely, the memorization of moral verities is believed by many Chinese to be a way to promote ethical behavior. Traditional education was based upon that very prem-

ise. In Imperial China the classics were held to contain the Truth concerning virtue. He who had committed these ancient texts to memory thereby *knew* the tools of correct behavior and would later be able to bring these tools into use as a magistrate. It was this that provided the rationale for selecting officals through examinations which tested candidates on their remembrance of the ancient moral/philosophical readings. The quantity of memorization that flowed from this principle was stupendous; it has been calculated that the textual material of the classics which had to be memorized for the imperial examinations would have required six years of memorization at the rate of a new 200-character passage every day (with interminable reviews of everything already learned).[3]

Such feats of memory are no longer called for. Mao himself opposed most types of rote learning—he called it "stuffing students like Peking ducks." But the underlying principle still holds. The passages in school primers that are most frequently memorized are those containing moral/political lessons. Thus when "politics" and attitude-formation received priority in the schools after the Cultural Revolution, this last reason for rote learning took on increased importance. The memorization of Mao's Works as the fount of ethical wisdom literally dominated classwork in 1968-70. What this memorized ethical education ideally entailed, even for young children, is illustrated by the following short story from a reading primer used in the early 1970s in the second grade elementary school classes of Guangdong:

> Lei Gang had an illness in his eyes. Reading was uncomfortable, but he loved Chairman Mao. . . . During the day he studied hard at school; at night after going home, he again attentively studied Chairman Mao's works. With a magnifying glass in one hand, pen in the other, he copied character after character. He kept on copying, and when tired sprinkled water over his head and continued to copy. In this manner he copied several tens of thousands of characters of Chairman Mao's quotations and filled several diaries with notes on [his efforts to] study Chairman Mao's Thought. He often said: "Mao's Zedong's Thought is a bright lamp leading the way. After reading Chairman Mao's books I can see everything clearly. Without having read Chairman Mao's books one cannot see clearly even with one's eyes!"[4]

This is all quite traditional. As in the schooling for would-be magistrates of Confucian times, a junior high school student of 1968-70 recalls being taught the saying, "When you raise a pole it casts a shadow." He was instructed this proverb meant that if he read and reread the essays by Mao until these were memorized, when he later had decisions to make the relevant passages would well up in his mind and influence his actions.[5]

In absolute terms, however, rote learning declined in China's elementary schools after the Cultural Revolution. This was because there was noticeably less daily memorization devoted to learning to read and write or to improving children's writing styles. As we shall later observe, education between 1968 and 1977 was used to level the gaps between children; and so instruction was aimed more toward the below-average and average learners in class. The pace of textbook learning was accordingly slowed down, which in turn meant smaller assignments to be memorized each night (and a noticeably smaller reading vocabulary by the end of the fifth year of primary school than in pre-Cultural Revolution times).[6] For this same purpose of leveling differences among children, the quality of the schoolwork of individual children after the Cultural Revolution was downplayed. A fine writing style or superior command of the vocabulary no longer was especially sought, and this too resulted in a reduction in the memorization asked of children.

But in learning to read and write, the teaching techniques of primary schools remained similar to pre-Cultural Revolution times: still the strong reliance on children's rote skills; still the frequent chanting of lessons in unison in the class; and, even though reduced, still what most foreign children would consider a formidable amount of daily homework. The teachers, just as before the Cultural Revolution, had to devise means to motivate their pupils to persist in the drudgery of this learning.

THE STRESS ON SCHOOL MARKS

Canton's schools in the sixties had made full use of a complex network of graded homework, formal commendations of good students, tests, and report cards. The teachers, if we may go by interviews, were convinced they needed such an extensive system to keep the children busily at their work, to pace the children in their progress, and to create a climate where the children's own peer group reinforced the importance of the school work.

This grading program inevitably created two types of problems, so far as the Party's educational leadership was concerned:

(1) As we would expect, children's attitudes apparently were influ-

enced in ways contrary to the spirit of cooperation they were taught in their storybooks. Occasional essays in the newspapers reflected the fear that this would nurture individualistic emotional needs, promoting a politically undesirable "careerism."

(2) Focusing the pupils' attention upon tests and grades helped to build a milieu in the primary schools where children who did well at their schoolwork received a high formal prestige and peer-group respect. There was a "class line" issue at stake here, since middle-class children tended to acquire a status and self-image superior to working-class children.

But the need to provide the teachers with grading tools overrode these qualms about the side-effects, and the grading structure itself was never altered. This included the *daily* grading of homework, to get the children to conscientiously do their two hours or so of daily homework assigments. To push the message that diligent work won teacher and peer-group approval, a small selection of well-done homework papers were exhibited each week on a classroom bulletin board, as models for the other children to emulate. To spur memorization, class tests and quizzes were also frequent—several each week. To oblige pupils to review scrupulously all the lessons they had done, twice each semester (i.e., four times a schoolyear) the children also had formal course examinations. These semester exams were devised jointly by all the teachers in a school who taught the same subject, and school heads used these exam results as a comparative check on the various teachers' performances. (This was true too of secondary-school course examinations.) Teachers pressured their pupils somewhat in turn, which reportedly did accentuate the amount of review-work and memorization that the primary school children put into these classroom examinations.

So too did the possibility of being failed. This was not *intended* as a threat. The official educational philosophy held that it was harmful to humiliate children in front of their classmates for poor schoolwork; and my interviews with former teachers and pupils alike suggest that the urban primary-school teachers almost invariably did use encouragement and praise rather than criticism or punishment to motivate children. In this, Chinese teaching methods in the 1960s differed greatly from schools prior to Liberation or in Taiwan today.[7] But the pupils in China's schools all worked at the same pace out of their schoolbooks, and in a class crowded with fifty children any who had fallen too far behind could only be helped through a repetition of courses. The established rule was, and still is, that those who scored less than 60 percent on the final end-of-year course examinations in both their arithmetic and reading classes were to be held back. By the end of primary school, a fifth or more of all the pupils had been retained at least once.[8] As a result, while the best pupils competed against each other to come out at the top of the class, many of the less able students were nervously cramming to avoid the humiliation of being left behind with children younger than themselves. Grades took on a very real importance to the very set of students who were least involved in any competition to get into higher education.

Since the idea was to use grades to spur pupils' rote learning, the report cards sent home from Canton's primary schools in the 1960s were rather elaborate affairs, with a *weekly* grade listed for the reading and arithmetic classes, adjoining a list of the children's mid-term and end-term examination results for all their courses and, finally, their overall semester grades.[9] But at the same time, for ideological reasons Canton's schools in the sixties were trying to defuse the children's competitiveness over grades. Repeatedly children were taught the rhetoric that the competition among themselves was wrong—that it was unsocialist; that they were to learn not for grades but to help the country; that they were always to cooperate with classmates in their studies, etc. As rhetoric often can, these phrases did to some extent influence pupils' attitudes and behavior. Interviews suggest that children who too obviously showed a competitive drive over their own and others' grades ran the risk of open peer disapproval.

Moreover, schools were backpedaling in the 1960s in their willingness to reward individual accomplishment. From the early 1950s onward the primary schools had held annual ceremonies to hand out prizes of pens and storybooks to the pupils who were best at given subjects and skills; as of the mid-1960s these award ceremonies had ceased. But the elementary schools (and the high school system) continued to promote schoolwide and citywide contests in math and calligraphy, in which children were supposed to "represent" the collective honor of their classroom. The most talented children reaped attention and honor from these contests, but the schools were not entirely averse to that. They did, after all, still want to grant prestige to the notion of doing well.

Central to this effort was a practice called "3 good" or, after 1964, "4 good" students: honors for pupils "good" in labor, academic work, attitude, and orderliness. This was a reward not just for studies (though success in schoolwork was always necessary), but for the child's "politics" too, which gave the scheme of titles more of an ideological justification. The "3 good" students were to serve as models for their classmates to emulate. And to promote this, from the fourth grade of primary school onward, they were always to be selected by their own classmates. This was in line with a strategy the Party normally has been careful to use: that conformity to official values is to be rewarded from *within* the peer group. The idea is not just to diminish the other group members' potential resentment of the models. More than that, the presumption is that in mulling over the selections, the peer group will itself be affirming the correctness of the official standards for "goodness"—and through this the peer group will come closer to adopting the official values as its own.

    All these various programs—the grading of homework, the tests, report cards, "3 good" titles, etc.—generally succeeded in keeping children orderly and oriented toward getting their studies done. For this reason, the primary schools after the Cultural Revolution still depended upon most of these pre-Cultural Revolution motivators. Every one of the six post-Cultural Revolution primary schools (both urban and rural) on which I have done interviewing with teachers continued to give tests and formal course examinations. Only one of the schools in my small sample ever did away with tests for any sustained period (while keeping term-end course examinations). But even this school reinstituted tests after 1972, since "without the tests the pupils weren't energetic in studying." For similar reasons the schools continued to grade homework daily, and these results continued to be included in detailed report cards. Of all the earlier mechanisms, only the schoolwide and citywide contests were eliminated.

TESTS AND MEMORIZATION IN HIGH SCHOOL

In junior high school, even in the 1960s, the grading structure always was less elaborate than in elementary school. Homework in junior high school was not graded by the teacher, bulletin boards did not publicize whose assignments or tests were well done, and report cards were less elaborate.

    But in all schools, even in the post-Cultural Revolution high schools, the basic mechanisms of tests, marks and report cards remained intact. After the Cultural Revolution, however, grades held little influence over high school students. Young children still did their lessons because their teachers and parents wanted them to and prompted them to through grading. But once teenagers, they knew perfectly well in the period of 1968-1976 that their accomplishments or nonaccomplishments at school would have no influence whatsoever on their futures. As we shall see in later chapters, students after the Cultural Revolution balked at studying for the merely symbolic rewards of grades—and were provided with few other reasons for studying.

But in the pre-Cultural Revolution key-point high schools students were well aware that hard studying was necessary for success. And since school tests were indicative of their prospects on the higher-school entrance examinations, a concern with grades, which had origins in primary school separate from any competition to climb the ladder, became increasingly (though never strongly) linked to this competition as students moved up into secondary school.

This did not mean, however, that the tendency to memorize became accentuated. For one thing, so far as the educational authorities were concerned the several special reasons which promoted intensive memorization in primary school had already been satisfied. The pupils had even already passed the phase of learning moral/political passages by rote: for it was only with the onset of the Cultural Revolution that the traditional precept of memorizing a worldview—in the present times, Mao Thought—re-emerged in China in full force.

As revealed in repeated articles in the press of the mid-1960s, the national educational leadership felt it was the high schools' role to encourage students to be able to think more flexibly in their postgraduation careers—that this is what manpower development entailed. They realized that the habits of memorizing textbook facts became *substitutes* for learning how to reason effectively, and they recognized that the system they had erected of tests and course examinations often promoted the very types of nonthinking rote effort that they wanted youth to abandon. This view percolated downward into the provinces and in turn into the schools.[10]

At the most prestigious schools, the response was relatively positive. Teachers there very much wanted to see their students do well on the higher-school examinations and have their own and their school's reputations rise in consequence. But at the same time, if we may go by interviews, they appreciated and intellectually agreed with the leadership's arguments against having their students prepare by blindly cramming textbook materials.

More importantly, teachers at these key-point schools were apparently aware that reducing the amounts of memorization would not be detrimental to their students' chances on the university examinations. The university selection examinations did not ask for memorized responses—except for the Politics exam section, which for that very reason was considered the easiest examination. In the other examinations the remembrance of facts could help, since knowledgeable answers to a series of essay questions had to be given. But it becomes evident when reading through the syllibi for the nine university entrance examinations for 1960[11] that the exams emphasized the *concepts* presented in the high school subjects. In the face of such examinations, there was little direct reason for an education oriented toward getting into a university to be dominated by the unquestioning memorization of facts. Effort and time could be better spent on other aspects of schoolwork. In fact, a 1964 conference of Canton teachers attempted to make this very point. Teachers read speeches on how their own efforts to reduce tests and to ask thought-provoking questions in class had been rewarded in improved results on their course-end examinations, which presumably were patterned on the university selection examinations.[12]

Nevertheless, there were various factors in the high school system conducive to memorized learning—reasons that had little to do with the pressures of a competitive ladder. Combined, these several factors assured a high degree of memorized study despite the leadership's desires and the shape of the university entrance examinations:

(1) Traditional concepts die hard, and many members of the educational field (including the teachers among my interviewees) continued to believe that memorization, when conducted properly, enabled students to comprehend their course materials more systematically. Such a method of study was called "living memorization" (*huobei*), which meant understanding the subject matter first and then organizing and ingraining the concepts through memorization. Teachers contrasted this with "dead memorization" (*sibei*), learning by heart without understanding. But in practice, when teachers left the door open to memorized daily study, many students did not bother to distinguish between the "living" and "dead" forms.

(2) This was because many students felt comfortable with rote learning. They had been taught to memorize by heart in primary schools, and found it still provided a safe and methodical method when in doubt or nervous about a test. A correct answer, after all, was equally a correct answer whether derived through comprehension or memory. It was the not-too-good conscientious students' means to overcome their more academically competent classmates' advantages. Some students (normally

girls) routinely and exactly memorized by heart all the key paragraphs in each textbook chapter. But this habit of study was more common among junior high school students than those in senior high. For one thing, since the youngsters who most frequently engaged in rote learning were not usually among the better students, they were less likely to get past the senior-high entrance examinations. And those who did continue into senior high school found that, as the courses became more difficult, their intensive memorization became correspondingly more difficult to practice and less fruitful in its results. "Dead memorization" and the stolid memorization of facts big and small diminished as the ladder was climbed, and was *less* prevalent near the most highly contested point of selection—the university entrance examinations—than during the earlier less "ladder oriented" phases of learning.

(3) Ironically, Mao's and the Party's overall influence in education supported the tendencies of students to try simply to commit the details of the textbook contents to memory—and even encouraged "dead" memorization. Even though Mao himself had condemned memorization and spoken in favor of more independent thinking from students, most of the nonscience subjects were based on the premise, a premise Mao himself pushed, that there was a single truth that should be taught—the "correct line." Hence, on all issues considered important in a nonscience course, students were simply to learn the correct interpretation and venture no further than that. Teachers were to try their best to help students comprehend the given truths, could show them the correct mode of analysis and how to make the proper deductions. But because there was a fixed "appropriate" answer, a student could just as readily try to learn the key points by rote as by comprehension.

(4) Since ideological issues were by definition present in the content of all the nonscience courses, the teacher's role was to a certain extent politically sensitive. Yet many teachers were not from good-class families, and they were not entirely trusted. To better assure that they taught in an ideologically appropriate manner, the schools required that all teachers prepare a detailed teaching outline for each class session, which occasionally would be checked by the school heads. Once written, many teachers found it most convenient to lecture woodenly from these notes. It was common for students to half-listen, jot down all the facts mentioned in the lectures, and simply memorize these for tests.

(5) A good many of Canton's teachers administered frequent tests as a means of controlling their classes. This probably provided the most important reason for the persistence of rote study. Interestingly, interviews

suggest that teachers at the poorer schools used such a technique more often than teachers at the key-point schools. Two reasons emerge from these interviews. First, at the poorer schools the teachers often were not as capable and found their own abilities were not up to handling classes without such controls; and second, their students were less likely than students at the good schools to have the strength of will to keep up with their assignments without the regular prods of tests. What is significant here is that poorer high schools which were *less* oriented toward the higher school entrance examinations tended nevertheless to be *more* test-oriented—and through this rewarded the rote learning of facts more.[13]

The following piece from a 1964 Shanghai newspaper shows clearly where the authorities thought most of the blame lay:

> Sometimes because students are not paying close attention in class, the teacher will lightly tap the lecturn and warn: "Students, listen to my lecture; on this section of it we're going to have a test next time". . . . An algebra teacher turning over a student's workbook will say: "See, you've already had tests in geometry six times; we've only had three. No wonder the students don't take algebra seriously. These next several weeks we must have tests two times". . . . The teacher in the latter example uses tests as a weapon to "contest on the battlefield" against *other* school courses. . . . At root, some comrades consider that if we increase the exams and tests, students cannot but seriously listen to the lectures, cannot but time and again review their lessons, cannot but carefully consider the question of grades, and therefore will remember, will read, will memorize, will practice, and from this they can raise the quality of teaching.
>
>   . . . This "cannot but" kind of talk says quite clearly that having students cope with tests "seriously" and "attentively" is due to a classroom situation that is forced and passive. And such tests themselves only let students cram in material without digesting it, stiffly memorizing their books and teacher's lectures. . . . They completely sink into a passive condition, reading life-less books and reading books lifelessly. . . . With exams to the right and tests to the left, it is easy to lead students to develop a one-sided pursuit of grades, as if studying were for tests, and tests were for winning excellent grades.
>
>   . . . Therefore, it is not permissible to snatch time or fight for territory by using exams and tests as a trick to spur your students. It is only through teaching reforms—thinking of all sorts of ways to raise the quality of classroom teaching and to lighten students' burdens—that we can stir students' initiative to take the right path in studying.[14]

These last sentences were more than rhetorical flourishes. From 1964 up to the Cultural Revolution, a continuous campaign was mounted in the newspapers and through conferences to convince teachers and school principals to reduce tests, homework, and memorized learning.

This campaign was tied to the increased politicization of the schools from 1964 onward. Editorials in the press expressed worries that too great an "academic burden" on the students would reduce their capacity and willingness to participate in political extra-curricular activities. The school principals were responsive to these worries, since they were usually long-time Party members who had often been selected to head the schools for that very reason. They exercised their leadership not through their titled position but rather through the school's Party committee, and this strengthened each one's self-image as the Party's representative in the school. While they wanted to raise their student body's success rate in the university examinations, as Party cadres they equally wanted to promote the Party's political goals. If the Party line called for students to spend more time away from their studies in labor classes and politically "activist" endeavors, the principals were inclined to pursue this. If doing so demanded fewer out-of-class assignments, fewer tests to prepare for, and less memorization, then the school leaderships were prone to support moves in those directions. The fact that the university entrance examinations did not require large amounts of memorized learning made their decision all the easier to take.

Their task in persuading the students to shift more of their attention over to political activities was simultaneously made easier by the fact that the university entrance criteria in the mid-1960s increasingly demanded that applicants possess "political" credentials. Students would not lose out by switching some of their energies toward classroom activism—in fact, quite the contrary. From interviews, it seems students ended up looking favorably upon the educational reforms that were introduced, which they saw would not harm their chances on the university entrance examinations, would not harm their academic prestige or standing among their peers, and at the same time would provide them with more spare time for "activist" endeavors that were helpful to them.

THE OPEN BOOK EXPERIMENTS

The educational leadership had a set of specific reforms in mind. These included the complete phasing out of tests in the less important (i.e., the nonexaminable subjects) and restrictions on the numbers of tests permitted in the major courses.

But the most prominent reform was open-book testing, inaugurated in about 1963. In this, students were permitted, both for tests and course-end examinations, to bring their textbooks and reference books with them to class and use them as they wished. A former student explains how the system operated:

> During both the tests and course exams we could discuss with our class-mates how to handle the questions, though your friends weren't supposed to literally copy from you. On these exams there were lots of *theory* questions, in which you had to explain the theories or apply theories in working out answers; or it would involve essays in which you were supposed to analyze some topic. The teacher looked at the procedure by which you'd derived your answers—at your reasoning—in determining how well you did. On some of these exams or tests, they'd announce the topic one or two days in advance and you could go to the library. You knew the questions, but you still had to go to investigate and think about them. I preferred these open-book exams to the closed-book ones. For one thing, it was less nerve-wracking. If it were open-book and you'd done your daily assignments and understood the material there was no need at all to worry. And it cut cown on the memorization.

This particular student was from an elite key-point school. Since it was not a matter of political "line," each school retained the discretion to decide whether or not to try open-book testing, and the less highly reputed high schools usually decided against plunging into the new venture.

Only the key-point secondary schools (and most of the universities) seriously experimented with it. The key points, after all, were *supposed* to pioneer new ideas; and their leaders seem to have been more alert to new trends and more confident of being able to successfully implement the innovations. For one thing, open-book tests were more difficult to devise appropriate questions for and more difficult to determine grades for, and it was the key points which had teachers more capable of doing both. Furthermore, their students could more readily handle the more analytical types of questions that the new open-book program necessarily was geared toward. Once again, the schools which were more concerned with the university entrance exams also happened to be the ones most willing and able to move away from the old test-oriented learning.

The type of test question the open book system posed most successfully was of the following genre: a class is taken to an empty rectangular granary with a pitched triangular roof-space and is asked to think up all the different possible ways to calculate from the ground the dimensions of the hall and the volume of grain that would fill it. Working in groups, the students have to put their knowledge of trigonometry and geometry to use in a situation similar to what they might face later in life. But such a test—calling for as many different creative methods to solve a problem as the students can devise—was far more effective in mathematics than in the social sciences. Chinese school subjects can be thought of as ranged between two poles: on the one side the politics courses, in which there is a single given method and fixed solution to every question; on the other, the pure sciences and math, in which more diverse modes of analysis were permissible. The more "political" the contents of a course, the less effective was the open-book style of testing. Not surprisingly, the great majority of the sample questions presented in the mass media to show the advantages of open-book testing concerned math and science.

The leadership was quite happy with the results achieved in the key-point schools' experiments, and from 1963-64 up to the Cultural Revolution a regular stream of articles in the national press tried to advertise the program's attractions. While there is no guarantee that the new test system actually fulfilled what was claimed for it, these articles proclaimed the following advantages[15] (my interviewees, both students and teachers, made much the same claims):

(1) That, as expected, the open-book tests allowed students to reduce the hours spent in academic work, enabling them to engage more in political activities and organized sports;

(2) That the new system sharply reduced the nervousness many students had previously felt towards tests and semester examinations;

(3) That in the old system of tests, since *factual* questions had been easiest for teachers to devise and grade, these had been the mainstay of classroom tests, and the tendency among students to treat their courses as the memorization of useless details had been accentuated. The new test method obliged teachers to reorient both their teaching styles and their own thinking;

(4) That the open-book test system forced students to concentrate throughout the semester on comprehending the concepts of what they were learning;

(5) That open-book testing promoted students' initiative in problem-solving; that the tests themselves became a creative learning experience; and

(6) That the new tests were close to the conditions in which learning normally is applied in a job. The students began to seek out reference

books and to consult with others on solving problems—work habits that should be promoted even before students graduate from school.

Ever-increasing numbers of schools took up the program during the three years prior to the Cultural Revolution. Even a few of the poorer schools had begun to acknowledge the leadership's desires. It is possible that if the Cultural Revolution had not put an end to the school system, the program would have been universally introduced into the high schools and universities. Already at least one province, Jiangxi, had converted its provincial senior-high entrance examination in politics to open-book.[16]

After the Cultural Revolution, the open-book tests were used widely in the secondary schools, but the focus was changed. The questions, rather than being difficult, became comparatively easy to solve, and the students' ability to consult the books and help each other enabled the poorer students to turn in passable results despite little study. In these circumstances, the open-book program seems to have helped level the differences between the more mediocre and the more capable of the students. But they still seem—from interviews with post-Cultural Revolution teachers and students—to have involved students in at least some thought-provoking problem-solving, group learning, and training in the use of reference materials. Most of my interviewees gave discouraging information on other aspects of schooling after the Cultural Revolution; but almost all thought well of the open-book test program.

Yet the program was not popular with everyone. The open-book system became identified in many people's minds with the lack of learning and disorder in China's new school system. Many parents and teachers looked fondly back toward a pre-Cultural Revolution era when serious and disciplined learning was accompanied by old-fashioned tests and worries about grades. A 1974 article from a Guangdong education journal indicates the shape of the popular backlash which had begun to develop:

> With the evil wind of negating the Cultural Revolution that had been whipped up in society, some people spread the idea that the quality of teaching today "was poorer than that of yesterday." They alleged that in [a certain Canton] secondary school, the students . . . acquired too little knowledge and that the senior high school students were no better than the senior primary school students. In the light of this reactionary trend of thought, some teachers showed new distrust in the open-book test system. These teachers said: "The [academic] foundation of the students today is poor; in fact, they are becoming worse" and "the quality of teaching will

not improve if we do not return to the old system of tests". . . . Therefore, whenever they had a chance, they would apply the old system of testing against the students, introduced shock tests, and vainly hoped that they could "control the students with examinations."[17]

A 1974 senior-high graduate from Canton recalls that in his own school the only test which had remained open-book by his final years of schooling was in his Chinese course, where at the course's end he had a take-home essay to write. To be sure, in at least some other high schools—"models" of the new education—the open-book method withstood the trends and remained fully in use.[18] But once the radicals fell, the method's future was further jeopardized by the loss of these political patrons and by the new moves of teachers to promote disciplined studies once more.

The open book system, though, still had powerful promoters. Though the open-book testing method had gained strong backing from the radicals, the system had been initiated in the 1960s not by Party radicals but by reformist educators—and these are now back in the bureaus. Many of them still view open-book testing as a salutary means to prompt students not simply to study but to think. In December of 1977, after the ouster of the "Gang of Four," educators in Guangdong took the one step likely to assure that teachers would still give weight to open-book teaching. Guangdong's new university entrance examinations were made predominantly open-book. (However, it was prohibited for students to confer with one another during the examinations.) In justifying this open book system, a high official of Sun Yatsen University explained:

> On the examination topics this time, the main points are to test students' independent thinking and independent ability to solve problems; the questions all will have to be figured out in a roundabout fashion, not learned by copying from books.[19]

When nationally uniform examinations were revived in mid 1978, however, these were again, as before the Cultural Revolution, closed-book. And reports from China suggest that students anxious to get into a university crammed by rote for the revived exams of 1978 and 1979 far more than had ever been true before the Cultural Revolution. But the leadership seems committed to less rote learning, and we can expect the pendulum to swing once more during the 1980s toward open-book testing.

CHAPTER FIVE

Student Ideals and Competition: The Gathering Storm

THERE WAS always a tension in the schools between what the State's political teachings wanted of the students, and what the educational competition rewarded students for doing. This intrinsic conflict between ideology and the educational contest had posed for some of my interviewees a considerable personal dilemma.

In this chapter we will explore how students acted out their political adherence in a manner that brought into the open this clash of interests and values. We shall be observing this against the backdrop of the narrowing opportunities in the 1960s to squeeze into higher education and the rising tensions which attended this. As a result, we will at the same time be witnessing the prelude to the student uprisings of the Cultural Revolution. We shall be examining the values and psychic needs they brought to the Cultural Revolution; the organizational forms which they already knew how to fit themselves into; and the passions, discontent, and interests which drove them into a ferocious civil war among contending student groups of differing class backgrounds.

THE IDEOLOGICAL CONTENT OF SCHOOLING

Any outsider leafing through the schoolbooks used in China is struck by the very heavy dosage of political content in the daily lessons. Even mathematics textbooks in the 1960s were peppered with questions asking the distance of enemy ships from China's shore, the rate of unemployment in America, and the compound burdens on the peasantry of rents in pre-Liberation China.[1] In literature classes, readings were chosen for their properly socialist flavor, and even the occasional poems in classical Chinese were put into a political context by accompanying annotations. When the students themselves wrote essays every second week in their literature courses, these were usually on explicitly political/moral themes: to describe the rural harvest-time labor in appropriately glowing terms; to describe their feelings on National Day; to give a picture of the pre-Liberation sufferings of the masses; to discuss growing up under the care of the Party. The students always knew what particular views they were expected to express, using precisely what sort of accepted phraseology. The schools believed in the power of constant exposure and reiteration to drive the political messages home to youngsters.

There was not, however, in any sense a systematic education in political theory. The Chinese, unlike some of the Western European Marxists, feel no great need to prove their credo or justify their political actions through rigorous intellectual constructs. For that reason, the secondary school politics courses were considered of limited importance in the curriculum, and were not paid much official attention. In their politics classes, students mostly learned how to follow the Party line through newspaper editorials, and were taught a smattering of Party history and some simple textbook explanations of Marxist thought. But even the senior high school students were never required to read any Marx or Lenin—not even the *Communist Manifesto*. Except for the ritual memorization of key political phrases and some rote learning of Mao's precepts, students did not have to study much for the course, and the tests were kept sufficiently easy that no one failed.

What weighed instead in the political teachings were the emotive and moral elements, and what counted here was how the students acted out these messages in everyday group situations—be it in student small-group sessions, or labor classes, or extramural activities. Accordingly it was this which influenced a youth's chances of joining the Communist Youth League, not one's understanding of the ideology or grades in political courses.

The messages which were to be acted on were simple and consistent. In fact the very same themes which children learned in their elementary school primers were repeated in an increasingly mature context all the way through senior high school. Other writers have already written analyses of these schoolbooks,[2] so I shall touch here only upon three of the themes in them that are particularly important for understanding students' beliefs and their political behavior:

Patriotism was then and remains today an especially prominent theme. It was a special type of patriotism. The sacred symbols of nationhood which the children were taught to cherish all served as symbols both for socialism and the Party: the red flag, the National Day on which the Peoples's Republic was declared, Tiananmen Square in Peking and Chairman Mao, who was portrayed in the school texts as the benevolent and sacrosanct father-figure of both nation and Party. The socialist cause and the Chinese nation merge in the books into a unified identity.

The stories which children and teenagers read in and outside of school promoted this linkage. Many were set during the struggles against the Japanese and Guomindang, and the storybook heroes were either youngsters helping out the People's Liberation Army or were soldiers themselves: and if so, very often martyrs who died for the revolution/ nation. Children were to identify with their heroism and to see the patriotic/socialist cause as worthy of their sacrifice. An implicit message was that a debt had been created through martyrdom that connected the patriotic past with the patriotic present. It became "glorious" to undergo similar sacrifice. A poem from a third grade primer notes:

> Without the [previous] martyrs shedding their blood,
> How can today's flowers bloom? . . .
> We are the next revolutionary generation
> [Who] take over the elders' rifles.[3]

With the triumphs and deaths of the past held as a mirror for the present, they were taught that China still is surrounded by external and internal enemies. The repeated message was that the survival and success of the nation and China's revolutionary mission depended upon the new generation's dedication and uprightness. Especially after 1962, when the split with Russia introduced the concept of "revisionism" into the political vocabulary of secondary schools, stress was placed on the question of whether the new generation would, in fact, be worthy successors to the historic revolutionary tradition.

Social action. The primary-school reading lessons also focused persistently on the daily behavior expected of socialist youths. Almost always these lessons centered on social responsibility, as in stories of children returning lost property or helping the elderly and infirm. But those who were helped were usually specifically depicted as symbolic of the proletariat or peasantry or nation. The story's hero is made aware that by performing the good deed he or she is serving the broader cause; and these good acts are explicitly portrayed as a proving-ground of the child's mettle and dedication to the wider cause. The storybook heroes never secure material reward or personal gains from their actions. Rather they feel inward satisfaction and the glory of being more intimately linked with Chairman Mao, the socialist mission, the proletariat, or the revolutionary heritage. Often this feeling of communion is portrayed as having been heightened by the fact that the heroes have kept their good deeds anonymous.

The primary-school stories also contain morals on appropriate classroom and peer-group behavior. They stress cooperation in activities; willingness to share possessions with others; a concern to improve others' moral or political behavior; and diligence, perseverence, and self-discipline in one's own work. But here again the proper actions are given legitimacy and rewarded in terms of the higher cause, with the story's protagonist being described, say, as a "good student of Chairman Mao."

At the same time, the overall thrust of the stories and essays makes it apparent that a youth should not simply try to adhere to the greater cause in a personal, individual sense. The notion of political *efficacy* becomes a central theme in a student's political education; and here, as in any Leninist political system, effective action is seen as organized action. It becomes the child's responsibility to boost his or her efficacy by getting into the Young Pioneers and, when older, the Communist Youth League. By secondary school, youth magazines are intimating that if you can join the select and elite League and—after the age of about 25—the Party, you become part of a pivotal organization that will enable you to play a vanguard, catalyst, leadership role. In such a context, you become considerably more effective than the organizationally unaffiliated "masses"; and as such you have brought yourself closer to Chairman Mao and the great cause.

Young Pioneers and Youth League members are to take their organizational affiliations very seriously. In many of the stories the child-heroes are trying to make sure that their actions are worthy of their affiliation. A child's sense of being integrated with the greater cause is to be expressed in the directly tangible terms of this organizational communion. The children in stories are not mere friends but Young Pioneer comrades-in-arms. From some stories, it seems almost as if comradeship within the organization was supposed to supersede friendship in a youngster's life.[4]

Political effectiveness, since it is organized action, requires discipline and a very high measure of voluntary conformity to group norms. It was supposed to be each youth's responsibility to "self-cultivate" his or her own character. Young people were to analyze themselves, stand watch over themselves, and struggle to strengthen and purify their performance.[5] As one example of this, students were supposed to introspect (fanxing) in daily or weekly diary entries, writing on their various efforts to improve their attitudes, on the good deeds they had done, on small faults which they were paying particular attention to correcting. During about the fourth year of primary school, teachers taught children how to keep such diaries, and some interviewees earnestly continued the habit even into adulthood.

Taking a Class Stand. In 1962 Mao published the directive "never forget class struggle" in an effort to reaffirm the "roots" of the revolution. During the several succeeding years stronger attempts were made in the schools to instill "class feelings" and "class hatred" in young people. From the first grade onwards, children's stories dwelt on the evils and injustice of the old pre-Liberation society and the comparative happiness of life in present-day China. To hammer home the message, children and teenagers began in 1963 to attend *yiku sitian* (recall the bitterness, contemplate the sweet) meetings, at which old peasants and workers recounted their personal stories of past sufferings. Children of "red" class background were supposed to have their "class feelings" fortified through these tales. Children of bad-class background were to be helped through the stories to "draw the line" ideologically between themselves and their parents.

Though China's students were supposed to hold to the ideal of "serving the people," they were to remember that this word "people" (renmin) most decidedly did not include all humanity. As Mao had written, there are the "people" on the one side and "enemy" groups and classes on the other, with antagonistic contradictions separating them.[6] In the children's stories there were pointed reminders that the persons being served were all part of the "people." In the classroom of one interviewee, a student inadvertently did a good deed for an elderly former landlord and was publicly criticized for not having been adequately observant; whatever his intentions, he had temporarily alienated himself from the greater cause.[7]

The wickedness of the old landlords and capitalists was depicted repeatedly as the main cause for pre-Liberation suffering. But their evil went beyond that. In many of the tales and comic strips set in present-day China, a villainous former landlord[8] remains secretly and viciously unreconciled to the revolution, and the child hero thwarts him in his evil efforts to connive with the Guomindang spies or carry out sabotage. The children were to learn that they should remain suspicious of the intentions of the toppled classes and never forget "class struggle."

The Chinese child was presented with a Manichean world; the perfect good of the proletarian cause pitched against the absolute evil of the enemy forces. It is a worldview which comes through nowhere more clearly than in a popular storybook that recounts (and reshapes) for children the adventures of Monkey, the hero of a famous traditional folk story and novel.[9] The new message of the tale may surprise some readers, and it is worth a synopsis. Monkey was the fearless guardian of a pious monk journeying to India to seek the Buddhist scriptures. In the new children's story a demon lays plans to feast on the monk and his disciples. To lull the pilgrims into complacency the demon transforms himself into a young pretty maiden. But Monkey, ever vigilant, recognizes the demon beneath the girl's innocent features and beats the maid to death before she can offer resistance. The demon tries again as a harmless old lady and then as a venerable old man, and both times Monkey takes cudgel in hand to slay them. The horrified monk banishes Monkey, only to find himself at the mercy of the hungry demon. A vindicated Monkey returns in the nick of time to kill the predatory monster.

In the 1960s and 1970s the morals of the tale were driven home to children at school. We must be ever vigilant against an enemy who can take what on the surface appears to be innocent forms: be it a young girl, elderly man or old woman. "Class enemies" such as former landlord families can appear harmless, but we should not be seduced into fraternizing with them, since they perhaps stand ready to destroy the revolutionary forces first. An activist youth can prove his dedication, if and when the time arises, as much by his "class hatred" and staunch ruthlessness in the face of the enemy as by his warm "class feelings" and good small deeds on behalf of the masses. Each type of activist performance complements the other: as it were, the reverse sides of the same coin.

The "class struggle" theme at school lent extra color to the notions, already implanted in the lessons on patriotism, of a movement besieged from without and within. In student activities even mundane conversations frequently became peppered with the high-blown terminology of war and "class struggle." The bad-class students were not direct targets, but as the rhetoric of class struggle escalated in the mid-1960s their situation, as we shall later see, did become increasingly uncomfortable.

ORGANIZING STUDENTS

These themes of patriotism, social action, and class struggle were played out in a considerable variety of student activities; and almost always these were *group* activities. The idea was to place young people in situations where peer-group pressures could be used to influence each individual student to abide by the official norms. As an example, naughty children were apt to find their behavior criticized in "small-group" (*xiaozu*) sessions of a dozen or so children.[10] In a similar fashion, after a high school labor session each classmate's efforts were evaluated in these small formalized student discussion groups. An insufficiently enthusiastic labor performance would come under criticism, and conformity to the officially recommended performance drew approving peer-group remarks. To a remarkable extent, through these and other mechanisms, the school authorities organized the students in a fashion that made them into the agents of each others' socialization.

Similar group-centered pressures are used widely even with adults. High school graduates invariably participated at their new jobs in labor-evaluation meetings not so different from those they had engaged in as students. By then they were adept at the difficult social arts of giving and receiving criticism. In this sense, through the intricate pressured activities at school, pupils were being taught not just values but also the social and political framework of their adult life.

Moreover, the group activities taught them—and still do in the schools today—how to operate in a *hierarchical* group context. They had to learn how to be willing and disciplined followers, and a minority of them had to learn also the attributes and organizational abilities required for grass-roots political leadership. These several different functions—the reinforcing of values, the learning of formal social skills, and a training in how to be both leaders and led—were intertwined in a great many of the same classroom activities.

By the time the pupils graduated from primary school, classroom structures of remarkable intricacy and sophistication had already been erected to promote these learning processes. As a first step, the first-grade primary school teacher tried to develop a close and positive relationship with her pupils, so as to be able to guide them to accept the values she taught them. Teachers tended to be gentle with their pupils, unlike the traditional teacher in China. Interviewees had had little fear of their class mistress as an authority figure.[11]

Since some pupils were more amenable to the teacher's influence than other children, the teachers used them as student class officers to help shape the behavior of the less obedient pupils. As one teacher whom I interviewed phrased it, these children served as "bridges" between a teacher and the other pupils. Each primary school classroom had between four and seven of these student officers: one as the overall class head, one in charge of helping the other children learn good study habits, another for leading the labor sessions, etc. They helped in addition to keep order in the class, especially in the teacher's absence. They also held the more general and difficult responsibility of behaving regularly in a model fashion—diligent in their studies and taking the lead in saying and doing the appropriate things in meetings and campaigns.

Besides these classroom officers, each class also had Young Pioneer officers, and each front-to-back row of seats had a row head who led rowmates in academic self-study sessions and helped lead small-group (xiaozu) discussions. These various types of student leaders all learned how to meet beforehand in committees to plan out and rehearse the activities they would lead. To an extent remarkable for children of such a young age, they already knew in primary school how to combine multiple organizational roles, how to cooperate in committees, how to form a united front of leaders, how to control meetings, how to help motivate the political education of classmates and push the "backward" students into conformity, and even how to sit properly in judgment of fellow primary-school students. They were learning also the prestige and "glory" of acting as a vanguard corps. They were, in essence, learning how to perform later as Communist Youth League members.

There was, though, a problem in the use made of such primary school pupils. China's political authorities, in trying to influence the pupils' peer-group milieu, were resorting to two somewhat conflicting formulas. On the one hand they created a stable longterm classroom group (e.g., the schools purposely kept the pupils together for all six primary school years, and the same teacher sometimes went up several grades with the children) and made heavy use of the tightly knit peer group's sustained pressures. On the other hand, they placed a minority of the peer group in the anomalous leadership position of standing partly outside the peer group so as to bend the informal childhood peer-group norms to fit the values and behavior desired by the authorities. At times the pupils as a whole had sufficient respect for the official norms, and sufficient numbers of students were amenable to playing the "activist" role, to make the formulas work. But if enough children in the peer group resisted, then the informal peer-group pressures worked to isolate the "activist" minority in a them/us situation.

By the final years of primary school the student class heads thus sometimes found themselves in an uncomfortable position. They were caught between their two different constituencies—teachers and peer group. They had to be on their best behavior, but that cut them off from participating in their friends' roughhousing. They held a special responsibility to keep order and reproach mischief-makers, but that inevitably aroused resentment. A couple of interviewees who had been primary-school class heads had found their playmates distancing themselves from them. They responded by playing up their roles as informal student leaders and downplaying their ties to the teachers. Whenever possible, for example, they neglected to report troublemakers to the teachers. A different interviewee, faced with the same sense of estrangement from the children below her, took the opposite tack. She nailed her sails to the teacher's mast, continued to report all wrongdoings to the teacher and looked entirely to the teacher for approval and reward. By the final year of primary school she had let herself earn a reputation as the "teacher's running-dog." As a result, in the fifth grade she was voted out of her post as class head in the semester student elections, despite support from her teacher.[12] But in the difficult effort to balance between formal duties and friendships, the two respondents who had preferred easy-going relations with their peer group had not fared much better. Both of them declined to continue in formal positions.

It is worth distinguishing here between those who set more store in serving as formal activists as against those who preferred the satisfaction of remaining informal student leaders. Their paths tended to diverge. Notably, the girl who had shown such strong proclivities to side with the authority structure and the official norms regained her leadership position in junior high school, fervently loyal not only to the teacher but also to the new official peer leadership structure of the Youth League. The Party "cultivated" just that type of attachment and upward loyalty, and this particular girl graduated into an adult cadre post. The interviewees who had opted to return entirely to the peer group, on the other hand, did not regain any formal posts in high school. This example seems in line with the general case.

ACTIVISM AND THE COMMUNIST YOUTH LEAGUE

Even more than in primary school, junior high school classes varied greatly in their acceptance of "activism." In some classes, schoolmates were inhibited from seeking League membership due to the great majority's insistance that the peer group's solidarity be preserved. In the classroom of one interviewee, only one student joined throughout the three years of junior high school, and did so secretly, revealing it only at graduation time. In other junior high classrooms, however, a substantial number of students, sometimes the majority, competed frantically to enter. Depending on which way the greater percentage in a class initially leaned, an atmosphere got set, and most of the remainder of the students got pulled into the orbit created by peer-group pressures. A respondent whose junior high classroom had been nonactivist remembers, "I just didn't believe in that League activism stuff; almost all my classmates weren't in the League clique and I didn't want to pass over the line to the other side." When he transferred to a senior high school which had a very high representation of activist students he, too, enthusiastically vied to be an activist.

Overall, my interviews suggest that the great bulk of the nonactivist classrooms were to be found in the neighborhood junior high schools; and the more activist junior high classrooms were concentrated in the key-point schools. One reason was that activism was promoted most readily when young people were placed for most of their day in a formal school-sponsored social milieu. The key-point schools were mostly boarding schools, and their students were on a school-organized schedule from early morning until bedtime. They even did their afternoon sports and games and their evening homework in formally organized groups. In the neighborhood schools, contrarily, almost half a youth's time was spent out of school among friends, and the informal group norms became more important than the discontinuous formal group pressures at school.

Secondly, the neighborhood schools held a high proportion of working-class youths who saw themselves headed for a factory. Such students had little motivation to become "activist." They knew that if they became League members they would be expected by the factory managers to help set a faster pace for the other workers. On the other hand, in the better schools, where the great majority of the students were trying to get into a senior high school, students competed avidly to build up good records in their political activities. In particular, they were trying to get into the Communist Youth League and were willing to follow, even if uncomfortably, the suggestions of an activist student leadership. Under such circumstances, by the final year of junior high the school authorities were able to shift the formal classroom leadership away from the elected class officers and into the hands of the nonelected political "vanguard," the League.

The desires to be activist and to join the League were related to a desire for personal achievement, but a considerable number of my interviewees were idealistic as well. It seems achievement-oriented youths often held to both types of aspirations more strongly than their peers. Admittedly, the claims to idealism of a couple of my respondents probably had served merely as rationalizations or camouflage covering an inner ambition for personal success. But for a large number, the desire to "serve the people" and to gloriously contribute to the greater cause seems to have been as sincere as their ache to be upwardly mobile. To a few interviewees who had joined the League, the League had been a "calling," even though they had knowingly angled for membership with a strategic purpose in mind.

Precisely because participation in the League was of personal advantage, many members felt it crucial to live up to the more idealistic aspects of membership. To have been considered a "phony activist" (*jia jiji*) who had entered for purely self-interested motives would have been humiliating. A non-member observes,

> They generally tried very hard to have good characters. For example, they cultivated the habit of trying to be as patient as possible toward others, never to get angry or bossy. These efforts to discipline themselves largely worked, because they paid strict attention to improving themselves. They often self-criticized their own actions, even small things. But they were behaving unnaturally, some of us felt. Their concern for us was for their own reasons, and they were too nagging (*pwopwo mama*).

League membership implied a duty to consciously impose values upon yourself, and to impose them equally on others.

League membership also meant entering into a separate social circle. By senior high school, the League members' spare time was occupied almost constantly by their "organizational life." Since all League affairs were kept secret by the rules of "organizational discipline," the League became a private inner sanctum which set League members off from those left outside the gates. The mystique of the League, born of its romantic image as the revolutionary Party's right hand, was reinforced through these daily personal experiences of shared secrets, duties, and powers. League members normally even purposely distinguished themselves from ordinary students by wearing the small League badge everywhere they went. League participants began to form their own League friendship groups. Though many continued also to retain their older friendships with non-League classmates, interviewees who were not League members recall a "gap" between themselves and their League-member friends. They held a certain uneasiness about League members in general.

For one thing, by senior high school the League members, and especially the League branch secretary, held substantial power over them. Voting secretly, the branch was empowered to grant or deny their application to enter the League. The League branch also appraised students on their small-group pronouncements, labor, and general behavior in and out of class. Based on this, the League branch would help the home-room teacher compose the other classmates' political reports, to accompany their university application.

Students who wanted to get ahead in life thus had to curry the League members' favor by behaving with "activist" propriety. But there were special tensions here. At the same time that conscientious League members were sincerely concerned (guanxin)to help their fellow students' self-improvement, these same League members viewed their classmates as competitors. Among other things the League members had to be models of good behavior, which entailed consistently being better than others. More than just performing well themselves, moreover, they had to seem righteously upright, and this could be demonstrated most readily by criticizing and publicizing others' flaws in small-group sessions.[13] This tendency was exacerbated by the fact that League members who stood as keepers-of-the-gate over others' entry to the League held a vested interest in keeping the branch as select as possible. They encouraged others to be activist, but at the same time wanted to keep most of their classmates firmly in place as not-quite-equal competitors. In small-group meetings League members who felt free to criticize others' performance often felt threatened if other participants reciprocated. Interviews indicate that applicants for League membership found it wisest to be competitively activist in relation to other nonmembers, but to be fawning toward those already in the League.

A few interviewees felt sufficiently uncomfortable with this humble competitiveness that they stopped trying to win admission to the League. But not many were deterred. In those schools where the great majority of the students were hoping to enter universities, the efforts to get into the League sometimes became ferocious.

This was so even though academic attainments, taken as an independent criterion for university admissions, always remained more important than political performance. Even working-class students, whatever their activist achievements, had difficulty entering university unless their scholastic work was up to the mark.

Yet there was little overt competitiveness in academic studies, as we saw in the preceeding chapter. Instead, the tensions among students almost invariably centered on activism and League entry. There were at least five salient reasons for this:

(1) The ideology that had been taught to students discouraged open competition over grades and placed any youths who tried to engage in such a contest in a bad light. On the other side, the political teachings supported the students' competition to be "politically" superior. Students could feel positively righteous about proving the latter.

(2) Each student's "class" designation was already set, with nothing that they themselves could do to change it. They were also aware that they and most of their classmates were already working hard at their studies, and that any further efforts would not very appreciably alter their entrance examination scores. But a more strenuous and convincing effort to be politically active might pay off in admission to the League. It would grant a qualitative leap into a high standing on that third criterion for higher-school entry, "politics."

(3) Moreover, in their academic work the students were *not* directly competing against any of their classmates to get into the next higher level of education. The examination arena for senior high school entrance was citywide and for the universities nationwide. This permitted classmates to cooperate in their schoolwork[14] and had been a major element in the success of the cooperative open-book tests. But the students *were* contrarily engaged in a direct competition to be activist. The authorities, in order to keep the League a select vanguard organization, had established quotas specifying the maximum number of recruits the various League branches might enroll each schoolyear. Furthermore, only so many students in a small group could be designated as "3-good students" or labor activists. With the arena for activism the size of the classroom or the small group, one student's gain often meant another's loss, and the students knew it.

(4) As the contest to enter a university intensified, increasingly stiff standards were being set by admissions officers—not just in examination results and class background, but also on that third pillar of admissions policy, a student's political record. More than this, the weight attached to this third criterion was growing in importance relative to exam show-

ings. As classmates accordingly began vying harder to win League credentials, they often discovered that, with a limited quantity of League
memberships available, each had to keep escalating his or her efforts to
keep abreast or ahead of classroom competitors.

(5) This activist competitiveness was further strengthened in the mid-
1960s by new government campaigns to politicize the students. As
China's split with Russia aroused fears among leaders that China might
slide gradually into "revisionism," exhortations began appearing in the
youth magazines calling upon the teenagers to demonstrate they were
not "hothouse flowers." The expanding movement to send youths to the
countryside was increasingly phrased in terms of the "glory" of "tempering," of young people proving themselves by voluntarily facing up
to rural hardships.

These strengthened appeals to ideology permitted the student peer
group to place their activist contest in a highly moral light. So much was
this so that classmates who preferred not to compete to be highly activist
were apt to find themselves chastised as ethically and politically backward. In most of the senior high schools and in the key-point junior highs
the activist contest accordingly gained a momentum which went beyond
students' attempts to improve their opportunities for higher education.
It became an effort to prove and protect one's status in the here and now.

On the other hand, at the third-rate senior highs, where the chances
of gaining university admittance were slim, there was a fear among some

Table 5-1. Percentages of League Membership in Canton Secondary Schools,
1962–66

	"Key-point" Schools			
	"Best" 4 schools	*Next best 8 schools*	*18 ordinary schools*	*Neighborhood jr. highs*
SENIOR HIGH	42%	42%	26%	
Number of classrooms surveyed	5	8	18	
JUNIOR HIGH	19%	19%	10%	7%
Number of classrooms surveyed	5	12	12	14

SOURCE: questionnaire remembrances. The sample of 74 classrooms is the same as in
Table 1-2.

of the students, expressed in interviews, that too much activism, especially Youth League membership, would put heavy pressure on an unsuccessful university applicant to take the lead in volunteering for the countryside. There was considerably less interest at such schools in engaging in "politics" and there were correspondingly fewer League members.

ACTIVIST DEEDS

At the better high schools and even many of the average senior highs, the heightened competition to obtain political credentials was focused on the spirited carrying out of small good deeds (haoren haoshi). In the 1950s this type of activity had been promoted largely in the political education of younger children, not in the secondary schools. But in 1963 a fullblown campaign had begun in China's schools glorifying Lei Feng, a soldier who had died accidentally that year. His diary, found posthumously, had revealed he had been a devoted doer of precisely such anonymous small deeds. Until Lei Feng, the model heroes for teenagers had been wartime heroes who had died on the battlefields. Now, coincident with the growing stress on political activism, new heroes were usually portrayed at pedestrian tasks, often dying glorious deaths at those tasks. The authorities were trying to press home the view that in the period of socialist construction such mundane livelihoods and sacrifices were the necessary counterparts of the romantic guerrillas of the anti-Japan, civil-war, and Korean War eras. Lei Feng's celebrated hope was to be a tiny but useful "screw" in the socialist machine. Not great deeds but the habitual performance of tiny acts of "serving the people" was to be the mark of the Lei Feng activist.

As the Lei Feng campaign engulfed the schools, students competitively set about seeking good deeds to engage in—preferably ones which could be done anonymously but which others might catch them at. With League membership or at least a good "activist" record at stake, they washed classmates' dirty laundry; they swept the school floors; they hunted for whatever ingeniously selfless good acts they could accomplish for their classmates or the janitorial staff. The problem was that there simply were not enough small chores on a school campus to go around. In a majority of the interviewees' classrooms, the efforts degenerated gradually into farce. Students at some boarding schools competed to wake earliest before dawn in order to get first crack at sweeping the floors anonymously. There were not sufficient dirty clothes on hand to give everyone the chance, so some students had to resort to rewashing fellow students' already clean laundry. The pettiness of such contrived activities inevitably embarrassed some of the students. And this discomfort was made worse by the fact that peer-group pressures and their own ambitions obliged them to engage in such games themselves.

Moreover, many of the activities became overlaid with hypocritical sentiments and play-acting. In the *yiku sitian* (remember the bitterness, contemplate the sweet) meetings, for example, interviewees recall having felt genuinely moved the first several times they participated. But since the meetings were attended by the entire class, there existed strong temptations among students to *show* that they were moved, even if they weren't. In order to demonstrate publicly the depth of their "class feelings," girl students became deliberately tearful.

Students found even their diary writing caught up in a calculated public show of commitment. Since candidates to the League were half-expected to reveal their diary secrets to their chosen League sponsor in "heart-to-heart" talks (*tanxin*), many of them were tempted to compose lengthy diaries replete with carefully fabricated feelings and artful self-criticism. Some students at the boarding schools resorted to writing long entries on their devotion to Chairman Mao and the Party (in the famous Lei Feng diary style) and then left such pages propped up open on their beds for passers-by to chance upon.

The Party leadership was willing to tolerate such play-acting. At times, the educational authorities seem even to have actively promoted the cant and the tears. The Party apparently felt that even if the posturing was phony, reiterating and performing the correct sentiments would gradually help internalize them. And though it must have been recognized that some of the opportunistic ploys could *only* teach students the art of pretense, pretense itself had become a legitimized part of Chinese political activity. Most Party campaigns have been built upon the mixture of truly felt values and play-acting. Among other things, this had the advantage of encouraging conformity and discipline even when the commitment is not inwardly felt.* The Party can have it both ways: it can make use of the activists' commitment; and it can expect activists to obey

---

* As one example, during the next decade and a half, a political activist could be relied upon to denounce and praise Deng Xiaoping's policies on cue as he rose and fell and rose again.

the Party line and to push through policies with a show of enthusiasm even when they harbor reservations.

In the Chinese senior-high classrooms the end results of the activist competition were not so far from what the Party authorities must have wanted: on the one side the young people absorbed, for the most part, the values and a large measure of the idealism that they were taught; and on the other, they conformed for the most part to the behavior patterns pushed by the school authorities. But at the same time, precisely because the formal values were real to many students and they wanted to make sincere efforts to carry out legitimate actions, the hypocrisy present in the classroom activities rankled. I do not, of course, want to make too much of this mood of dissatisfaction. Most students happily went along believing most of what they were taught; and they equally willingly engaged in play-acting either to put themselves on the safe side of the peer-group pressures or to serve their own futures, or both. But other students did feel a quiet unease. It did not shake their belief in the values they were taught. In fact, the net result of the petty activism was that they yearned all the more for an opportunity to act out their commitment in a genuine manner—and grandly, in counterpoint to the trivialized acts at school. It is notable that the several interviewees who had most strongly felt qualms about playing the activist game at school sought later, as Rebel Red Guard leaders, to fulfill the activist creed at purposeful risk to their own and others' lives. They recall that when the opportunity first came to rise up, the feeling of release from the constraints of trivialized activism had been exhilarating.

My own attention, and that of my interviewees in retrospect, was drawn so strongly to these frustrations of competitive student activism precisely because the Cultural Revolution did break out. Had it not, the weight of my writing here most likely would have been on the success of the schools in educating and politically socializing students. The high schools taught students an idealism and dedication sufficient to reconcile most of them, if need be, to the prospects of hard lives in the countryside. Their schooling showed students how to engage in complex organizational activities that would be beyond the capacity of most western university students. But it becomes difficult now to perceive these results without reference to the Cultural Revolution: as difficult, say, as to study a seemingly stable France of the late 1780s without repeatedly asking, why the imminent explosion? Unbeknown to anyone at the time, the idealism and dedication which the students had learned were to be played out in disturbing ways in one of the larger domestic upheavals of this century. Their organizational and agitational skills were to be put to unexpected use in Red Guard organizations. The activist role-playing, the rhetorical overkill and the Manichean worldview of "class struggle" were to take exaggerated shape in the violence of "defending Chairman Mao."

When seeking the social origins to the violent student uprisings and the internecine student warfare of the Cultural Revolution we must also look again and more closely at the competition in these classrooms. There were more explosive elements present than merely the frustrations of trivialized activism. The growing strength of the class line was influencing differently the opportunities of the different class categories of students, and these different class-groupings would end up acting out their dedication at each others' expense. In the Cultural Revolution they would be coming openly and violently into conflict.

STUDENT ACTIVISM AND THE CLASS LINE

On the whole the children of the former middle classes had tried harder to be activist than had students of other class backgrounds. This had been true throughout the 1950s and 1960s. For one thing, unlike the bad classes they were never directly discriminated against by official policy, and so had not felt deterred from seeking leadership positions in school. In fact, the rather mild political doubts imposed by their family background had spurred some of them to vie in school to prove that they personally were as truly red as their better-class schoolmates, and some to prove that they were even more devoted. And when it came to winning activist credentials, the middle-class students, especially those who were academically very good, normally had held certain advantages. Since a successful activist and in particular a League member had to "take the lead" (dai tou) in group situations, he or she had best have a fair degree of articulateness, for which the middle-class students' family influence provided an edge. Moreover, since League members were to serve as models for others, among other things it was best that they be conscientious in their studies, and preferably successful at them. After all, if students poor at their studies were admitted to the League, classmates might privately look down on them, and this would affect a League branch's reputation.[15]

Abilities at their academic work thus helped middle-class students to improve their "political face." As China became more politicized in the mid-1960s, a middle-class youth's best strategy was to give just as much emphasis as in earlier years to his academic work, while stepping up his or her more directly "political" endeavors. A fair number of students could not find adequate time for both, and according to newspaper reports of the period exhausted themselves in the effort.

The brighter of the middle-class youths tended to think very well of themselves. A good percentage of them had already tasted leadership in primary school and felt they deserved to continue to hold a high political as well as academic status. They often had gotten admitted to the best categories of secondary school.

There, as expected, they found rivals in the children of Guangdong's political leadership. A fair number of these children, especially if from military homes, had been to special boarding primary schools, where they had been shown deference by nurses and teachers and had learned that very high expectations were held for them.[16] But when such children entered secondary school, they found themselves in ironically unhappy circumstances. Due to their sterling red-family backgrounds they had obtained easier access to the better schools than had other children. Yet this meant that a revolutionary-cadre youth of above-average scholastic ability had to struggle to keep abreast with the very *best* of the students from middle-class homes. Likewise, cadre students of below-average academic standing found themselves at above-average schools. Rather than endure a low-status position, some of them refused to accept academic achievement as an important criterion for social esteem. Instead, they claimed "politics" as the significant standard, since their own red blood gave them preference there. But even in terms of political behavior, their middle-class schoolmates could perform as well as they and frequently better. So the revolutionary-cadre students instead often chose to define political standing in ascriptive terms—in terms of a red birth.

The end result was that the middle-class students on the one side tended to envy their revolutionary-cadre classmates and on the other to look down on them due to the cadre youths' poor academic showing. They felt that these classmates were unjustifiably "arrogant" (*jiao-ao*). The revolutionary-cadre students for their part found cause to look down on the others, at the same time resenting those who did well at their studies. They similarly found their classmates arrogant.

As if to deny the relevance of academic standings, some of the children of *high*-level cadres purposely declined to study seriously. They could feel increasingly sure of getting into a university on their parents' credentials alone. The children of senior military officers in particular had few worries; they almost invariably were recruited into the PLA (both sons and daughters alike) to begin careers as a second generation of officers. Though these high-level cadre children normally sought to join the League, it was not so much out of ambition for their own futures. Rather it was to shore up their standing and authority *vis-a-vis* the other students and to vindicate their contention that activism was a "natural" role for someone of their own origins. Within the League they sometimes formed their own tight friendship groups, keeping the other League members outside their own "superior" circle. In the early period of the Cultural Revolution, when they found better ways of expressing their status and authority, they were willing to abandon and even turn against the League for being "impure."

The children of *lower*-level revolutionary cadres could not take their futures as much for granted. They were trying, like other students before the Cultural Revolution, to put together as good a record as possible both academically and politically. Frustrated by their lack of academic success, they saw the possibility of leadership in the League based on their red origins as a means both to recoup their prestige and to boost their chances of squeezing into universities.

Many of the cadres' children felt that, having been brought up by the workers' and peasants' liberators, their own "natural redness" was superior; and some of them were more than willing to let the worker-peasant children know these views. The muted resentments which arose would later promote a rift in the Cultural Revolution between these two different types of "red origin" students.

The worker-peasant students who had succeeded in getting admitted to senior high school sometimes were placed in schools better than their schoolwork might have warranted, but only slightly. The class line was not benefiting them to the same extent as the revolutionary-cadre youths. They thus had somewhat less reason than the revolutionary-cadre youths to feel irritably at odds with their academically capable middle-class schoolmates. But they shared the revolutionary-cadre students' desire to see good-class background rewarded with high formal prestige; and they similarly had reason to share the notion that they, more than the middle-class youths, possessed genuine "class feelings" and hence as a group were more politically advanced.

To a certain extent, the middle-class youths had to be in agreement. It was part of the worldview which they too had been taught. For this reason, at all times students of good-class background did not have to show nearly as much enthusiasm (or have as good grades) to enter the League as youths of middle-class background. A former junior-high League member of middle-class (medical doctor) family origins recollects in a tone of approval,

> In our classroom even if students of good-class origins didn't demand to join [the League] we persuaded them to apply and to strive to meet the standards. We felt that because their class background was so good, they should become awakened. The country needed youths of "red" origins to be revolutionary successors. . . .Because I wasn't of pure class background, I placed a lot of pressure on myself to stand on the side of the proletariat. I was well aware, and said publicly, that my own family influence wasn't so good.[17]

Such thinking placed the *bad*-class students into a very awkward position, especially during 1963-65 as the official class-line rhetoric strengthened. In the student small-group sessions their activist classmates of middle-and good-class origins, in tones similar to the mass media, had begun persistently urging them to join forces with the proletarian cause by "drawing the line" against their parents. Though the activists' advice was prompted in part by the opportunity to chalk up a political good deed, it also seems from interviews that in many cases the urgings were genuinely intended. But such advice placed in high relief the distinction between the better-class small-group members and the bad-class students. The pride of the former was heightened by performing the comradely deed; and the feelings of personal integrity of the bad-class students were placed in jeopardy.

A portion of the bad-class youths did end up yielding to the peer-group appeals.[18] But for many others the humiliation imposed by such sessions made it all the more difficult to accept the official values. Even to take the first demonstrable step in expressing their support for those values would involve them in a denunciation and betrayal of their parents. They were caught in an anomalous situation. They were alienated from their peers if they refused to mouth convincingly the proper criticisms of their home background; yet they did not gain their classmates' respect if they did strongly "draw the line" against their parents, since they would be breaking the code of filial loyalty by which most Chinese still abided.[19] A bad-class youth who seemed activist would not, in fact, be fully believed or trusted by his or her classmates. This was particularly so because the bad-class youth had to make an especially concerted effort of it, entailing more of the phony petty displays than students normally engaged in.

The majority of the bad-class youths never made the attempt. They gave only ritual renunciations of their parents in small-group sessions, and as much as possible tried to melt into the background in class activities. As awareness of "class" heightened, the system of politically "educating" them did not push them toward activism or a stronger commitment to the national values; it pushed most of them in the opposite direction. They *did* generally believe in the broader values that imbued the classroom, but were forced into a certain degree of political cynicism by their need always to proffer a ritual support. The system itself was boxing them into the stereotype believed of them: that they were not full-throated supporters of the new world.

If they were to some degree good at their schoolwork, their strategy was to concentrate all their real energies on their academic studies. They reasoned their only real hope for upward advancement lay in scholastic achievements of such high order that admissions officers would be willing to overlook their handicaps. At the same time, they were careful to make a show of participating adequately in all the small campaigns. They labored hard during the two annual work stints in the countryside; they tried never to quarrel with classmates; they remained carefully modest about their academic talents. Yet even their gestures of quiet modesty did not entirely safeguard them from the envy of good-class students who found their own studies too difficult. During the first phase of the Cultural Revolution, some of these bad-class students found themselves under attack; and one of the charges flung at them—on the face of it, fairly— was that they had striven to be "white experts, not reds."

The schools had always urged students to become both red and expert: on the one side they were to study conscientiously, since the country needed manpower skills; and on the other side they were to strive to absorb the proper attitudes and class stand. But during different political periods, the relative importance of these two roles had varied. Whereas at the height of the Leap in 1959-60 the informal slogan at school was "redness takes command," within a couple of years (1960-62) the pendulum had swung[20] and essays almost solely pushed China's need for "experts." The League's own newspaper proclaimed in 1961 that the "ambition of wanting to be famous and an expert" was to be encouraged even if unaccompanied by any explicit evidence of redness.[21] Within a few more school terms such a notion was again to become a political anathema.

From interviews and Cultural Revolution documentation it becomes apparent that the different categories of students, rather than altering their own private perspectives each time the climate changed, almost without thinking simply adopted as their personal views whichever red/expert weighting benefitted them most. Bad-class interviewees had believed that what counted for China was economic progress; that if given half the chance they could serve the nation better than anyone else, simply by studying hard and becoming experts; and that the shifts after 1962 were all deviations from the proper Party line. Middle-class interviewees, on the other hand, adhered to the official Party interpretations of the mid-1960s: one needs to possess both expertise and redness in order to be truly effective. The good-background students—the revolutionary cadre children most so—were not only inclined to give greatest significance to "redness." They went further as the "class line" and "politics" became more important after 1963-64, and began pushing the view that academic success was *contrary* to redness. By the eve of the Cultural Revolution, as a middle-class student recalls,

> The cadres' kids in my classroom considered those who were good academically as sprouts of revisionism. According to their way of looking at things, success in academic work could influence a person's thought transformation. They weren't satisfied with their own standing; they felt their weak points—their difficulties with the coursework—were the result of "oppression."[22]

The cadre youths' interpretation was not to become the official perspective until after the Cultural Revolution, especially in the years 1968-70. However, from 1964 onward the red-family students did find firmer grounds to press the argument that it was difficult to be absolutely sure of a student's genuine beliefs from mere observations of his or her surface behavior. On the one side they could point out that they themselves had, almost by definition, imbibed true proletarian class feeling as infants and that their own public show of adherence to the revolution could accordingly be taken as genuine. In the League evaluations of new applicants they could imply, on the other hand, that those of bad or petty-bourgeois (middle-class) family background all too often could and did shield opportunistic motives behind activist espousals. And in the years after 1963, as many of the students flung themselves into the types of petty small deeds and hypocritical play-acting which we earlier noted, there seemed foundations for leveling such an accusation. Some good-class students became prone to doubt the intentions of all non-good-class student activists.

The middle-class interviewees contrarily were and still are today convinced that attitudes can be reshaped and that school and society were more influential than parents in a person's character formation. They agreed that there was a deplorable degree of opportunism and play-acting involved in students' efforts to show themselves activist and get into the League. But they believed (correctly, I think) that this resulted from the fact that the League had become an avenue to educational promotion and that the League organization itself had rewarded the bouts of petty conformist posturing. These interviewees suggest that if the mid-dle-class students did tend to exaggerate their petty good deeds slightly more than the red-class League aspirants, this was because League entry was made harder for them. But they see their own personal credentials and integrity, and their own desire to act in behalf of the higher cause, to have been as great as any other student's—greater, indeed, than what they considered to be their pompous soft-living revolutionary-cadre classmates.

After 1963 these middle-class students frustratedly were finding it progressively harder to enter the League. In support of the strengthened class line, directives in 1964 from the higher echelons of the Youth League had made it clear that more good-class background candidates ought to be recruited, and even the League members of middle-class origins had obediently hurried to "cultivate" more red-class background classmates. The following table drawn from questionnaire remembrances lends support to the impressions given by the official documentation of the mid-1960s: a near-majority of the "veteran" League members, who

Table 5-2. The Changing Pattern of League Enrollments, 1962–65

New Enrollees, by Year	1962–63	1963–64	1964–65
Revolutionary cadre	30%	32%	38%
Working-class	24%	26%	38%
Middle-class	37%	34%	21%
Bad-class and overseas Chinese	9%	8%	3%
	100%	100%	100%

SOURCE: questionnaire remembrances
NOTE: The figures for the 1965–66 schoolyear (not shown) are incomplete, since the spring term was disrupted by the Cultural Revolution. The figures suggest, though, that higher percentages of middle- and bad-class students were again getting into the League in 1965–66.

had joined back in junior high school, were of non-red origin, while the new recruitments were topheavy with good-class credentials. Moreover, within the League itself the non-pure-class members were increasingly being displaced in the branches' leadership positions by the good-class members: mostly by revolutionary-cadre students in the best schools and worker-peasant students in the average senior highs. The middle-class students had reason to feel increasingly resentful.

In 1965-66 the League's national leaders applied brakes to these League enrollment trends. They had apparently become mildly disturbed by the growing dissatisfaction and frustrations of the middle-class students. They had become aware also that the bad-class students were being pushed back into the arms of their parents. The national level of the League now decided to reverse itself, in a new line proclaimed to a National Student Congress in January 1965 by Peking's mayor, Peng Zhen:

> Inasmuch as the Party, in dealing with young people with different family origins and experience, *attaches importance to their performance*, those who resolutely follow the Party will not lose their bearings but will have a bright future.[23]

In the months which followed, actual performance rather than "class origins" was again intended to become the major criterion for League admissions, in a new "emphasize performance" (*zhongzai biaoxian*) movement.[24]

Related to these efforts to reencourage the non-red-background students, the Party provided a new hero alongside Lei Feng. Lei Feng had been an orphan of poor-peasant birth, and good-class youths had been able to cite him as an exemplary case to support their own claims that redness sprang from origins. The middle-class youths had not only been injured by this play upon class, but also had difficulty relating their own reasons for activism with Lei Feng's "gratitude." Moreover, Lei Feng had been *successful* in his own lifetime as an activist. He had been admitted to the Party, had become a nationally publicized model soldier, and as such had been selected to attend a National People's Congress. Young people who were discouraged and filled with self-doubts over their lack of activist recognition could not readily look to the simple-minded and all-too-successful Lei Feng as a guide on how to cope with their own predicaments.

They were now introduced to the soldier Wang Jie, a hero of middle-class (middle-peasant) origins. Like themselves, Wang Jie had never personally suffered. But he had been genuinely moved by the tales of good-class fellow soldiers and had taken the activist road as a result. He had tried to enter the Party, yet was rebuffed. He had harbored self-doubts. He had blamed some of his disappointments upon his classification as a middle peasant.[25] But he had proven his dedication in the summer of 1965 in the grandest way possible. To save others' lives, he had hurled himself heroically on an accidentally released grenade. The martyr's diary appeared in bookstores in November 1965 and 30 million copies were sold within two months.[26] He was the only model hero of the sixties who came near to rivaling Lei Feng in popularity. A young woman of middle-class origins observes:

> He was better than Lei Feng because he was only a normal person. No one paid attention to him. He had many misunderstandings with his immediate superiors. But he still wanted to do good—and not just for the reason of showing others. Only after he died and they read his diary did they realize the type of person he was. Maybe in China there are very many such people from bad families, who feel responsibility toward the country and don't have the chance to be cultivated, but who are still loyal to the Party. Yes, there are many persons like Wang. I really admire that. Their level of thought is higher than those who are admired. . . . Wang Jie was a model for us middle-class people.

The middle-class students had had their hopes raised by the "emphasize performance" campaign, but they still felt rather anxious over their status and defensive over the questioning of their revolutionary integrity. At the same time, the new official sympathy for them did not sit well with their good-class schoolmates. As the class line in other spheres of life was still being stressed, the red-origin students felt justified in resisting the new national League policy. In classrooms where they had come to dominate the League, they often continued to lay a very strong stress on "class" in selecting new members. In some cases this posture seems to have held the tacit support of school officials and teachers of good-class blood, who were themselves suspicious of the integrity of the middle-and bad-class activists. In other cases, classroom teachers who supported an increase in middle- and bad-class enrollments found themselves at loggerheads with their classroom's League branch, which by senior high school was no longer under the teachers' strong influence. The animosities and tacit alliances generated during this period between school administrators, teachers, and different constellations of students would soon take more violent shape. School officials and teachers who had taken either side in the issue were to find themselves the targets in the Cultural Revolution of aggrieved students.

In short, in the months before the Cultural Revolution erupted the schools and students were caught in tense and uncertain circumstances. The signals from above had been wavering, and the students' present statuses and future prospects were at stake. If anything, the "emphasize performance" movement had served only to put some of the red-origin students aggressively on the defensive.

SUMMARY

Since about 1963, in line with the tightening competition to enter higher schooling, the disquietude of the student body had been growing: over the question of promotion into higher education; over the frustrations and hypocrisies of student activism; and most divisively over "class." On the eve of the Cultural Revolution the classrooms were split in diverse ways: "veteran" League members against the newer red-origin contingent; the League members as a whole as against non-League members; the unsuccessful rivals for the League jostling each other and pushing against the nonactivists; the academically good students as against those poor in their studies. Most important of all, the class line was pushing students into four increasingly self-aware groupings with opposing interests: the cadres' children; the worker-peasant children; the middle-class children; and the bad-class background children.

Within months, as the Cultural Revolution began to take shape in the schools, students would be acting out their competition, tensions, and worries along these various cleavages.

CHAPTER SIX

The Cultural Revolution

IN THAT spring of 1966 the tensions, conflicts and schisms in the student body were pronounced; but they did not necessarily portend a Cultural Revolution. It could reasonably be argued that the latent hostilities in China's high schools might have persisted for decades and never have surfaced in expressions of violence had it not been for the catalyst of Mao's attempt, as a charismatic leader, to oust his Party opponents by turning to the schools.

In two important respects, though, China's high school students held a high potential for violent conflict once the floodgates were opened to them. First, as we have seen, the students in China had already wanted and needed to express fervent "activism"; their competitiveness had already moved outside a competition over schoolwork, had already been thrust into a semipolitical context. Second, the "class" differences among Chinese students had been transformed by the Chinese state into an *official* categorization of students, in a manner which crystallized and aggravated the students' awareness of their differing backgrounds and interests. Piled atop the growing competitiveness in the schools, these twin factors provided a kindling that all too readily could be set aflame once a political match was struck.

THE OPENING ROUND

China's urban students had been asked in that early spring of 1966 to participate symbolically in a campaign that Mao was launching against two of his Party critics, the playwright Wu Han and the Peking editor Deng Tuo. For the first time in their own experience, the students were being provided with an opportunity to exhibit their activism in terms of the national political stage. They responded with enthusiasm. They did not know what the issues were and had great difficulty deciphering Wu Han and Deng Tuo's critical allusions opposing Mao. But what mattered to them was that they had been called upon to defend Chairman Mao's line against enemies, and that they held the mission of writing posters to exhibit this support. If there had been too few small good deeds to go around in the Lei Feng campaign, now there were to be more than enough.

Preparation for final exams and for the senior-high and university selection examinations still commanded much of the students' attention. But especially at the key-point schools, students found the spare time to scribble enormous numbers of denunciatory posters. The wording was copied almost verbatim from newspaper essays. In some of the schools, posters were soon pasted from floor to ceiling, and when the students ran out of room they overlaid new posters on the posters of the preceding days. It became a frenetic activist competition between informally organized small groups to see who could produce the greatest quantity.

In May, when classes were suspended and the repetitive copying became a full-time occupation, boredom began to set in. Trapped in activities that had become increasingly trivialized over the weeks, the students were eager for the new and ill-understood campaign to move on to a phase that demanded from them more direct action.

Then on June 1 a big-character poster by a philosophy teacher, Nie Yuanzi, was publicized at Peking University, and was hailed almost immediately by Mao. The poster had attacked Peking University's administration. Within days some of the revolutionary-cadre students at Canton's most prestigious school, having had word of the new events at Peking University through their parents, pasted up their own declarations against teachers and the school administration. Since their parents were of considerably higher political status than even their school's Party head, they already stood little in awe of the teachers' and the school head's authority. By their militancy, the revolutionary-cadre students took over the leadership of the student body, nudging the Youth League aside. As news of the new wall posters spread to the neighborhood high schools, these too quickly became plastered with big-character posters criticizing teachers.

With their academic classes dismissed, a good political performance seemed more important than ever. Students began criticizing teachers for not emphasizing politics or the thought of Mao Zedong enough, for laziness in labor, for the teachers' styles of clothes, or any slips of the tongue a teacher might ever have made.

In laying such charges, some of these students felt exhilaratingly liberated from the confines of petty activism. Yet the students were not "rebelling" *per se*. They were all aware of previous campaigns in China, where specified categories of people who had made "political errors" had been struggled against by the "masses." Now they too would show their adherence to the highest political authorities—above all Chairman Mao—by attacking people whom they believed had been placed by the campaign in a politically disgraced category. In short, the students were still locked into an activist competition with classmates and were eager to conform to the demands of the new campaign.

At the same time, however, the campaign was providing them with new opportunities to give vent to the tensions and grievances which the previous years of competition had aroused. In particular, some of the red-class students were finding it easier to pursue "class line" arguments. Peking's mayor Peng Zhen and the Peking Party and Youth League Committees had just been toppled by Mao's widening campaign, and the red-class students in Canton began using this as a pretext to attack in wall posters the "emphasize performance" position with which Peng Zhen had publicly been identified. In their attacks against teachers, they arugued with increasing vehemence that the teachers had placed undue stress upon examination results; that teachers had shown unconcealed preference for the middling and bad-class students who did well scholastically; that they had not been sufficiently concerned with the children of cadres, workers, and peasants; that many of the older teachers possessed a "bad-class nature." There was nothing novel to such charges; they were part of the "class" lexicon of struggle campaigns. But there was an emotional impetus to the attacks. Many of these good-class students, having had difficulties academically, felt a grievance against teachers whom they thought had looked down on them. In the excitement and militancy of the times they sometimes physically assaulted the isolated teachers. The tensions of the previous months were now coming disturbingly to the surface. Some of the middle-class students began to feel a bit uneasy about the intensifying class-line charges.

In most schools the Party committees encouraged this emphasis upon the "class" issue. They had observed that a few of the Party committees at the best schools had become targets of high-level cadre children, and they were apparently worried their own turn might come. A Central

Committee directive of May 16, pushed through by Mao, had already contained disturbing intimations that the campaign nationally might move not only against bad-class "reactionaries" but also against portions of the Party.[1] In such circumstances, even the Guangdong Party leadership felt it wise to keep student attention fixed on the "class struggle" against bad-class teachers. When the Party secretary of one junior high school tried in early June to protect his school's bad-class teachers from threats and physical assault, students went to the municipal Education Bureau to complain, and the school head was made the object of official city-wide ridicule and abuse.[2]

Mao himself initially supported the campaign's class-line and class-hatred overtones. On June 13 he pushed a directive on education through the Central Committee, and the report in *People's Daily* announcing it argued,

> We must warn those anti-Party and anti-socialist bourgeois "authorities" who are entrenched in the educational world: . . . You have taken the offspring of the reactionary classes to your bosoms and in a hundred and one ways have thwarted, spurned and attacked the children of the working people. You have collaborated with and encouraged the anti-Party and anti-socialist bourgeois "specialists" and "professors" to spread bourgeois and revisionist poison. With so much wickedness to your account, with such a debt that you owe the people, can we possibly allow you to continue your misdeeds without exposing you, without criticizing you, without fighting you?[3]

At the Cultural Revolution's end, the shaken educational establishment would, as we shall see, go overboard for several years to assure that they would not be accused again of standing on the wrong side of the class line.

Trying to turn the heightened play upon "class" directly to their own interests, high-level cadre children in early June had begun making concerted efforts to have the senior-high and university entrance exams abolished and replaced by admissions procedures heavily weighted toward class background. Revolutionary-cadre students at one of Peking's elite schools sent such a petition to Mao and received the Chairman's private commendation.[4] As word of this had spread south in early June through the high-level-cadre grapevine, the cadre youths at Canton's most prestigious school, the South China Attached Middle School, circulated similar petitions among their classmates. As might be expected, none of the school's middle-class students would sign, and some staged a walk-out in protest.[5] But within the week the offensive proposal became official national policy. The middle-class students' chances for a university education had all but collapsed. The Central Committee decision of June 13 put through by Mao explained:

> Beginning this year, a new method of [university] enrollment, a combination of recommendation and selection in which proletarian politics are right to the fore . . . will go into effect. . . . The old examination system is a serious violation of the Party's class line. It shuts out many outstanding children of [pre-Liberation] workers, [former] poor and lower-middle peasants, revolutionary cadres, revolutionary armymen, and revolutionary martyrs and opens the gates wide to the bourgeoisie to cultivate its own successors.[6]

The Guangdong Education Department, following suit, extended this class-line principle to senior high school recruitments.[7]

Yet once these directives had been announced, they caused little stir among the non-red-orgin students. They were caught up in June and July in efforts to prove that they too were dedicated to Mao's line and that they too had "class feelings." The incidents of hypocrisy and petty opportunism of previous years lent added impetus to their attempts now to demonstrate that they themselves were neither opportunists nor careerists. Once the elimination of entrance examinations had been laid down by Mao as official policy, they were in no position to admit openly that they were against it. Rather than contest the issue, they simply refused to recognize it as an important question in the Cultural Revolution. By mid-summer, differences over examinations and educational priorities therefore dropped almost entirely from sight as a point of overt contention between students.[8]

THE WORKTEAMS

Workteams of Party cadres had begun entering the schools in mid-June, under the national direction of Liu Shaoqi, to guide and control the campaign among students. The workteams took over complete control of most of the schools, and the school Party committees had to "stand aside." Initially the workteams turned to the League branches for detailed information on the student bodies and on the movement in the schools. But like the citywide and school Party committees, the workteams were intent on directing the movement along "class" lines. They sought out students of good-class origins to act as their closest aides.

The workteams insisted upon a more orderly program of "struggle." Instead of allowing the students to attack teachers and school authorities indiscriminately, the cadre workteams narrowed the scope of attack to selected teachers, mostly older and of bad-class background. But at many of the schools it was under the workteams' auspices that the attacks upon teachers for the first time turned ugly. Until then the accusations against the teachers had been based on whatever petty incidents students could recollect. But at Girls High in Canton, for example, one of the workteam's first steps was to release to the students the official dossiers of some of the targeted teachers. These were all older teachers who had had "historical" problems: ones who had been given bad-class labels at Liberation, or had been Guomindang members, or had been declared political "rightists" when 1957's Hundred Flowers Movement was repressed. Students were shaken to find that these various dangerous "historical" elements had been hidden in their midst as their own teachers. As if applying what they had learned from stories like the Monkey, the students labeled such teachers "demons and monsters" (!), devils cast in humanlike forms.[9] The abuse and violence mounted as students frenetically competed to prove their revolutionary spirit through the pitilessness of their hatred. The workteams transformed some of the classrooms into makeshift jails. The targeted teachers were confined there at night and dragged out in the daytime for humiliating "struggle meetings" and bouts of hard labor.

The students were no longer trapped in an activism of petty deeds. They were part of a grand drama, made all the grander by the revolutionary violence. Some were chagrinned that particular teachers whom they personally liked were under attack, and some shrank uncomfortably with awe and fear from the incidents of student brutality. But few felt much pity for the targets. These teachers had been placed beyond the pale, no longer "people." Moreover, in a heightened atmosphere of "class struggle," many of the middle-class and bad-class children were under pressure to show their "class stand," and it was far better to do so by "drawing the line" with already discredited teachers than to have to make criticisms of their own family upbringing. If the middle-class students at the better schools felt increasingly frustrated, it was because the good-class students, but not themselves, were permitted to fully express their activism. "In my own school," recalls one, "we didn't beat those teachers very much. Maltreatment definitely existed, but only a comparatively small sector of the students were permitted to mete out such maltreatment. Those duties were regarded as very glorious. The ghosts and demons were guarded and controlled only by people of good origins." Another student recalls that "The red origin kids argued that previously when the classrooms were dominated socially and academically by the kids of professionals, they hadn't had the opportunity to show their true activism and worth. They said, 'Now we'll show you how active we can be.' Were they ever!"

Up through July 1966, the middle-class youths continued to strive hard, when given the opportunity, to participate side-by-side with the good-background students in the struggles against class enemies. The middle-class League members even voluntarily pursued the trend set by the workteams; relinquishing some of their own authority to good-class students reaffirmed the genuineness of their own "class stand." But as one non-League middle-class student observes: "I felt the workteam was no good. They relied on the high-level cadre kids, and we were made to seem low class." He wanted his fair chance at defending Chairman Mao's line. Yet the Party workteam was denying him this right. And then word sifted through in early August that in Peking workteams were being pulled out of the schools, and that the workteams' legitimacy had been thrown into dispute.[10]

In retrospect, we know that Mao felt the workteams were beginning to restrict his campaign. Partly it was because he was not just after "scholar-tyrants" and "bourgeois academics" but also conservatized Party members. But perhaps more important at this stage of the Cultural Revolution was Mao's displeasure at the workteams' conventional manner of carefully controlling and orchestrating the students' activities. As the workteams in Peking began withdrawing from the schools he pushed through the "16 points" of August 8, which he intended as the guide to his Cultural Revolution. It declared, in part, that "In the Great Proletarian Cultural Revolution, it is the masses [at this juncture meaning students] who must liberate themselves. We cannot do the things for them which they should do for themselves. We must trust the masses, rely on them and respect their creative spirit. . . . We must not be afraid of disorder."[11]

A relative handful of the middle-class youths sensed they were to be given their chance. When reading the August documents their eyes skipped the references to "class" and fastened on the phrases about the masses' liberating themselves and about "capitalist roaders in the Party." This small minority of excited middle-class young people thought they saw the schools' Party committees being shifted into the same vulnerable category as the teachers. Without much consideration for the possible adverse consequences to themselves, the boldest among them pasted up posters denouncing their school's Party leaders even before the work-teams had completely packed up and gone. By doing so, they in effect were trying to push the campaign away from "class line" issues and symbols. They were also temporarily taking the initiative away from the red-class students.

Yet they quite often had no special grievances against their school Party committee, just as their earlier attacks on teachers had not normally been fuelled by concrete grievances. Interviews bring this out well. A middle-class student who took the lead in attacking a retreating workteam for shielding his school's Party committee and who then urged that the Party committee be struggled against, still has difficulty explaining why he had opposed the school committee:

> Actually, . . . hm . . . the basic problems with the Party committee weren't big. I thought it had done some wrong things . . .(pause) . . . such as something bureaucratic . . . (pause) The school principal was lazy, I thought . . . (pause) . . . Actually when talking about him or the Party committee, there weren't many concrete problems . . . (pause) . . . but how could we know that inside the committee there were no problems? Especially after reading the 16 Points I was convinced. . . . At that time the spearhead was pointed against the teachers instead. I thought that was wrong, that it should be against the Party branch. So I criticized the work-team [and implicitly the good-background youths and League] for making a mistake in direction.[12]

This interviewee was not one who stood confusedly at the fringes of the Red Guard rebellion. He was later to become the deputy commander of Canton's high school Rebel Red Guards. Other students seem at that early time to have had as little or less notion than he did of any broader ideological issues. Students like him were simply responding to their need for action, and were interpreting Mao's directives in a manner that was most favorable to their "class" circumstances. In large part, they hit out at Party committees because they were being thwarted in participating in struggles against the lesser targets. Only at a rather later juncture did the activities of some of them become tied to ideological values and principles.

Those who tried to wrest the initiative from the good-class students in August were acting several months too soon. The newspaper editorials in August still indicated that the thrust of the Cultural Revolution in the schools should be on "class struggle" against bad-class elements. At a majority of the senior high schools the red-class students, in particular the cadres' children, had already moved firmly into the positions of student body leadership by the time the workteams had withdrawn. In some schools, the red-class student leaders opposed and smothered any efforts to attack the Party members. In other schools, they themselves sometimes initiated the attacks, but played up arguments that the school authorities had "oppressed" the youngsters of worker-peasant-cadre background prior to the Cultural Revolution. Having recently helped push the campaign along class-line tracks, these schools' Party committees now ironically found themselves among the class-line targets.

THE GOOD-CLASS RED GUARDS

Mao on his side provided a stamp of approval to the pure-background students' claims to exclusive student leadership. In early August, high-level revolutionary-cadre children at several of Peking's most famous key-point secondary schools had put together their own youth groups, whose memberships were based upon young people of pure origins. They called their little organizations the Red Guards. On August 18 Mao reviewed a massive rally of good-class students, and a *People's Daily* photograph of the event pointedly showed the Chairman accepting a Red Guard armband from the daughter of a high-level cadre.

Within days the title and the concept had been taken up by the revolutionary-cadre youths of other cities. These new student groups provided a means to bypass and repudiate the Youth League, where "performance" had counted heavily and where power and prestige had had to be shared with non-red-origin classmates. With the formation of the Red Guards, the vestiges of the League's power in the schools collapsed. The frame of reference which some of the red-class students had formed even prior to the Cultural Revolution, that family origins should count for everything, was to find extreme expression in this new Red Guard movement.

On August 25, only a week after Mao had publicly endorsed the Peking Red Guards, the revolutionary-cadre daughters of Girls High in Canton established their own exclusively good-background Red Guard grouping. The inaugural meeting was held out-of-doors in the evening. One of my interviewees, a middle-class 15-year-old girl named Wang, had climbed secretly to the school roof to watch the event. Spread out below her, seated on the grass, were three concentric half-circles of girls. Wide swathes of empty ground carefully demarcated each of these ranked groups. At front-center sat the new Red Guards, all of good-class background, along with honored guests—revolutionary-cadre students from several other schools. The second ring of girls was composed of good-background youths who had not yet been permitted to join the Red Guards. Though they had claimed to be of working-class family origins, the new Red Guards were demanding a reinvestigation to ensure that their fathers had not actually been urban artisans or coolies before Liberation, occupations not purely "proletarian."

The outer circle of girls was composed of students of non-red families who were anxious to participate in the Cultural Revolution. They were to be allowed to become aides to the Red Guards. At most schools this adjunct grouping of middle-class students was called the Red Outer Circle (*Hong-wai-wei*). At Wang's school it included a noticeably high number of middle-class League members. League members had "cultivated" themselves to be conformist and politically obedient; most of them had been willing to put up with the class-line trends; and, now, by aligning themselves with the good-origin students and gaining permission to enter the Red Outer Circle, they would be able to salvage for themselves a higher official status than other middle-class students.

Good-class student emissaries from Peking had brought word that in the capital the cadres' children had begun turning against the students of enemy-class families. Having based their new organization upon the premise that inherited class feelings counted for everything in determining attitudes, they had concluded that an irremediable "original sin" was conversely attached to classmates of bad-class parentage. The red-class students already felt a diffuse antagonism towards these classmates, generated by frustrations with their own coursework and annoyance that so many of the bad-class students did so well academically. For Girls High's inaugural Red Guard meeting, a group of bad-class students was to be cursed at by schoolmates eager to prove their activist ardor. By bad luck, as the participants whipped themselves into a revolutionary anger, my interviewee Wang was sighted on the roof. She was called a spy and made to line up with the targeted group.

In the days that followed, in a series of struggle meetings conducted in her classroom, Wang was accused of having been too arrogant before the Cultural Revolution and for having shown dissatisfaction with the class line.

I had to make self-criticisms. I felt it was true what they claimed, that I had previously not been concerned (guanxin) for the workers' kids. I felt ashamed before Mao for this. When I saw Chairman Mao's portrait I often cried, for having looked down at workers' and cadres' kids. I felt several different ways all at once, all confused. When I read Mao's works for guidance, he said you must care for the people and must help even capitalists change their minds. I felt, I am certainly a part of the "people." I did not believe Chairman Mao wanted them to oppress me like that.[13]

Wang's confused sentiments were shared in a less emotional way even by middle-class students who were not under attack. They did not quite know that summer how to respond to the class line. On the one side, it was strongly supported by Mao himself. But on the other, it was corroding their own status in a way that seemed unfair.

The revolutionary-cadre youths' perceptions of class were becoming progressively more extreme. They had found their ideologue in Tan Lifu, the son of a deceased high-level cadre, who had gained national attention through an August 20 speech which propounded a "blood-line theory" as the basis for judging all youths. Though Tan did not put it so crudely, the gist of the message was expressed by two "blood-line" couplets which went up on the walls of schools throughout China in September 1966, reading

If the father is a hero the son is a good fellow;
If the father is a reactionary the son is a bad egg;
If the father is middling, the son sits on the fence.

and

A great dragon gives birth to a dragon,
A phoenix gives birth to a phoenix,
A rat gives birth to a child who only burrows holes in the ground.

At Wang's school the Red Guards themselves developed a strict pecking order: the children of high military cadres stood highest, then the daughters of factory and administrative Party men, followed by worker- and finally peasant-background youths at the bottom of the organization. In some schools the high-level cadre youngsters even wore armbands of velvet or silk to distinguish themselves from lesser-born Red Guard colleagues.

The red-class youths themselves gradiosely titled this phase of the

Cultural Revolution the Red Terror. Wang remembers,

They had struggle meetings in every class night and day, and everyone not from red families was forced to self-criticize. Some were treated harshly, others not at all, but all were cursed. The red-background kids commanded even those League members who were supporting them to engage in some self-criticism; but when the Red Guards struggled against those of us under attack, these League members joined in.

I was beaten and yelled at. They forced me to study Mao Zedong a great deal. In the middle of the night they disturbed me in my sleep and forced me to the playing-field where I'd be cursed at till morning. They even used sticks.

But Want was largely spared physical abuse. Though a target, she was after all middle-class. In those schools where systematic violence occurred it was the "hidden demons"—the targetted teachers and the "blackest" of the black-class youths—who were subjected to the competitive activist terror. Usually it was among the immature teenagers of the junior high schools (shades of *Lord of the Flies*) and especially in the competitive key-point junior highs that the worst reported outrages occurred.

Even during this period the bulk of the middle-class students did not feel threatened. They remained "among the people." Accordingly, when the Destroy the Four Olds movement began in late August and early September and students went through the city searching for decadent bourgeois objects to destroy, some of these middle-class students tried to regrab the initiative by launching their own search-and-destroy missions against black-class homes. But the red-class students soon denied them the right to a leading role, while embarking all the more furiously on the searches themselves. It rapidly became evident that it was an exercise tailor-made for their own purposes, since the furnishings and books which were destroyed as decadent were similar to those contained in middle-class intelligentsia homes. The message to the middle-class students gradually became clear; their own credentials were being further placed in doubt by this indirect discrediting of their upbringing.

MAO AND THE RISE OF THE REBEL RED GUARDS

The blood-line theory's extreme interpretation of "class" received at least a fair measure of high-level Party approval. Leaders such as Tao Zhu and

Tan Zhenlin apparently regarded the blood-line proposals as an assurance that rather than seeing the "spears pointed upward" toward members of the leadership in this campaign, the spears would be deflected downwards towards bad-class or bad-historied teachers and students. They must have seen too that defining "redness" in class terms, with "revolutionary cadres" as the reddest of all, strengthened their own legitimacy. And they knew that the sons and daughters of the revolutionary cadres would not be so likely to turn the campaign against the middle and higher levels of the Party. To do so would be to endanger their own parents and to undermine their own claims of superiority. In fact, Tan Lifu's famous August speech had contained a general defense of high-level Party cadres.

But by autumn, for the very same reasons, Mao and his close supporters in the leadership were beginning to turn against the activities of the Red Guards. These leaders had no inherent objection to a "class struggle" campaign, and on educational issues, as we have seen, Mao himself supported a stronger class line. But even though he initially had been satisfied to put the leadership of the student campaign into the hands of the red-origin youngsters, Mao apparently had not expected that the pure-class children would use the campaign primarily to erect a rigid caste system favoring themselves, or that the campaign would become altogether stuck in the groove of attacking bad-class enemies.

Mao by the mid-sixties had come to feel that the greatest *immediate* danger to his political vision lay with the new Party bureaucracy rather than the old "bourgeois" classes. In the Chinese Marxist conceptualizations of "contradictions" and the dialectic, it is necessary to determine the most significant contradiction of the moment and to concentrate on building alliances that are focussed on correctly resolving that particular contradiction. Accordingly, the Maoist leaders repudiated the blood-line theory in the autumn of 1966 in order to revamp the campaign. They were ready to make use of any groups of students, class background notwithstanding, who were willing to hit out at Party "capitalist roaders."[14] As just one among many examples, in a speech to student groups Lin Biao proclaimed, "We must replace the blood-line theory . . . and unite all those who can be united. . . . Our Party has always maintained that revolutionary youths are entitled to equality."[15] In December Tan Lifu, the university student who had authored the blood-line theory, was placed under arrest by the Public Security Bureau as a "counterrevolutionary."[16]

Yet at the same time, Mao and his radical followers in the leadership did not repudiate all the good-background students who had led the movement in the schools up till then. Mao was not even opting to drop entirely the theme of the literal "class struggle" against bad-class people. What he *was* doing was insisting that the Cultural Revolution be considered principally a "political line struggle" campaign rather than simply "class struggle." At least for the time being the "class" terminology was to be taken as a metaphor for political stances, and the targets were to be Party "capitalist roaders" rather than "capitalists," and "representatives of the bourgeoisie in the Party" rather than actual members of the bourgeoisie.

"Line struggle" and "class struggle" bring into relief one or the other of the two axes of the Chinese Marxist perspective on "redness." When "class struggle" is emphasized and the targets are defined in literal "class" terms, the accusers tend to define themselves as righteously "red" due to their pure-class backgrounds. But when a "line struggle" campaign gets mounted, not only do the targets get redefined; the scope also widens as to who can claim to be the "red" accusers. Taking the proper political line is then what counts. Accordingly, the more that the non-good-class students could claim the Cultural Revolution to be purely an attack on Party leaders who had taken up the wrong political line, the more they could declare themselves "red" by virtue of their own attitudes.

Later in the Cultural Revolution, some of those with an analytical bent even developed a political argument supporting *permanent* emphasis on "line struggle" at the expense of "class struggle." This theorizing culminated in the influential postulations by Sheng-Wu-Lian, a Rebel Red Guard organization in Hunan Province, which redefined the Party bureaucracy itself as a perpetually dangerous "new class."[17]

But the great majority of the middle-class students never dared to think such thoughts. They never even dared to repudiate the literal notions of "class." Their own claim to political legitimacy was that they were championing Mao's cause; and when Mao himself had begun in the early 1960s to develop new perspectives on "class" linked more to attitudes and to the rise of new life-styles and new social groupings in "revisionist" Russia and post-Liberation China, Mao had in no way discarded his prior conceptualizations of "class." Thus the commander-in-chief of Canton's high school Rebel Red Guards—a young man of middle-class background—continues today to protest:

No, we didn't go against the class line. The Party's class line was correct. What we were against were those blood-line couplets, against the way those revolutionary-cadre kids were doing things, against their not believing in the masses. We never said we were against the class line. That kind of thing seemed to have come with life. I just had never thought it was wrong. I was born like this and so I am like this.[18]

But by stressing "line struggle" and the revived official slogan of "emphasize performance," and by playing up their own willingness to die in violent defense of Chairman Mao's line, such students could convince themselves that their own activism as middle-class youths was of a purer moral quality than the young people whose activism claimed closer ties to "class." Wang, for one, became a confirmed believer in this:

Though I admitted to myself that there was a family influence at work, I felt people could change themselves and could cultivate themselves to become revolutionary. I felt that those from good-class background also had to cultivate themselves to have the correct stand and world view. But I came to feel in addition that the good-origin classes' reasons for being revolutionary weren't for the very highest of reasons. They were thankful to the Party merely because they had benefitted from the revolution. Yes, the workers and peasants were thankful to the Party, and too, very often, were their sons and daughters. They saw that their parents, who had lived such miserable lives before, had benefitted, and that if the revolution hadn't occurred they themselves would today be occupying their parents' pre-Liberation shoes. But this is a "low-level" feeling. A truly good revolutionary, and a truly good person, still believes and still is activist even if he hasn't benefitted personally from his beliefs and actions. The kids I admired most were some of those who as Rebel Red Guards were willing to endure oppression and suffering for what they considered the truth.

Mao had not stipulated or probably even intended that two antagonistic Cultural Revolution factions would emerge among the students. But Wang describes the new turn of events.

Suddenly in October student representatives from Qinghua University and other Peking colleges came to Canton and to our school. They announced that the class-line policy being used by the red-origin kids was really the tool of reactionaries sitting at the Party's center who wanted to sidetrack the Cultural Revolution. They declared that the revolution must utilize more people, and we must concentrate our struggle-power against those taking the capitalist road. When they told us that Mao Zedong's line was to trust the masses and believe in their creativity we were exhilarated and leaped forward to join the Cultural Revolution. One reason was to liberate ourselves. And we felt Mao was in danger and was giving us the power to participate and to protect him and to follow him to make revolution.

Some of the good-class youths of Canton had already begun leaving Canton on what they called "great link-ups" (*da chaunlian*) to Peking and other cities, to "share revolutionary experiences." But previously they had not given the non-red-origin students permission to go. Now the middle-class students cut loose from the schools and embarked on the sight-seeing pilgrimages themselves. Traveling in small groups and meeting students of their own backgrounds and circumstances from oher parts of the country, they had the opportunity to vent their feelings in discussions and to begin defining themselves more on their own terms. When they drifted back to their schools in late December and early January, they formed their own independent Red Guard groupings, which were subsequently labelled "Rebel" Red Guards. The successors of the initial pure-background Red Guard groups became known colloquially as the "Conservative" or "Loyalist" Red Guards.

The developments of the autumn had presented the largely middle-class Rebel youths with an advantage. They could claim that by their militant attacks upon "Party capitalist roaders" they were proving themselves the true followers of Mao. Their attacks also provided them with the satisfaction of revenge; the targets included the parents of the revolutionary-cadre youths. The Loyalists for their part maintained that Mao had said repeatedly that most cadres were good and warranted respect, whilst only the minority were "capitalist roaders." For them, the faithful pursuit of Mao's line demanded that a smaller number of local "authorities" be overturned and the remainder be protected.

Hence as the scholar Hong Yung Lee has shown; while the new-born Rebel Red Guard groups tended to attack the highest leader in an organization, the Loyalists concentrated more on the organization's number-two person. One reason was that the Rebels were attacking the Party powers-that-be by way of the top person, whereas the Loyalist Red Guards tried to imply through their attacks that there were merely a few rotten eggs *inside* the organization. A second factor was that the second-in-command of a unit often functioned as the "expert," whereas the top person was the more trusted Party functionary. Each, to the differing student Red Guard groups, became symbols of *what* should be attacked.[19]

CHOOSING SIDES

During the first months of 1967, most of the students had gravitated into one or the other of these two opposed Red Guard camps. In statistical terms, as seen in table 6-1, their factionalism was tantamount to class warfare.

Table 6-1. The "Class" Composition of Canton's Two Red Guard Factions (1967)
(N = 50 classrooms)

	Red-class	Middle- and Bad-class	Total
East Wind Red Guards (Loyalists)	81%	19%	100%
Red Flag Red Guards (Rebels)	26%	74%	100%

Table 6-2 shows the divisions more precisely, and shows also where the new Rebel groups and the reconstituted Loyalists were able to draw adherents across class lines. Such shifts had been made easier once the issue had slid from one simply of "class" to the question of how broad the attacks on Party committees should be.

Interviews suggest why these crossovers in factional allegiance occurred. Among other things, as seen in an earlier chapter, many of the working-class youths had never gotten along well with the revolutionary-cadre students. Though they justifiably had had complaints that many of the middle-class students had looked down on them due to their academic difficulties, they had been just as aware that the revolutionary-cadre students felt superior to them on the basis of "class." Similarly, though the blood-line theory had given most of them access to the initial Red Guards and they had gone along with the rigid class-based hierarchy, they had resented being placed at the very bottom of the pure-blood organization. If anything, it had sharpened their antagonisms with the cadre youths.

Those working-class youths who had done reasonably well academically now saw little reason not to swing over to the side of their middle-class schoolmates. They had little cause to oppose the renewed emphasis upon performance and were not particularly averse to attacking the Party's "revolutionary cadres." Frequently they were joined by working-class schoolmates whose good-class origins had been denied by the initial Red Guards. During the Red Terror, at least some of the workers' children whose *grand*fathers had not been industrial workers had been given

Table 6-2. Red Guard Alignments, by Class Origins
(N = 50 classrooms)

Official Class Label of Father	Factional Alignments of Students (%)			No. of students
	Red Flag (Rebels)	East Wind (Loyalists)	Non-participant	
RED-CLASS FAMILY BACKGROUND				
"Revolutionary cadre" (listed below by father's status, 1966)				
high-level PLA officer	10%	80%	10%	62
lower-level PLA	6	86	8	66
high-level civilian Party	30	65	5	60
middle-level Party cadre	32	61	7	79
local civil-war guerrilla (still mostly rural leaders)	11	78	11	18
Working-class (as of Liberation)				
industrial worker	36	41	23	442
poor or lower-middle peasant	23	36	41	95
MIDDLE-CLASS FAMILY BACKGROUND (as of Liberation)				
Non-intelligentsia				
peddlars & store clerks, etc.	40	10	50	250
middle peasant	40	10	50	52
"Intelligentsia"				
white collar & professionals	61	7	32	562
high level (scientists, professors, etc.)	60	7	33	102
BAD-CLASS FAMILY BACKGROUND				
overseas Chinese Merchant	42	12	46	96
capitalist	31	1	68	140
Guomindang official	58	4	38	50
rightist	31	4	65	26
rich-peasant	17	0	83	18
"bad-element"	7	0	93	14
landlord	33	3	64	39
counterrevolutionary	31	0	69	16
Total number of students in the surveyed classrooms				2,187

insulting non-red-class labels by the ultra-class-purist cadre sons and daughters.

Moreover, in the working-class neighborhood junior highs, where most students had never striven to be activists and where resentments against ambitious activists were sometimes strong, larger numbers now seized the opportunity to go against the activist classmates who had led them both before the Cultural Revolution and during its initial phases. Further numbers of these working-class junior-high students attached themselves to the Rebel side simply because in the gathering chaos the Rebels seemed to offer a better climate for disruptive excitement.

Tabel 6-2 illustrates also that the revolutionary-cadre youths were hurt even by internal divisions. Some of the children of the local civilian Party cadres had resented the superior status assumed by the military-cadre youths. The latter were mostly northerners who spoke little Cantonese and who had usually kept to their own tight-knit friendship circles. Some of the local cadre youths now began to defect, especially if they had been able to keep up academically and if their own parents were not under threat from the Rebel Red Guard thrusts against local Party leaders. They were joined by cadre youths whose parents were in Party organs which had swung over strategically to the radical side;[20] and by the misfits among the cadre youths who had never been permitted by their good-class peers to join the League.

The newly formed Rebels could hence be considered a grouping of disparate types of students who shared individual or group antagonisms toward the initial Red Guard leadership. Within this loose coalition, in fact, some of the red-class Rebels preferred to operate their own Rebel units, keeping the Rebel students of lesser breeding at arm's length. The new Rebel organizations' main numerical base of support, however, and almost all the leadership, was drawn from the ranks of the middle-class students.[21] On the other side of the battle-lines, their pre-Cultural Revolution rivals for classroom prestige and upward mobility—the revolutionary-cadre youths—provided the most active support and most of the leadership for the Loyalist Red Guard groups.

The bad-class students stayed largely on the sidelines. Their parents had taught them from an early age onward to avoid being put in an exposed position, and the Red Terror had very recently reaffirmed their need for caution. As table 6-2 confirms, most of them went quietly home for the Cultural Revolution's duration. As the data also show, when such students did participate it was almost invariably on the side of the Rebels.[22] But if their family origins were truly "black" their school's

Rebel groups sometimes denied them formal membership and consigned them to informal and sporadic participation on the fringes of the movement.

Students who had been highly motivated before the Cultural Revolution tended now to be the most activist and dedicated during the upheavals. The leadership of both factions emerged largely from the dozen best schools in the city; and the fighting tended to be fiercest at these schools. They had been competitively involved in trying to get into universities, had been more eagerly engaged in trying to get into the League, and had in consequence been more frustrated by the "petty deeds" of the classroom activism. They were now more eager for the "big deeds" of the Cultural Revolution. Conversely, interviews suggest that at the less prestigious schools students of almost all class origins tended to be more lackluster and inconsistent even when they participated. In short, youths who in pre-Cultural Revolution high-school days had been less ambitious—who, for example, had wanted to get manual jobs after graduating from junior high—were also less eager now to join in the Cultural Revolution struggles.

Generally, too, as table 6-3 shows, students who had been Communist Youth League members were more apt to participate in the Cultural Revolution's events than the average student. Again, pre-Cultural Revolution activist efforts were carrying over into Red Guard activity. This table reveals also that the controversy over "class" versus "performance" had swung the middle-class League members over to the Rebels almost en masse. But as we observed, a fair number of these League

Table 6-3. League Members' Affiliations in the Cultural Revolution
(N = 50 classrooms)

	Canton Students in General				League Members			
	Nos. of students	Rebel	Loyal	Non- part.	Nos. of students	Rebel	Loyal	Non- part.
Revolutionary cadre	285	19%	73%	8%	142	21%	73%	6%
Working-class	537	34%	40%	26%	146	35%	51%	14%
Non-intelligentsia middle-class	302	40%	10%	50%	25	56%	12%	32%
Intelligentsia middle-class	664	61%	7%	32%	120	77%	11%	12%
Bad-class and overseas Chinese	399	36%	4%	60%	37	62%	8%	30%

SOURCE: questionnaire remembrances

members had earlier also joined the Red Outer Circle. Having been more emotionally attached than most of their schoolmates to obedience, conformity, and political hierarchy, these League members were not particularly enthusiastic about wholesale attacks against the local or provincial Party committees. They now generally attached themselves to the more moderate of the Rebel groups.

The Rebel faction had adopted the slogan that it did not matter when you had become a Rebel so long as you were one. But in reality the students who had rebelled earliest and with the greatest noise—who, for instance, had led the abortive attacks on their school Party committees in August 1966 or had dared to speak out against the subsequent Red Terror—now commanded the greatest respect and more often than not became the Rebels' leaders. In this, the Rebel Red Guards were unconsciously emulating the Communist Party itself, where a member's stature is normally measured in accordance with how early he or she had joined the pre-Liberation revolution.

ALLIANCES AND ISSUES

The organizational abilities that the Red Guards had acquired as students came in handy. They had learned since childhood how to divide duties, how to work through committees, and how to coordinate activities. Through this, they were able eventually to paste together loose citywide coalitions.

The university students brought them into a yet broader coalition. The university Rebels had sought out allies also in the factories, among labor crews of demobilized soldiers, and among personnel in the urban administrative organs. In January 1967, with the Party organizations and city administration on the verge of disintegration, these university Rebel Red Guards, though in existence only several months, had sufficient strength and gall to move successfully, in alliance with their new-found older and younger allies, to topple Canton's leaders and momentarily take over the seals of public office.

The issue of class line had not held any great importance for most of the university students. They had already passed successfully through the competition to enter higher education and were already largely slotted into designated careers. Even during the months of Red Terror in the high schools, therefore, the good-origin students at the colleges had not given the blood-line theory strong support. When the university students split into two major camps of Red Guards, the division primarily had been between the "red" students and the "expert" students.

The experts were those students who had emphasized their studies in order to become China's engineers, etc; whereas the so-called red students had put much of their time and attention into League and Party activities, aiming for careers as political/administrative supervisors over the experts. Good-class students took the red route more often than other students—first, because some of them had entered university with lower educational attainments; and second, because their access to a red career was made easier for them than for other students. Thus, even in the universities the lines were drawn somewhat along class lines, but indirectly.

In the Cultural Revolution, the red students (who either already were Party members of were Party acolytes) tended to side with the university Party committees. Many of their classmates asserted their own dedication to Mao (and their own antipathy for the controls which had been exercised over them by the red-student activist leadership) by launching attacks against these university leaders.[23] Their subsequent alignment as "loyalists" or "rebels" often depended upon whether the provincial Party committee had backed or opposed their attacks on the college administration at their own particular campus. Because the university students were not directly preoccupied with "class line" problems, they latched onto the issues and rhetoric that interested the Party center more quickly and more readily than the high school students. By the early winter of 1966-67 their secondary-school allies in Canton were eagerly following in their footsteps.[24]

The high school Rebel Red Guards profited from this shift in issues. They knew they could not win out in the end if the themes they fought over were still related to "class," with themselves of worse class origins than the Loyalists. Consistently they exhibited rather greater concern than the Loyalists to develop new issues to bolster their cause.

In particular, they came to see themselves not only as fighting in a hazily defined "defense of Chairman Mao," but also to establish permanently the Cultural Revolution's "great democracy" (da minzhu). This Cultural Revolution catch-phrase came to mean the right of grassroots groups to freely criticize local Party committees and to help determine policy through the free expression and arguing out of ideas. To quote Wang, "Great democracy meant you were against being repressed in what you did. Of course it didn't mean you could criticize Mao or the legitimacy of the Party; but it meant you could criticize the Party personnel and the basic levels." These semidemocratic espousals came to serve almost as an ex *post facto* justification for their near-indiscriminate attacks on local Party organs. But this does not negate the fact that "great democracy" became a genuine conviction of burning importance to some of the young Rebels. The Loyalists meanwhile held more to the Leninist faith in Party hierarchy.

The small minority of intellectually oriented idealists in the two Red Guard camps, who wrote many of the tracts, defined themselves and their own faction in contradistinction to the other. In their violent competition they came to see each other as polar types. With different interpretations of how a youth's "redness" should be defined, of what targets should be attacked or protected, and, finally, of how tight or loose Party control should be, the students came to feel they were engaged in a Manichean struggle in which they themselves were the defenders of Mao's line against the demons. They felt they were battling for causes that transcended themselves.

In this respect, the Cultural Revolution adhered to a crudely "Marxist" progression: individual interests becoming "class" interests and in turn becoming ideologies. As such, the students' ardor was the greater and their resistance to ending the Cultural Revolution stronger: for their continued fighting did not depend upon whether there was something "in it" for themselves. Whatever the origins of their factionalism, it was in this new context that at least some of them killed each other or willingly sacrificed their own lives.

The issues and maneuverings of relevance to us had largely been played out within the first year of the Cultural Revolution. We need not concern ourselves here in detail with the ensuing twists and turns of the Red Guard conflict. These have been more than adequately described elsewhere.[25] But it should be noted that it was only a minority of youths who continued this idealistic combat of accelerating violence. Larger numbers dropped out. Their needs to prove themselves were not usually strong enough to sustain them through two years of violence.

Even before the Cultural Revolution ended, indeed, there were indications that a "lost generation" syndrome was forming. With the student fighting still in progress, Canton's *Southern Daily* in March 1968 complained that some of Canton's student population had turned apolitically anarchic, and that others had adopted the view that "indolence is justified"—a pun on the Red Guard slogan "to rebel is justified." *Southern Daily* complained that many such youths cared little any longer about anything: be it the country, the Chairman, politics, their own futures, or a job.[26]

For some of the Rebels who had kept fighting, the disillusionment would be even greater. Having, as it were, flown higher, their spirits had further to fall. When the PLA in Canton intervened in the summer of 1968 it crushed the high school Rebels' remaining force of some ten thousand armed students. That the army, if and when it entered the fray, would move to suppress them must not have surprised them; after all, our questionnaire shows fully 84 percent of the army officers' teenaged children had enrolled actively on the Loyalist side of the lines. But insult soon became added to injury. When all of Canton's secondary-school students were forceably herded back to their schools in the autumn of 1968, the PLA teams that were placed in charge of the schools made them reenact the first "class struggle" phase of the Cultural Revolution. The same teachers who had been attacked two years earlier for bad-class or "historical" faults were now to be the targets once more for weeks of struggle meetings. The point was being hammered home: the Rebels had been defeated in Guangdong.

More than that, it seems Mao and his radical followers in Peking were willing once more to throw their backing behind stronger class-line policies that favored working-class young people. The radical leadership measured events as part of an evolving dialectic. During the Cultural Revolution the "major contradiction," as defined by themselves, had involved backsliding within the Party. It had been legitimate and necessary to shape alliances to combat the menace. By the Cultural Revolution's end, however, the historical circumstances had altered: the Party machine, let alone humbled, had been all but destroyed temporarily. The new "major contradiction," the radicals believed, concerned the persisting influences of "bourgeois" practices and personnel. Policies were now to be geared toward weakening the status in society of the middle-class professionals. They and their children were to be the Cultural Revolution's losers.

THE FORCIBLE RUSTICATION OF THE RED GUARDS

The Red Guards had been brought back to their schools in the late summer of 1968 to be disciplined and allocated to jobs. Almost all of them were told to consider themselves junior or senior high school graduates. Only some of the youngest of the first-year junior-high students and a chosen few of the second-year students of pure red origins would be permitted to renew their schooling for one final year. All the remaining high school desks were needed for a younger generation.[27] At the same time, because the two years of Cultural Revolution turmoil had brought industrial expansion to a halt, there were very few factory jobs available for the recent Red Guards. There was considerable irony in this, for the struggles in the Cultural Revolution had sprung in part from their prior contest to secure upward mobility. Now instead the great majority of the former Red Guards of both factions would have to settle in the countryside; and they were told it most likely would be for life.

Whereas before the Cultural Revolution all of the rusticants from Canton had been volunteers, in this new program of 1968 it was a matter of being *forced* to go. The PLA teams and the Worker Propaganda Teams which had entered the schools had the power arbitrarily to determine which students could continue their schooling, who would be assigned to urban jobs, who would be conscripted into the military, and who would be sent to join agricultural production. These decisions became a measure the Red Guards themselves used in determining whether they had "won" or "lost." And it can be seen in table 6-4 that the choice assignments were distributed largely on the basis of the class line.

In addition, separate tables, not shown here, reveal that a pre-Cultural Revolution League membership was of some help to a youth in obtaining a nonrural posting, but that a Loyalist affiliation in the Cultural

Table 6-4. Postings of Former Red Guards, 1968–69
(N = 55 classrooms)

	Entered PLA	Urban jobs	Continued studies	Total not going to countryside	Total going to countryside
Revolutionary cadre	26%	12%	4%	42%	58%
Working-class	3%	20%	8%	31%	69%
Non-intelligentsia middle-class	0%	5%	0%	5%	95%
Intelligentsia middle-class	0%	3%	1%	4%	96%
Overseas Chinese	0%	1%	2%	3%	97%
Bad class	0%	1%	0%	1%	99%

Revolution was of considerably greater advantage; for each "class" category a substantially higher percentage of Loyalists was able to evade the countryside than was the case generally for their class-category cohort. Most of the students who were sent to settle in the countryside accordingly had reasons to feel aggrieved. They considered they had been discriminated against for either factional or class reasons.

All in all the official newspaper statistics from Canton reveal that three-quarters of all the city's former secondary school students—75,000 in all—were assigned to the countryside during those four autumn and winter months of 1968-69.[28] These new rusticants constituted more than twice the total numbers that had been mobilized to go during the entire decade prior to the Cultural Revolution. It was an exodus of more than 5 percent of Canton's total population, and most of one generation.

The young people of Guangdong's smaller cities and market-towns, which had experienced slower industrial development, were even more severely hit. All told, a third of a million of the province's urban youngsters were sent at a single time into the villages to settle for life.[29] As shall be seen in chapter 8, the already overcrowded countryside could not readily absorb so many.

LOOKING BOTH WAYS

The Cultural Revolution and its immediate denouement help to illuminate the tensions separately faced by the pre- and post-Cultural Revolution school systems. As we saw, the campaign violence had reflected the competition and conflicting interests of different groups of students over questions of upward mobility. We observed how these issues in the sixties were complicated by the class line and the frustrations over entrance to the League. In the Cultural Revolution, armed factions had been formed and ideologies had eventually developed from these initial tensions and fractures.

The post-Cultural Revolution students would not be facing similar competitive tensions. The school system in which they would participate no longer would let their futures be determined by either their academic standing or political performance. But they would inherit from the Cultural Revolution a sense of confusion and aimlessness, and also would inherit job prospects made both worse and more realistically fearsome than their elder brothers and sisters had faced.

The Cultural Revolution thus provided a watershed for Chinese education. But it was a watershed in the sense that it was a divide between different types of problems, each created by the shape of the educational system and the job market. The Cultural Revolution turmoil not only propelled to power a new set of radical makers of educational policy; it also contributed to the unsettling new school milieu and dire job situation that would help defeat their new "revolutionary" reform efforts.

PART II

After the Cultural Revolution: The Disastrous Leap into a New School System

CHAPTER SEVEN

Back to School, 1968–1970

IN 1968, most of the leaders who opposed the views of Mao's disciples had been swept away or politically weakened. New leaders such as Yao Wenyuan and Zhang Chunqiao, who became Mao's representatives in educational affairs, were presented with a clean slate on which to try to devise a new system. They had never thought through the precise details of the educational reforms they proposed, but they did hold fixed notions of the general type of educational system they thought best for China. From the newspapers of that period, from Mao's own earlier talks, and from the actual school system which was erected after 1968, it is possible to deduce what they sought and why.

THE "RADICAL" EDUCATIONAL IDEOLOGY

Before the Cultural Revolution the regular senior high school system's principal responsibility had been to feed the universities with youths properly prepared to become China's high technical and professional personnel. The other half of this bifurcated senior-high system, the technical/vocational schools, were to help produce middle-level vocational expertise. In both instances, the concern of the educational leadership had been to develop an advanced industrial infrastructure.

The followers of Mao, on the other hand, saw less need to use the senior high schools (or in turn the junior highs) to help sort and prepare a corps of higher-trained personnel. In part this was because they wanted a different approach to economic development. The Party's left wing was oriented more toward a development strategy that relied on smaller and technically less sophisticated factories. They argued that with such an industrial program it would be adequate simply to develop greater numbers of politically reliable "socialist laborers" with on-the-job resourcefulness in handling nonadvanced technologies. The radicals wanted to gear the new schooling in the sciences and mathematics almost exclusively toward such low-level technical familiarity: how lathes operate, the principles of levers, etc. It was to be a knowledge geared not to theory but toward the tangibly practical and the easily practiced. In many of the high schools, systematic courses in chemistry, physics, and mathematics were entirely done away with. They were taught instead in a simple combined "industry-agriculture-military" course. to be linked to the labor the young people did.

The radicals' preference for this kind of learning was congruent with their class-line perspectives. Neither the bourgeois experts nor their offspring were to be allowed to excel in the schools or the factories at the expense of the workers and their children.[1] The radicals wanted equally to prevent the rise in power of a technocratic "new bourgeoisie," regardless of class background. The development of sophisticated industries augmented the status of "experts," and the technological complexity of factories promoted their hierarchic control over the blue-collar work force. The radicals hence wanted as little industrial "modernization" as was feasible. Even the future university-trained technicians were to see themselves simply as skilled workers, not a group set apart as a separate social stratum by way of their training, professionalism, on-the-job status, and life experience.

The Party radicals seem initially to have thought that they could pursue these lines in education and industry without adversely affecting economic development. This optimism was rooted in their belief that knowledge was purposefully "mystified" by experts to bolster their professional status. With a simple commonsense approach, mingling plain explanations with practical demonstrations, the secrets of science could be made easily and quickly comprehensible to a layman.[2] "Bourgeois" expertise was, in short, something of a con game.

None of this should imply, however, that the Maoists wanted to focus education principally on vocational training. Instead it was to center on character building, through the emersion of young people in Mao Thought.[3] The radicals were both "redder" and more traditional than the Party moderates: they seemed almost Confucianist in their belief that the schools' principal purpose lies in the teaching of morals.[4]

The students' labor was to play a special role here. The Party's radical and moderate wings had been agreed that young people could best learn skills and concepts by combining schooling with practice; that such work sessions promoted the integrity of labor; that it acclimatized young people to the manual jobs most of them would hold after graduation. But we saw earlier, when discussing the rural half/half schools, that the Maoists had felt that the significance of labor in education went beyond this. They believed that when linked to political teachings and conducted in the proper group environment labor had a morally purifying quality; that those who were not steeped in it would degenerate in their worldview; that it helped instill "proletarianism."

The proposed school curriculum therefore was to include greatly increased amounts of both labor and political content. But the near-elimination of "theory" meant that the academic part of the curriculum could be very markedly reduced. So great were these reductions that schooling through senior high school could now be shortened to eight or nine years. Before the Cultural Revolution, in the 10-year Experimental School program, the initial and unrealistically optimistic notion had been that a majority of the young people would be able to absorb sophisticated science and mathematics in highly concentrated doses. In the post-Cultural Revolution school system there was contrarily to be a tacitly pessimistic appraisal of the learning capability of the working-class young people. The new shortened secondary school program was to be pitched at a level and pace where almost everyone who tried could do almost equally well; education was to become an egalitarian leveller among youths. In this respect, the purpose of schooling was to be contrary to that of all other school systems, where educational structures purposely sort and stratify students.

In fact, under the new system China's competitive educational ladder was entirely eliminated. All secondary-school graduates were to be assigned directly to jobs—without taking into account their academic records when deciding job destinations. The choice of who went on to higher learning would be made at the workplace, on the basis of one's on-the-job performance. Class-line principles were well served by this new selection process. The good-class Party leaders at the work unit could be expected to take class very strongly into account when appraising the dedication of applicants.

There were other major reasons, too, for divorcing academic achievement from career prospects. The Maoists wanted a leveling of *aspirations*. They felt that by entirely cutting off at school the routes to upward mobility, they would be better positioned to reorient achievement-minded youths away from the "corrupting" personal ambition they had absorbed from their parents. The kinds of calculations we observed students making prior to the Cultural Revolution would now be impossible. Related to this, the radicals felt that by removing the educational ladder's reinforcement of the concept that there were "higher" and "lower" vocations, the virtues of the working-class occupations could be better appreciated by students. Moreover, the Party radicals were concerned that the very mechanisms of academic *competition* in the classroom bred individualistic and careerist values that were at cross-purposes with the schools' political/ethical mission.

Finally, the radicals felt that if some young people entered university direct from school on the basis of their academic abilities and subsequently moved into specialized careers with the status of "experts," their life-experience would have put them out of touch with the political interests of the masses. They would become too prone to erroneous value-judgments in their work: too prone to put "expertise" and "economics" in command. In the years after the Cultural Revolution, the derisory term "bourgeois technician" became a commonplace catchphrase, referring even to technical personnel who had come from "red" homes.[5] The new means of recruiting China's higher-trained personnel—chosen in reward for good *blue-collar* work—was supposed to help assure that they saw themselves as "proletarian technicians."

In light of all of the above, the reopened schools of 1968–69 were to organize education along the following lines:

(1) Schools were to teach concepts that were relevant to industrial and agricultural work, and were to downplay the systematic teaching of theory;

(2) A student's academic excellence was no longer to be rewarded or even permitted to be an important source of informal prestige in the classroom. Among other things, learning was to be simplified and slowed, narrowing the gap between good and poor students;

(3) Overall, the shaping of attitudes was to carry far greater weight in the education system than the imparting of knowledge;

(4) Learning was to be combined with more labor than before;

(5) Urban schooling would be shortened to a universalized eight or nine years;

(6) School graduates would be assigned directly to jobs, and the work units would hold the right to determine which of their young personnel deserved a university or technical-school training.

THE "MAOIST" ADMINISTRATIVE REFORMS

The radicals also were concerned to revamp the organizational framework and the loci of decision-making in the school system. No longer was the "domination of our schools by bourgeois intellectuals" (as Mao phrased it)[6] to be permitted. The educational system was to be placed more firmly into the hands of the "reds" and the "proletariat," not the distrusted professional educators and administrators.

The radicals' organizational proposals were related to a long-term debate over how China should be administratively structured. In terms of education, for example, should control over the schools be centered in the provincial departments and national ministry of education? Or should there be decentralization, with considerable decision-making powers placed in the hands of a grass-roots Party-dominated committee? If we wish to place our fingers on the central difference between pre-Cultural Revolution China and post-Cultural Revolution China, not just in education but in almost all spheres of activity, it was this transfer of authority from ministerial and professional channels into the hands of local "red" Party personnel.

There was a terminology to distinguish the two competing organizational forms. The one, in which the ministries hold the decision-making powers and directives come down through the hierarchic administrative chain-of-command, was called "The Branch Dictates" (*tiaotiao zhuanzheng*).[7] The other, in which a local district's Party committee holds authority over the multifaceted activities within its boundaries, and each lower unit's Party committee holds direct responsibility for decisions affecting that unit, was called "The Area Dictates" (*kuaikuai zhuanzheng*).

When the Branch Dictates had been followed most strictly (as in the first half of the 1950s and 1961–62), the intradepartment chain-of-command was strengthened, and the administrative heads of each level were granted greater responsibility at the expense of the Party committee at that level. For example, in the "conservative" early 1960s, many of the school principals and university vice-chancellors and deans were granted the day-to-day powers, and the school Party committee retained merely an advisory/supervisory role. The Branch Dictates even helped the professionals outside the Party who earlier had been distrusted. In 1961–62, for instance, the older generation of teachers had absorbed some of the powers over school affairs which the Party committees gave up, and their prestige had consequently risen measurably. In the Cultural Revolution it was this short-lived trend of 1961–62 which most heatedly came under retrospective attack. The Party leaders of the Sun Yatsen Medical School in Canton were toppled and even driven off into labor-reform camps for having let the specialists obtain too much say in school affairs—for more than just those two years—and for having let the Party committee perform too much like a mere organ of the school administration.[8]

There were personnel within the education system, in particular at the universities, with strong interests in pursuing such attacks; and it was they who emerged from the Cultural Revolution with considerably strengthened powers. An interviewee has described, for example, how in his own university department the political instructors (fudaoyuan) had always been somewhat at odds with the academic dean and the teaching staff. These political instructors had been employed as "reds" by the school's Political Bureau, under the university Party committee and outside the normal administrative structure. In the Cultural Revolution, according to this interviewee, these political instructors attacked and gained ascendancy over the academic deans, explicitly arguing that the Branch Dictates had to be overturned in favor of "politics in command." Within a university department, their rise in power meant that more radical prescriptions gained favor. In particular, it encouraged the primacy of political studies (their own speciality) over academic studies.

In similar fashion, within top university leaderships there was a flow of increased power to the non-"expert" fulltime Party officials. The Party committees achieved this concentration of power in the 1970s by placing themselves directly in charge of the school's administrative leadership (the new Revolutionary Committee). All policy decisions now had to be passed by the Party committee. This constituted an Area Dictates situation, in that the Party committee, standing directly above the Revolutionary Committee, interfered with the re-formation of a hierarchic administrative chain-of-command reaching into the ministries. Through this restructuring, the state and its ministries and bureaus would not hold any powers in education. In fact, the national Education Ministry was not even reestablished until January 1975;[9] and at the provincial level it was not until February 1975 that Guangdong became the first province to reveal it had reestablished a Bureau of Higher Education.[10]

What policies get vigorously pushed depends upon *who* controls policy-implementation in a unit. As we have seen above, the Maoists in Peking not only proposed a set of "red" educational policies in 1968; they also implemented organizational reforms geared to give dominance to people sympathetic to these new programs.

This was not the first time the Area Dictates formula had been tried. In the Great Leap Forward a somewhat similar decentralization into the hands of Party committees had occurred.[11] But the radicals had learned since then to distrust the Party professionals. The just-ended Cultural Revolution had been directed against conservatized Party officials, and Mao's followers wanted to be sure than an Area Dictates type of decentralization did not strengthen the hand of these same Party officials.

They were particularly sensitized to this unwanted possibility in the sphere of education. After all, at most of the secondary and primary schools it was not a question of a phalanx of "reds" wanting to capture authority from "experts." The same Party secretaries/principals who had carried out the detested pre-Cultural Revolution policies would have to be placed back at the helm; and worse yet, under the Area Dictates formula the hierarchic administrative supervision over such men would be weakened.

The radicals' answer was to have the Party secretaries/principals held in check by the participation of the "masses." Though at first army officers were brought into the schools as political supervisors,[12] the longer-term solution, in the radicals' eyes, was to place the primary and secondary schools under the jurisdiction of nearby factories. In this particular Area Dictates policy, the factory reds would run affairs across branch lines. Workers Propaganda Teams, squads of workers from the controlling factories, entered the schools in mid-1968. These Teams were to be there "for a long period, ensuring that all power in the schools is directly and firmly grasped by the working class."[13]

But a single factory normally was not large enough to handle the responsibility. So control over a school often would have to be shared by several smaller factories, or together by the factories and the local urban Neighborhood Committee or, in the suburbs, even shared with the local agricultural commune. These organs were also to serve as "proletarian educators" of the students, who were to rotate between school and factory and farm to perform their all-important labor. A Canton directive of December 1968 instructed, in fact, that the "courses in the schools will depend on the equipment and size of the factories with which they are linked."[14]

For the first year or two after the reopening of schools, the Worker Propaganda Teams did hold real decision-making powers in the schools' leadership and even took over some of the teaching. But their influence gradually receded over time. The team members were handicapped on too many counts. The industrial managers had been most willing to spare their nonskilled personnel from the factory shopfloor, and thus the veteran workers who got sent were often no more literate or numerate than the children they were supposed to help teach. Not surprisingly they encountered difficulty holding the pupils' attention and respect.[15] Most of them retreated voluntarily from the teaching podia as soon as there were sufficient regular teachers to take their places. Their contacts with the students were soon limited to the regular "recall bitterness" lectures plus supervision of the schools' tiny industrial workshops.

Their role in the school's leadership organs similarly declined. Since they were to remain workers, the Propaganda Team members stayed at a school no longer than two years before rotating back to their factory. They never gained the experience to know quite what to do in the school committees they sat on.

Furthermore, their factories did not give these Propaganda Team workers much backing. Nor did the factory leaders pay much attention to their own personal responsibilities as members of the school leadership organs. It is evident from the documentation of the times that the factory managers did not *want* to be involved in running schools; they had enough problems getting their own factories operating again. Moreover, the Cultural Revolution was fresh in their minds. It had taught them that educational issues were politically explosive; that students were potentially volatile; and that anyone responsible for schools was likely to be directly in the firing-line if another mass movement arose.

The school Party secretaries/principals, on their own side, seem to have favored having these outside supervisors withdraw. The presence of the factory representatives and Worker Propaganda Teams not only complicated the principals' administrative duties but also inserted men into the schools who held the power and the knowledge to damage them politically in the future. The factory leaders were more than happy to accede to the school heads' desires. Thus by 1974–75 there were only a few Worker Propaganda Team members left in most schools, down from a high point of twenty to forty team members. The Maoists were dismayed by the trend and tried to sustain the factories' and Worker Propaganda Teams' roles in the schools, but it was a losing battle.[16]

During these same years the Guangdong leadership was quietly reviving Canton's Municipal Education Office and gradually letting it take over responsibility for the various schools' programs. The school heads could increasingly look to this branch-type city education department for directives and support. As we shall presently see, the entire school system had been floundering in terrible confusion for two years. Almost no constructive education had been carried out. The middle levels of the educational bureaucracy had *had* to be rebuilt. The end result was that the Area Dictates formula not only was collapsing from within, but was also being pushed aside by the hesitant but growing reassertion of branch-type leadership.

THE INITIAL HANDICAPS FACING REFORMS

Even had the reforms proposed by the Party radicals been well-conceived and practicable, in the traumatic aftermath of the Cultural Revolution it would have been near-impossible to successfully implement them. As it was, the efforts to push the radicals' ideas through an entirely new and untested organizational framework assured that the schools would be plunged into considerable chaos between 1968 and 1970. The reasons for this chaos were several:

(1) *The political fears of school administrators.* Given the initial weakness of the basic-level Party committees and the coalitional nature of the school Revolutionary Committees, there was often no unified leadership at the basic levels; and to the extent that a school's leadership *was* unified, the decisions rested with the old principals/Party secretaries. Most of them could be expected to be unsympathetic to the reforms. They would go along with the new programs only grudgingly, and might even occasionally resist them through passivity, dissimulation or subtle sabotage.

Beyond this the reforms faced a second and perhaps more serious problem. The destruction of the middle levels of the education bureaucracies ironically meant that the very groups necessary to structure and organize the Maoist educational reforms were lacking. The bureaucracy would have provided a transmission network that would enable successful experiments and techniques at various schools to be certified as feasible, and for such experiences to be circulated, retested, and regularized. Without a bureaucracy to *process* reform, the school-administrators/Party-secretaries were genuinely confused.

They were left to concoct their own curricula—and even those among them who might have been favorably disposed to the radicals' ideas were understandably chary to proceed. To carry out the "wrong" reforms or to make "errors of political principle" could spell serious political trouble for them the next time a campaign came along. It was best to implement the reforms in whatever manner seemed politically safest; and as the cynical saying of the time went, it was safest "always to be left, left, further left." Errors of a "leftist" nature would at least ward off the possibility of being labeled a "rightist." An educational document of 1970, reporting on a Guangdong high school, noted that:

> some members of the school's Revolutionary Committee expressed their views in these terms: "Academic courses may get you into trouble. To place attention on the academic course work is to put effort into vocational study, and you'll run the danger of again putting 'intellectual training in first place.' It is better to concentrate more on political work and concern yourself less with the courses. This is the way to avoid risks." [17]

They left the teachers holding the bag.

(2) *The reticence of teachers.* In the first years after the renewal of schooling, the news media repeatedly noted that the teaching staffs felt "the work of teachers is dangerous." Many teachers were trying by any means possible to escape the profession. [18] Little wonder; their very vocation tended to blacken them as "bourgeois intellectuals." [19] Those who were literally of bourgeois or petty bourgeois class background were daily reminded in 1968–69 of how vulnerable they were, since a fair number of discredited former teachers were still sleeping in makeshift jails at the schools and performing humiliating janitorial work by day. [20] Most of the older generation of teachers felt tarred by the same brush as these unfortunate jailed teachers—by birth, by training, and by having taught when the "wrong line" had prevailed. As a news report from that first school year of 1968–69 observed, regarding one of Peking's most famous high schools:

> They were afraid and thought only of "struggle, criticism, and running away." Accordingly, some of the teachers had no intention of resuming classes. . . . Some of the students, too, did not treat their teachers correctly. They erroneously thought that since all the teachers were trained in the

old schools, they could bombard them any time they liked. So some of the teachers were unable to hold classes.[21]

Even more than the school administrators, teachers had good reason to take the safest tack possible. Many had no particular concern whether the Maoist reforms made sense or whether the reforms succeeded. Their concern was simply to avoid being placed in an exposed position; they "cherished an idea of avoiding mistakes by speaking less, showing their aptitude less, and doing fewer things."[22] Since "it is safe to teach politics but dangerous to teach knowledge,"[23] it was best to include a preponderance of Mao quotes in your teaching, regardless of the course; and to teach those quotes with as little commentary as possible, so as to avoid making slips of the tongue. But it was best not to make the students seriously memorize these quotes, since they might resent that. It was best just to go through the motions. Even if the end result was that the students were bored and disruptive, so be it. Safest of all—and a means to avoid the classroom anarchy—was to get your students assigned as many labor stints as possible, preferably outside the school and under the responsibility and supervision of someone else.

(3) *The unruliness of students.* The students would have been difficult to handle whatever the new school system. They had been out on the streets running wild for two years, and many of them were little inclined to return passively to their school desks. In the first year of renewed schooling, students at Canton's No. 12 High School went so far as to remove their desks and chairs from the classrooms and bury them in the school pond.[24] At a second anarchic school, according to a Canton magazine of 1969, they "came late, fought, sloughed off discipline, read "yellow novels," and remained indifferent to criticism."[25]

From interviews it seems that this younger generation did not share the bitter sense of disillusionment which now infected some of their older brothers and sisters. But in the past two years they had witnessed a world of social conflict that was still being played out among adults in post-Cultural Revolution recriminations and retaliations. The high levels of truancy and juvenile delinquency in Canton's newly reopened schools reflected the general sense of confusion and disorder in urban China, which was at its strongest in 1969.

Though they were almost all too young to have participated politically in the Cultural Revolution, they had at least been old enough to identify vicariously with one Red Guard faction or the other. The educational authorities were aware that these lingering factional identifications might transform individual acts of disorder in the reopened schools into more organized forms of student disturbances. The authorities therefore were careful to separate the children from each pre-Cultural Revolution primary-school class into different classrooms and even into different neighborhood schools—to the point that some students were assigned to schools well beyond the boundaries of their own neighborhood. Before the Cultural Revolution, the school system had purposely kept classes together year after year, so that peer-group pressures would have greater impact on any students who did not conform to the official norms. Now, after the Cultural Revolution, the schools were taking quite the opposite tack. The need was to weaken the peer-group influence and the young people's organizational links.

Even so, one respondent reports that when she entered her new junior-high classroom, purposely separated from her former schoolmates, some of the children sought out factional sympathizers among the other newcomers. Gang fights had erupted by the close of the first day. The factionalism did not die out until the beginning of the third year of her schooling, 1970–71.

These peer-group hostilities were encouraged by the pressures impinging on the schools from outside. The ideology of "class struggle" permeated Chinese society during these years, and almost literally meant struggle. In a couple of the classrooms which I have surveyed, this stress on "class" actually dissipated the Red Guard factional identifications, and recreated in their stead the divisions of the early phases of the Cultural Revolution—with all the red-background youths (worker and revolutionary-cadre children alike) demanding superior statuses and ranged as a group against their impure-background peers. In the worst school in my interview sample "the students of different class origins in my classroom composed two enemy camps."

It was not to the interests of the schools or teachers, of course, to let the fisticuffs and feuding take this antagonistic "class-based" form.[26] But their effort, as always, was to take the politically safest course, and that meant showing divisive favoritism to good-background youngsters: it was better once more to be overly "left." In classroom criticism sessions and small groups, red-class youngsters were permitted to mount criticisms against non-red-origin classmates but rarely vice-versa. In many schools, too, for the first couple of years only good-background youngsters were permitted to become classroom officers; leadership was to be in the hands of the "proletariat."

Family background similarly became the major means to determine who could join the "Red Guards." These new Red Guards bore no resemblance to the Red Guard groups of the Cultural Revolution. The name had simply been appropriated by the schools for a new elite organization, to provide a surrogate for the still-disbanded League. As it was, half the schools in my sample were unable to set up such groups until several years later. They were as yet too disorganized and had too little control over their students. In the school which was most orderly, the first batch of members was initiated in 1969–70; but the school leadership was so afraid of admitting a non-good-origin student—so afraid, indeed, to admit any student on its own authority—that it required all applicants to submit a letter from the father's place of work authenticating the youth's pedigree and the father's acceptable political standing.

One result of such "class line" policies was that the sons and daughters of the revolutionary cadres—or rather, those among them whose parents had not been disgraced[27]—asserted renewed claims to innate superiority. But this time, most of them did not link their re-found arrogance to any activist pretensions.[28] They normally were as unruly as any of their peers, yet were beyond the control of their teachers, who almost always bore the handicap of less pure origins. To a lesser extent, workers' children similarly were able to use their class origins as a means to avoid disciplining.

The teachers were able, however, to take advantage of the class line in one respect—to enforce a degree of obedience upon the non-red-origin students. And with the other students, the teachers held the advantage that there were as yet few inklings as to how the postgraduation job assignments would be determined. Teachers played upon both these levers as best they could.

> In my own class the kids behaved okay. Those of non-good origins did because if they didn't listen they'd be "struggled" against. Of course, if a good-background kid did something bad, the school wouldn't even let the students know, so they weren't necessarily controllable. But they did want to go to senior high school at the end of the school year rather than to the countryside, and it was rumored that if their behavior were really bad even their class origins wouldn't save them. . . . Yes, we non-red-family kids knew all along that we'd end up in the countryside, and all of us had rather low spirits in school. We felt like dying old men. We had no hopes for the future.[29]

In the end, none of the youngsters in this classroom got sent directly to the villages. All the students were sent on for a year of senior high school; and when they were assigned to jobs in 1970 they discovered their behavior at school had not in the least influenced their allocations. After 1970, as younger students became cognizant of this, the teachers lost the most effective weapon of control they had held.

NEIGHBORHOOD SCHOOLS
IN AN OVERCROWDED SYSTEM

All the incoming students in 1968 had been assigned to neighborhood high schools. No longer in China were there to be elite schools, or entrance examinations. In the new neighborhood schooling, the quality of the school and of the teachers was to be determined purely by the accident of residence.

The radical leadership saw a system composed solely of neighborhood schools as an egalitarian leveler of education in three respects. In the first place, under the new system there could no longer be educational competitiveness to win entry to a "good" school. There would hence be less cause for children to strive for "selfish" reasons to do better in their schoolwork than others, and less reason for them to acquire self-images of superiority or inferiority based on their varying academic work. In the second place, neighborhood schooling seemed fairer in class-line terms: no longer would the former middle classes be able to acquire educations at better schools than working-class youths. And for the third part, the system of neighborhood schools was quite explicitly meant to help hinder the perpetuation in China of a "new bourgeois" stratum of privileged Party officials. The Party radicals in Peking had been disturbed by the all-too-easy access the revolutionary-cadre children had had to the best secondary schools. They had been disturbed too by the special boarding schools which had been set up by the military and the central government bureaus for the children of officials. Mao himself had worried aloud that the Party leadership's children had become nonthinking, pampered, and soft.[30]

Yet in the end the new program of neighborhood schooling did not actually produce an appreciably greater mixing of children from different types of homes. The reason was that different social classes predominated in different neighborhoods. The dormitories for the officials of administrative bureaus were in particular neighborhoods, and so their children, even more than before, congregated together. The traditional blue-collar districts continued to send their children to neighborhood schools filled largely with other laboring-class young people. But now, at least, if a former key-point school was in a working-class neighborhood, it would serve the children of the local residents. Ironically, however, most of Canton's key-point schools were disadvantageously situated. A striking example is the South China Attached (to the Teacher's College) Middle School, which is situated in the suburban college district. In visiting the formerly elite school after the Cultural Revolution, I was struck by the high proportion of university staff members' children amongst the students I talked with.[31] In Peking, many of the most famous schools are located in the districts where state cadres live, and visitors to those schools were similarly struck by the high representation of Party officials' and professionals' children.

Moreover, in Canton and elsewhere, the Maoist program of neighborhood schooling did not succeed in closing every one of the schools run by the military and civilian bureaus for their own children. The Railway Administration, for example, had operated its own respected system of primary schools and a high school in Canton for the sole benefit of employees. Now, under the Area Dictates formula of linking schools to economic units, it sought successfully to preserve this school system. Some of the various national bureaus similarly were able to hold onto at least some of their boarding schools, on the grounds that personnel who were assigned to temporary posts around China needed to leave their children in the care of the bureau's home office (normally Peking). And once retained, reports circulated in China that these schools were catering fulltime to the children of high-level officials. It was not to the same extent as in pre-Cultural Revolution years. But the main effect of the new neighborhood system seems to have been to bring the middle and working class youngsters more together, now that the chance of a middle-class child in a mixed neighborhood going to an elite school had been eliminated. It did not affect the high-level cadre children as much.

Almost all of the reopened local schools ran into difficulties physically accommodating their new student bodies. Canton's population of school-aged children had continued to increase during the Cultural Revolution, and now 700,000 young people in a city of three million had to be squeezed into the school system.[32] The primary schools were better able to cope, because the birth rate in Canton had begun to taper off by 1960 and because elementary schooling had been shortened to five years.

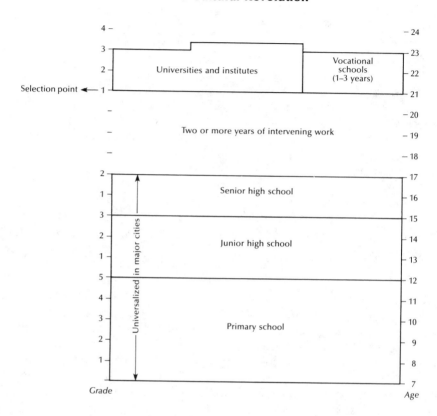

Note: Compare with the illustration of the education ladder of the Sixties, figure 1-1.

Figure 7-1 Canton's Ladder of Education, 1974–77

But the high schools were faced with serious headaches—and these headaches became more severe as the years passed.

In 1968–69 the secondary schools had only three grades' worth of students to deal with. But in 1971–72 the curriculum was extended by a further year, to a total of nine years of schooling. Through this the older officials who had begun coming back into office hoped to provide Canton's students with at least somewhat more book-knowledge before they graduated. But perhaps a more pressing reason was the peasants' complaints that the teenagers who were coming to settle in the countryside were too young to live independently or do a grown person's work; on this excuse, villages had been trying to refuse to take any more school graduates. In 1974–75, Canton added a tenth year of education, and probably for much the same reasons. Other major cities in China, though at a slower pace, similarly lengthened their high school curricula.

The end result was that the Canton high school system, which before the Cultural Revolution had offered three years of universalized schooling, now had to provide five years. By 1973–74, the secondary schools were desperately trying to accommodate practically twice as many students as in 1965–66 (!)[33]—and the city had not yet even inaugurated that tenth year of schooling.

Doubling the student body created an acute shortage of qualified high school teachers. These shortages were compounded by the disgrace and dismissal in 1968 of many of the older teachers with "historical" problems.[34] Very large numbers of fresh teachers were needed, but under the new Maoist policies these were not to be selected on the basis of "bourgeois expertise." The Canton schools were obliged to take in a large body of "reds" recommended by local units.[35] These new teachers tended to have had inadequate educations; and there were not even enough such people willing to take up the thankless tasks of a teacher. The school system therefore had to turn to new high school graduates— simply assigning some of them to stay in the school system as teachers. Those who were picked sometimes tried to get themselves de-selected, on account of the precarious status and practical difficulties of teaching. They had hoped and expected to become workers instead.

These young people were barely older or more knowledgeable than the students they would have to teach, having themselves received only eight to nine years of schooling. Moreover, interviewees report that they were chosen more for their pure family background and political activism than academic ability. They sometimes did get the chance to attend a teacher-training school. But this was only for a half-year or one-year "short course," because of the crush of new teacher recruits. The schools, hence, became caught with two types of teachers: older and qualified teachers who were reluctant to conduct academic classes; and "redder" new teachers who frequently were not *competent* to teach. When, later in the mid-1970s, the Canton school system tried to give greater play once more to schoolwork, many of these younger teachers resisted the new trends. They felt they would not be up to the new requirements. Almost inadvertently some became champions of the "radical" position, wanting to continue playing up political study and labor at the expense of learning. (Since the fall of the "Gang of Four" the older faculty members have been urged by the newspapers to take their younger colleagues in hand and give them needed academic lessons.)[36]

The severe overcrowding of students in the schools was as serious a problem, but at least here politically acceptable solutions could be devised. As early as the autumn of 1969, Canton's education authorities had hit upon the idea of erecting rural branch schools, and Canton became China's model city in running these schools.[37] They were built on uncultivated stretches of rural wasteland by the students themselves. Every one of Canton's 79 secondary schools had established its own branch school by 1970, and these provided desk space for 40,000 high school students. Classes were sent out to them in rotation for periods ranging from two months to half a year at a time,[38] and like clockwork students from the branch schools were rotated into the vacated urban classrooms. There was also a further advantage to the program. The branch schools' fields provided the teenagers with a place to do their politically requisite labor; the peasants adamantly had refused to accept swarms of troublesome young people on their own fields except during the peak days of the harvest season.

But in the longer run the branch schools created more problems than they resolved. Reportedly some of the peasant villages were dissatisfied that the branch schools took up agricultural land, no matter how infertile that land might be. School administrators eventually complained that their urban school facilities were deteriorating because funds had been siphoned off to construct and maintain the branch schools. Teachers complained that the time spent at remote mountain schools had been detrimental to their students' studies. In 1978, therefore, Canton announced that all the branch schools would be abandoned.[39]

During 1968–70 Canton's schools had relieved their classroom shortages also through contrived labor outings. By managing such forays efficiently, one of the schools in my sample—the one shortly to be discussed—was able to rotate two or more different classes through a single classroom. School heads must have been doubly happy to organize such labor stints since, as we have observed, these happened to be the safest politically of all educational activities.

SCHOOL DAYS, 1968–70

One young interviewee, Lee, lived in the district of Canton least affected by the turmoil of the Cultural Revolution. As early as February 1968 the district's military and civilian leadership was able to get the younger children off the streets and back into the classrooms. But during his first two years of revived schooling Lee saw little of his own neighborhood junior high school.

—During February and March the 13-year-old Lee was at the school, though studies had not commenced.

—In April and May, his class was at an engine factory working half days. They also had three hours of daily classes in a converted workshop.

—In June, they were in a village. Classes continued only sporadically.

—July and August they were let out on vacation.

—September and November were spent back at school.

—In December they went to work in an umbrella factory in their neighborhood. There was no place to hold classes, and there were none.

—In January 1969 they performed labor in a rural village, sleeping in the village brick factory. Lee's first year of junior high school drew to a close.

—Three weeks of vacation in February before the start of the second junior high school year.

—Late February and March, at school.

—April through June out in the countryside laying bricks for his school's rural branch school. Morning classes under a tree.

—July, back at school.

—August, vacation.

—September, at a second and smaller umbrella factory, with eight hours' daily labor. No classes.

—October, helping bring in the late harvests. No classes.

—November–December, back at school, with regular classroom hours.

—In January 1970 they remained at school but without any academic coursework. Instead the entire class held daily meetings to convince each other to accept whatever job assignments they might receive. As it was, the students already knew that only five of them were too old to enter senior high school the next year and would be going to jobs instead. Three of these five had been allocated to factories by the school and two had been asked to settle in the countryside. All fifty students in the class spent an entire month helping convince these two to volunteer!

With only four years of primary education before the Cultural Revolution to add to these two recent years of schooling, they were all declared junior-high graduates.

This was, notably, the best experience of junior high school education in my sampling of Canton schools for those years. The expeditions to the countryside and to factories had provided these particular students with a structured and disciplined environment and had helped reestablish the classroom community. There had been little classroom teaching, but then there were few available textbooks anyway.[40] The other schools in my sample had not had the organizational skills to arrange nearly so much labor. Yet with the paucity of textbooks and the reluctance of teachers to push academic classwork, their students had had scarcely any more real book-learning.

The worst school in my survey was the former Guangdong Provincial Experimental School—where four thousand students were squeezed into buildings which formerly had housed only eight hundred. The new and largely working-class student body spent only six months out of these two years away at labor sites. The remainder of the time pandemonium reigned. The school had four textbooks devised by the city: in arithmetic, Chinese language and literature, industry/agriculture/military, and politics. But even the arithmetic book largely contained Mao quotes. The only informative book, it seems, was the industry/agriculture/military text, with its lessons on machines and crops. But even here, students didn't listen. Some boys regularly played poker during class periods; others skipped classes to play ball or rough-house instead.

If anything, high school students during these first two years showed up more frequently to the politics classes or the sessions purely involving Mao quotes than to classes containing any academic work. They were, after all, more liable to be criticized for neglecting ideology than for ignoring coursework. But their disdain for academic classwork had deeper roots than this. They saw it as of no real use to themselves. They knew their futures would no longer be determined by their academic performance, and they knew too, through their own labor experience, that most manual workers had little need for any learning. A student from that same chaotic school, the former Guangdong Experimental School, claimed in an article for a 1969 education journal that

> we thought that studying was of no use because we would be going eventually to the countryside to work with a hoe anyway. That was [one reason] why we set no high political aim, became undisciplined and studied carelessly.[41]

By 1971, the school curricula at Canton's schools were better organized. The turmoil and confusion of the Cultural Revolution was receding into memory. The textbooks were filled more with nonpolitical information. Yet even so, students continued to ignore their schoolwork. They continued to play truant, and many of them continued to be rowdy. Students were graduating from high school both semiliterate and—significantly—with decidedly nonactivist attitudes.

Interviews and documentation suggest that the principal reasons for this continuing malaise centered on the twin problems raised in the above quote—the inability of students to positively influence their futures; and their fear and discouragement at the prospect of rural settlement. To understand the persisting turmoil in Chinese education, it becomes necessary to investigate the government's policies on job assignments and rustication.

CHAPTER EIGHT

Down to the Countryside

NOT ALL of the young people who had gone to the countryside in 1968–69 were dissatisfied with their lot. Many were, perhaps the majority. But it also seems from interviews with rusticants that at least a sizable minority were initially somewhat enthusiastic about going. During the Cultural Revolution they had heard the complaints of those who had gone down during the 1960s, but many of the Red Guards had discounted these tales as the self-interested exaggerations of selfish malcontents. They had been taught to regard settlement in the countryside as a testing ground of their political dedication; as an experience of tempering that would strengthen and purify their own characters; and as a means to contribute to the economic construction and cultural enlightenment of the rural districts. Within a relatively short time, though, many of these optimistic new settlers were learning a series of lessons that disabused them of any romantic notions.[1]

The first lesson was that generally they were neither wanted or needed by the peasantry. They could have hoped for a welcome only in villages lacking labor power or the skills of literacy and numeracy. But with hundreds of thousands of urban young people dispatched into Guangdong's countryside in 1968–69, many of the villages acquired more youths than they could readily accommodate. In parts of Guangdong this point had been reached even prior to the Cultural Revolution. Since the Chinese countryside is divided into peasant production cooperatives whose members share in the proceeds of the land, adding unneeded urban youths simply meant that the peasants would have to feed more mouths from limited harvests, and many peasants naturally resented this. As the post-Cultural Revolution high schools annually began sending new crowds of graduates into the countryside, the relationship between the urban youths and peasants further deteriorated.

The discomfitting circumstances of the sent-down youths were made worse by Mao's directive of December 1968 that "It is absolutely necessary for educated young people to go to the countryside to be reeducated by the poor and lower-middle peasants."[2] With the media chorusing the refrain, the young people were placed in a position politically inferior to the peasantry. Their urban origins became a handicap. Young people could no longer fantasize that they were "glorious" revolutionaries for having come to the countryside.

The urban youths found too that there was little scope for them to exercise their school-learned skills. Almost all the villages needed accountants, team cashiers, teachers, and Mao Study leaders, but they could absorb only a fraction of the sent-down youths. Making matters worse, the expanded rural school system of the 1960s had begun turning out local graduates who could compete with them for the posts.[3] The peasants naturally preferred to give the positions to their own children rather than to the outsiders; and the Mao directive and "class-line" arguments porvided the rhetorical justification.

Even rusticants who have left China are quick to concede, though, that on the whole the peasants were tolerant of them and individually were often quite decent to them. But the peasants did not like having to subsidize the sent-down youths, and some peasant cadres tried by hook or by crook to minimize the drain on local incomes. For each sent-down youth the province had allotted 230 *yuan*—more than many peasants could earn in a year—to help build dormitories, buy farm tools, and to provide foodstuffs for the rusticants' first eight months in the countryside.[4] But in the cases of half of the six youths from whom I solicited this particular information, some of this money had simply been expropriated by the local peasant production-teams as compensation for the long-term losses the collective would suffer. The youngsters had to make do with extremely makeshift quarters.

Even after the young people had managed to settle in, they often had difficulty sustaining themselves. Agricultural labor in south China is gruelling. The urban-raised youths were not used to heavy manual labor and did not have the peasants' stamina. Exhausted by day's end, the rusticated young people could not till their private plots diligently after work and so were unable to supplement their diets. Many of their parents had to begin sending money. Factory wages had largely stood still since the early sixties, and with the new monthly drain parents found that in middle age their own standard of living was actually declining. Caught in this unexpected bind, they had good financial reasons to be antagonistic to the rustication program. Some whose children had been assigned to especially poor districts even calculated that it might be almost as cheap to keep their children illicitly at home sharing the family's rations. More and more parents refused to let their children go.

Word had gotten back to China's cities that a small proportion of rural cadres had taken advantage of the social isolation and vulnerability of rusticated girls and that there had been cases of seduction or rape. With this as a pretext, many parents became especially adamant in refusing to let their daughters sign up for the countryside. Among other things they hoped that their stay-at-home daughters would eventually marry young men with urban jobs. The brides would gain a permanent urban status and would even become eligible to work in a neighborhood workshop for housewives. In 1975, Guangdong province finally moved to close this escape-hatch by denying stay-at-home daughters the right to wed.[5]

Mao was aware of the urban discontent with the program,[6] and in the spring of 1970 he had issued a strong nine-point directive. It ordered that rusticating youths be given the full monthly grain rations due them, that they get equal pay for equal work, that they receive adequate housing, that they not be excluded from the local health-care system, and that rural cadres who forced themselves on urban girls were to be severely punished. In short, the six or so million youths who had gone to the countryside since 1968 were to be protected.[7] It was even stipulated that some were to be elected as local cadres.[8]

The circumstances of the sent-down youths did begin to improve after 1970. But the peasants remained reluctant, even under pressure, to sustain the losses caused by the unwanted new arrivals. When dormitories were built, in several of the villages of interviewees the new structures closely resembled granaries and barns. Village leaders evidently hoped that the youngsters would not be in the village forever.

For their part, many of the young people feared that they would be trapped in the countryside for life. They saw themselves facing a lifetime not just of hard work and tedium, but also of celibacy. To marry and raise families the young men would have to get their own private house built, and that would cost about a thousand *yuan*. Even in a well-off village, this was equivalent to three full years' earnings from collective agriculture. The young urban-raised women did have better opportunities. They were sought after as brides by the young peasant men—especially since the young women's families in the city would not demand the traditional expensive bride-price. But marriage foreclosed any possibility of their being recalled to the cities. This rule applied even if both parties to the marriage were sent-down urban youths. It deterred many from marrying even when they could afford it.[9]

The young people were aware there did exist *some* possibilities of being recalled. Beginning in 1970 a number of factory posts in the county towns and Canton, some of the openings at Canton's universities and technical schools, and some to the PLA were reserved for rusticated youths. By mid-1975, 23 percent of the urban youths from Guangdong who had been sent to the countryside had been able to find a way out.[10]

The government's directives to rural cadres stipulated that these selections were to be made largely on the basis of work enthusiasm and political activism. According to interviewees, this policy did convince some of the sent-down youths to labor energetically and competitively. But in the long run this policy of providing urban outlets had serious drawbacks. In particular, it was common knowledge that the children of officials got unfair priority due to their parents' influence. For its own smooth functioning, the Chinese economy requires extensive networks for trading favors among economic and administrative units, since needed supplies and spare parts are not consistently available through legal channels. The officials now found it all too easy to make personal use of these networks to secure contacts and reach bargains in their own children's behalf. Bad-class or even middle-class youngsters seemed to have almost no chance of selection—at least in their own eyes—while the children of the powerful seemed merely to be stopping off in the villages for a year or two to acquire a "gold-plating" helpful to their future careers. Referring to this phenomenon, a rusticant of 1964 who had remained a fervant political activist till the early 1970s observes:

> Ha! Those cadre's kids got out in no time! Though I didn't think this when I went to the village, afterwards I realized that it was "bad" people who got left in the countryside. If the policy really had been that everyone equally had to go down, I'd have been willing to sacrifice. If to work in the countryside were really glorious (*guangrong*), I'd be glad and happy to be there. But it's become the antithesis of glory; and I want nothing to do with it.[11]

This capacity of officials' children to leave the countryside "through the back door" was becoming a sore point for many urban Chinese. The best-known articulation of this discontent was by a schoolteacher in Fujian province, who found the courage in 1973 to write an angry letter to Mao Zedong. He complained that despite the measures of 1970 his son was still getting short-changed and he himself still had to assist the boy financially. It was entirely unfair, he wrote, that the kids of ordinary folks got shipped to the villages for life, while those with influence escaped. The letter reached Mao, who responded with a quixotic gesture by publicly sending the father some money from his salary as Chairman.[12] The schoolteacher's letter became required reading for Party meetings throughout China; the Central Committee shortly thereafter passed a decree raising the settlement disbursements to Y500 per youth;[13] and a campaign was begun publicizing the rustication of the children of ranking Party officials. But rustication remained singularly unpopular. The sudden ballyhoo surrounding the departure of the cadres' children to the countryside reportedly only sharpened the scepticism.

JOB ALLOCATIONS, 1969–75

Especially now that so many students had to be sent to the countryside, the job-hunting free-for-all of the 1960s had been ended once and for all. From 1969 onward, the high school administrators had been given the task of designating precisely where each graduate would go. Each school received a number of slots at specified urban work places and, based on guidelines handed down by the city, the school determined who was eligible. Similarly, the school received a list of rural destinations from a new Municipal Rustication Arrangements Office.

The rusticating students in most years were offered at least two choices—a commune or a state farm. On the positive side the state farms provided a fixed and reliable monthly salary of about Y25 and a social life among fellow urban youths, in contrast to the vicissitudes of a village income and the possibilities of a more lonely life among the peasants. On the negative side, the state farms frequently were run by the PLA and held a reputation for imposing a suffocatingly regimented style of life.[14] Moreover, most of the new state farms in Guangdong were concentrated on Hainan, the large tropical island off Guangdong's southern tip. Hainan Island soon acquired a very unenviable reputation—backbreaking clearing of jungles in a malarial frontier area, too far from Canton to return home even on annual visits. Despite the growing distaste for both choices, as the years passed rusticants opted in increasing proportions for the easier life of the villages.

But the key question that bothered Canton's young people was *who* would be selected to rusticate. It was a problem that continued to trouble the authorities too. What criteria could be used that would not seem unfair or increase dissatisfaction with the program? In 1969 and again in 1970, the teenagers sent down had been almost entirely from the middle and bad classes. But this only strengthened the feeling among young people that the villages had become a dumping grounds for second-class citizens. It was not an image the authorities wanted to promote. Guangdong therefore decided in 1971 that class should no longer be a determining factor.

Nor, for much the same reasons, could a student's political activism at school be permitted to affect allocations. Settlement in the countryside was something a dedicated student activist was supposed to *want* to do, not something to avoid. Nor, finally, could a student's academic record be allowed to enter into the decision. That was precisely the standard that post-Cultural Revolution education no longer was supposed to reward.

Apparently as a way out of these dilemmas, Guangdong decided in 1971 that, rather than juggle with those three long-used criteria, a graduate's chance of going to the countryside would be determined solely by reference to the proportion of his or her brothers and sisters who had already gone to the countryside. If a certain proportion of the siblings had not gone, the graduate went. In this way, the onus of failure was to be removed from rural assignments.

For the year of 1971, this "sibling" policy dictated that the graduating student would have to rusticate if half or more of his or her brothers and sisters were still at an urban residence. For the most part, this meant the older children in each household now had to face the prospect of rural lives. But the parents were assured that at least the younger children, when they came of age, would be granted urban postings and remain near home to support them in their old age.[15] It was patently an equitable policy, and seems to have been recognized as such. But it was nevertheless difficult for Chinese parents to accustom themselves to it. In Chinese society the eldest son traditionally held special responsibility for the care of his parents and the continuance of the family line. Now it was the younger children who were likely to hold those responsibilities— and in many households a daughter!

Despite this new "sibling" criterion for assigning the young people, the schools did continue to possess a modicum of discretion as to whether any given student would be placed on the urban or rural list. Parents took advantage of this. From 1971 onwards, low-salaried parents with a goodly number of children were able to argue that the soon-to-graduate eldest child be given an urban assignment, so as to provide immediate help to the straitened family budget.[16] A former teacher from a factory-managed school in Yunnan Province observes that, in contrast to the "back door" advantages enjoyed by officials in getting their children *out* of the countryside, here it was those at the bottom of the factory hierarchy who were better able to *prevent* their elder children from rusticating.

The deal in these cases was that a younger child would later rusticate in the elder borther's or sister's stead. Sensing that the rules for allocating youths had been changed almost annually, many of these parents hoped to save the elder child without sacrificing the younger one. Some fathers even adopted the strategy of exaggerating their own ill-health so as to retire early. Their sharply reduced income would then oblige the school to come up with an urban posting for a child about to graduate, or even to provide an urban job for a child already in the countryside. The rush of parents trying to wangle early retirements became so great that the Central Committee had to pass strict regulations in 1973 to curtail the maneuver.[17] Some other families, left only with younger daughters, tried to marry them off quickly into families that lived at a distance. They could then claim that the household's loss of the girl to another family warranted a son's return from the countryside.

The proportion of graduating students who had to rusticate each year was determined by the annual manpower needs of the urban sector.[18] In years of quickened industrial growth more new graduates could stay in the cities; in years of industrial stagnation the schools might have to send all graduates who were not the "last child."[19] For the first several years after the Cultural Revolution turmoil, as Canton's industry revived, between one-third to two-thirds of the graduates, depending on the year, were able to stay in the city. But in 1973, following a recession and industrial retrenchment throughout China, the Canton city government recalculated its future manpower requirements and decreed that henceforth all but one child in each family would have to go.

By this time, however, parental resistance to the rustication of their children had become pronounced. In 1969 and 1970 it had been easier to bring pressure to bear on parents to make their children volunteer, particularly since they had been predominantly of middle- and bad-class background. Two respondents, both from bad-class families, report that their own parents had been brought to school and sujected there to daily "study sessions." Sometimes their parents were even forced to sleep at the school overnight, until they submitted and made their children sign up. But if they could weather the school's barrage of strictures (and eventually the schools learned to shed this duty as quickly as possible) their case was handed over to their Neighborhood Residence Committee and local militia. These units had little desire to try to "persuade" the annually growing numbers of teenagers and their parents to give in. This was especially true after 1970, when the majority of the affected families were of solid working-class background and could not so readily be addressed in threatening tones. The numbers of young people sitting idly at home began rising sharply as discontent with the program hardened.

New "mobilization" methods were needed. In 1973, the responsibility for convincing the young people to sign up for the countryside was handed over to the father's place of work. It was no longer the duty of the school or neighborhood. Apparently it was calculated that the work-unit would have an easier time of it. That was where the father had to participate politically in all campaigns and where his dossier was kept. In short, it was where the family was most vulnerable to pressure. The heads of factories now had rustication targets to meet, and from 1973 onward parents who resisted were sometimes subjected to grueling "study sessions" at their work-units.

The young people whom the schools had already earmarked for rustication were supposed to assemble first at the parent's factory, and from there go to the countryside in a group composed entirely of the factory employees' children. To assuage parents' fears, factory cadres accompanied these groups—to help the young people adjust to rural life and to ensure that the peasants did not discriminate against them.[20]

Moreover, all of these new rusticants were dispatched to sites within traveling distance of Canton. No more youngsters were to be sent to Hainan Island or other frontier districts. Similarly in Peking, Shanghai, and other major cities, the policy of sending youths to the frontiers was sharply cut back from 1974 onwards. In the first half decade after the Cultural Revolution, more than a million youths had been assigned to settle and pioneer the frontiers. This massive program to use China's younger generation to develop the borderlands had now proven too costly in urban discontent.

At the same time, though, many of Guangdong's villages were refusing to accommodate any more of Canton's young people. So the slogan of the rustification program, that young people should "unite with" and be "reeducated" by the peasantry, quietly was allowed to lapse. The groups sent out from the factories increasingly were settled in their own separate "youth points" on patches of rural wasteland. But placing the youths in these isolated youth points necessitated prolonged supervision by the factory cadres. Coming for a year or two in shifts, these cadres now had to help control the young people and prevent them from slipping back unchecked to Canton.

Rusticated youths of earlier years—destitute, bored or disgruntled—already were illegally stealing back to Guangdong's cities by the tens of thousands. A teacher from a commune high school in one of the poorest Guangdong counties recollects that all but fifteen or twenty of the hundred urban youths who had been settled in his immediate vicinity had drifted off by 1971 to the cities. The urban Neighborhood Committees and local police offices turned a blind eye to such youths so long as they lived quietly at home and were not of overly bad-class background. But there were thousands of youngsters whose parents could not or would not support them. Without work permits, ration coupons, or urban residence cards, some of them had to turn to petty thievery or prostitution. The city's rate of crime, which before the Cultural Revolution had been negligible, began rising rapidly, according to interviewees.

Yet the national government still felt it economically advantageous to pursue the rustication program. The more than fifteen million young people shipped to the countryside since the Cultural Revolution (10 percent of China's urban population!) had at least been able to contribute *something* to agricultural production, even if marginally. In the cities they would have been merely an idle, highly concentrated, and perhaps politically volatile body of unemployed.

But the heavy price paid for the program had included more than the rising tide of urban crime and the discontent among the sent-down youths, peasantry, and urban parents. Perhaps more serious, as we shall observe in the next chapter, many of the teenagers in Canton's schools who were earmarked to settle in the countryside were refusing to pay any attention in class and were fomenting disorder in the schools.

GUANGDONG'S ABOUT-FACE

Most provinces retained their rustication programs; but surveying the damage, Guangdong's leadership decided that the costs far outweighed the advantages. In the spring of 1975 the Guangdong Party Committee terminated its "rustication for life" policy. More surprising, it decreed that almost all the former Red Guards who had gone to the villages in 1968–69 at the end of the Cultural Revolution and almost all the pre-Cultural Revolution rusticants—close to 400,000 Guangdong young people *in toto*—were to be recalled rapidly from the villages.[21] These rusticants flooded back into Guangdong's cities during the summer of 1975. The generation of young people who had gone to the villages after 1968–69 were told that within a few years they too would be returned to the cities. Only the settlers of state farms were left behind in the countryside without any assurances of being recalled.[22]

1975 was an apt time for the Guangdong Party's new moves. The recent expansion of Canton education from eight years to ten meant that for two recent years no new graduates had entered the Canton job market. Through this, temporary labor shortages had been created. The returning rusticants were assured further job openings when Guangdong decreed in 1975 that almost all of Canton's newly graduating students would be assigned to the countryside for a two to three year work stint.[23]

In the five years between early 1970 and the end of 1974, only 85,000 youths from Canton (and 260,000 province-wide) had actually been persuaded to rusticate.[24] Now under the new policy the authorities calculated that in 1975 fully 80,000 additional Cantonese youngsters would have volunteered by year's end.[25] The volunteers apparently came not just from the newly graduating class, but also from graduates of past years who had previously resisted. Their objection had never been to the notion of working in the countryside, but to working in the countryside for *life*.[26] According to interview reports, they now went willingly, knowing that only by rusticating would they later be able to obtain urban jobs.

In 1978 the national government finally admitted what Guangdong had acknowledged in 1975—the rustication-for-life program had backfired. Declaring that "many rusticated urban youths have become listless and dejected, and the masses discontented,"[27] the government promised that as China modernized many more of the young people would be recalled to the cities and far fewer graduates would have to be sent.[28] One province after another quietly had already conceded the rustication program's defeat and had called its own youths home. By mid-1979 only 6 or 7 million young people remained in China's countryside out of the 18 million who had been sent since the Cultural Revolution.[29]

But the peasants obviously were not happy about supporting even this reduced burden. So in 1979 the national government announced that *all* the urban youths who were still in the peasant villages gradually would be shifted out of the villages into "youth farms,"[30] similar to Guangdong's earlier "youth points."

China's cities have faced severe difficulties accommodating the millions of youths who have been allowed to come home. Factories have been able to provide jobs for only a fraction of them, and the government's policies severely curtailed other types of job possibilities. City governments since the fifties had been ordered to reduce urban costs by closing down large numbers of urban shops and by cutting back sharply on service-trade personnel.[31] In addition, the drives to promote socialism had decimated the traditional cottage handicraft industries; and the workshops that took their place in the 1960s (which were engaged mainly in subcontract work for the state-run factories) offered employment mostly to housewives, not new school graduates. But in the late 1970s, with the unemployment rates among returning rusticants disturbingly high, the national government finally reversed all of these job policies. Three quarters of all the urban jobs provided to China's young people in 1979 were in these formerly neglected sectors—traditional handicrafts, retailing, services, and small profit-sharing cooperatives.[32]

Canton and other cities are playing for time. They know that the present all-too-large generation of young adults is a product of the urban baby boom of the 1950s. With a declining urban birth since the early 1960s and a halt to urban immigration, the crisis in the urban job market that has plagued Canton and the rest of urban China since the early sixties will eventually recede of its own accord.[33] In historical perspective, the massive rustication campaign of the late 1960s and the 1970s will be viewed as a temporary demographic expedient—obviated by the Pill.

CHAPTER NINE

Troubled Schools, 1970–1976

THE BACKWASH into the schools from the "last sibling" rustication policy was profound. The knowledge that their futures were beyond their own control made most students feel it was "useless to study." With no other topic of enquiry did I receive interview responses of such uniformity. Regardless of whether they were legal emigrants or refugees, or whether they still felt loyal to the government or not, the former students and teachers were in accord—that the allocation policies of 1971–75 provided the *main* reason for the students' continued lack of interest in schoolwork.

In my initial research hypotheses, there had been the supposition that if an educational system could be divorced from the competition for careers and if the threat of selection examinations were removed, students would be better able to learn for intrinsic reasons—interest in a school subject, or a general love for learning, or for the practicality of what was taught. The evidence from Canton and other cities provides no support for such suppositions. If anything, during the first half of the 1970s, despite renewed stability in the administration of education and the gradual improvement of textbooks, the students' interest in learning declined. A former student from Fujian Province who graduated from senior high school in 1973 and was assigned to a temporary job as a "monitor" in one of his own school's junior-high classes remembers:

> These younger kids' attitudes toward study were even worse than my own class's. It was really chaotic. Each class had two or three of us monitors,

but it made little difference; the kids yelled and horsed around even when the teacher was trying to teach. They didn't know why the heck they were in class. They said studying's useless because their level of achievement wouldn't have any relationship with their futures. I got to know a girl there, whose dad's in the Foreign Ministry and who was a good and very willing student. I asked her why, and it turned out she felt she'd have the opportunity to enter a university through her father. The teacher kept on telling the other kids, "Study to construct the country." Some students were willing to, partly because they also happened to be interested in studying. Most were unwilling.[1]

Occasionally rumors circulated that academic achievement once again would count, and in each recorded case the desire to study temporarily came back into vogue. The student from Fujian recalled that in his final year of schooling (1972–73) the transitory nationwide trend away from radicalism that year inspired erroneous conjectures by his school teachers:

Those final semesters before graduation the study attitudes of the students improved. The teachers that year taught a lot of material. For one, things generally were more stable that year, which encouraged more stable schoolwork. Second, though no one did end up going directly to a university, the teachers had hinted to them that this year some could. This spurred the desire to study. We organized math and science small-groups, where the good students helped the bad. There was a study-group organized by the students themselves, twelve classmates in all, in which I participated. We met at each others' homes at night. But not that type of stuff now: the students get worse and worse each year. Because students again feel they have no opportunity: when last comes to last, they still have to go to the countryside.

Interviewees report that students who knew they would be holding urban posts were generally more inclined to open their books than classmates who felt destined for the countryside. The latter students argued to their teachers that they would only be able to utilize rudimentary skills in the villages. Why pay attention to mathematics beyond the multiplication tables when rural accounting methods used no math beyond that? Why bother even to learn to recognize rural pests or how to plant rice when they would be learning that anyway once they were peasants? It was partly that they felt little preparation was needed for the countryside. But according to respondents, it was also that the students did not want to lead the hard and poor life of a peasant. They were consequently refusing to orient themselves toward such a future while still at school. In class some of them openly vented their frustrations and resentments. "The final year of senior high school was the worst to try to control," observed a high school teacher from Yunnan Province. "When kids imminently are facing settlement in the countryside, sometimes on purpose they"ll sabotage the class-period. Kids who are well behaved in senior high 1 can be impossible suddenly in senior high 2."

Students who were heading for urban job postings were less obstreperous. But they were only slightly more prone to give any attention to their schoolwork. "If permitted, I'd have tried to become a doctor," observes one interviewee, "but I felt I'd be assigned to a factory, so why study?" Most other factory-bound students had even less reason to concentrate on school lessons; they *only* wanted blue-collar work. In earlier times, a production-line job had seemed to middle-class youths like the sort of work one took when there were no other opportunities. But now that graduates were faced only with the stark choice between becoming a worker or a peasant, the blue-collar urban posts had taken on a considerably rosier image. Beyond that, workers after the Cultural Revolution held a high political status as members of the "proletarian" occupations and could lead comparatively stable lives in a period when intellectuals were vulnerable and sometimes harassed. Workers also had secure incomes, which stayed about the same whether or not they became skilled, and whether or not they stayed workers or became technicians. The higher standing which this gave to ordinary blue-collar work probably attracted a fair degree of working-class support. But the adverse side-effect was that for students who were reasonably content to be production-line workers with no career goals beyond that, most of their school subjects did indeed seem useless.

At the same time, though, the new desirability and improved status of industrial employment aroused among students a strong interest in the modern mechanical crafts. This was even true—in fact, especially true— of young people fated for rural assignments, probably because the hobbies represented the type of urban jobs they desired but would not be getting. Students who generally paid little attention to schoolwork often gravitated, out of school, toward radio-building, woodworking, model-plane-building, and the like. Such hobbies were considerably more popular now than in the 1960s. At the Fujian school, where these skills could be practiced in "hobby groups," the interest of students was so great that the school was able to get some of the students to behave better by denying participation to any students who were rowdy during classtime.

Some of the students who would be staying in the city had their own reasons for pursuing such hobbies. In their work stints at factories, say interviewees, they and their classmates had become aware of the monotony of routine production-line work. In reaction, the hobbies reportedly reflected a desire for *interesting* blue-collar work, as shopfloor mechanics and the like.

The students' views had become *more* utilitarian in many respects than the school system—and many young people rejected school on these very grounds. They were refusing for pragmatic reasons to pay attention to most of their classes, while at the same time wanting more modern craft skills than they could obtain at school. The radicals who until late 1976 were in charge of education had mixed feelings about encouraging the type of vocational training that the hobbies represented. They had decried the old educational system for being un-utilitarian, but simultaneously they did not want to orient education toward the development of "expertise." They felt that such an orientation was linked to inegalitarian social values. Before the Cultural Revolution, they pointed out in editorials, the high regard for expertise had propped up the prestige and salaries of the old petty bourgeois professional classes.

Whereas the Fujian school had encouraged technical craft hobbies, the teacher from the more politically radical province of Yunnan observes of his own high school:

> Kids who had hobbies such as building radios might be criticized. Though there was that old slogan of "red and expert," such a kid might be suspected of being white and expert. Before the Cultural Revolution there had been a connection between technical skills and the incomes of workers, and the more highly trained personnel still today get better salaries. The school wanted to prevent this type of thinking. Instead, ideological remolding is to be in first place, technical stuff in second place, and science in third place [each taking precedence over the ones behind]. More time is to be spent in political studies. But the kids didn't become more activist, and some are still more interested in skills. . . . There are still struggles in the leadership over this [this interview was in 1975]. Deng Xiaoping's line is to encourage students to have interests in such skills.

LABOR

To a certain extent, though, the radical-sponsored labor expeditions to factories did serve as a genuine sort of "practice" in technical skills, once these programs got properly organized after 1969. When the students did a fortnight or month's labor at the larger and more sophisticated factories, they sometimes had demonstrations of machinery, occasional lectures from skilled workers, and lessons in reading blueprints. Their regular classroom work moreover was supposed to tie into these visits; as we observed earlier, the sciences had been scrapped as disciplines and replaced by an Industrial-Agricultural-Military course. This sector of their education conformed to the type of schooling which students could be expected to find relevant.

But even here, major problems emerged which all but erased the students' interest. Canton is a city principally of light industries, and only a small number of the factories were sufficiently large and sufficiently modernized to offer an informative work program. Most of the students' industrial labor had to be nonmechanized assembly work with little chance to "learn" anything. From interviews it is evident that this factory work—and the farm work—did give students a realistic appreciation of what a day's labor entailed; taught them they had no reason to fear dirtying their hands; and taught them too that they could accustom themselves to the strains and fatigue of the hardest manual labor. This was all to the good; but it was not what "interested" students.

Moreover, many factories—and in particular the more modernized ones—began resisting the intrusions of students after 1971. The factories were already overstaffed on their production lines, and the last thing they needed were hundreds of unskilled and undisciplined young people swarming through the workshops.[2] Blocked increasingly from the factory gates, the schools no longer had a ready means for relating the textbook on industrial knowledge to any practice, nor any means for providing their students with enough of the politically requisite labor.

Many of the schools responded to this predicament by establishing their own small industrial workshops. Second-hand machinery was imported from the factories with which the schools were associated. Skilled workers from the same factories were seconded to manage the workshops and to provide a continued "linking" of education to the proletariat. These school-run enterprises normally had subcontracts with the "fraternal" factory and, since the labor of the students was free, the workshops even provided a modest source of income for the schools. However, two difficulties arose: first, the industrial processes which factories assigned to the school workshops were usually of the most simple, tedious, and labor-intensive variety, so that there were again few skills to be learned or "lessons" that could be devised; and second, the school workshops could accommodate only modest numbers of the school's students. The formula which had evolved by the early 1970s was that schooling should be 70 percent classroom work and 30 percent labor time[3] but even with their new school workshops most of the schools apparently had difficulty abiding by this.

COURSE CONTENT

Another major problem lay with the format of the new industrial knowledge course. Though it contained lessons on science and math, these were jumbled together in one book. The scientific explanations, being tied to discussions on production techniques, were not presented in any systematic progression, and the former students whom I interviewed had found the materials too fragmented and the underlying concepts difficult to understand. In 1971–72, encouraged perhaps by a series of articles by "moderate" Party educators and scientists who had defended the teaching of science theory,[4] Canton's school system quietly dropped the course—and returned instead to the teaching of chemistry and physics as separate disciplines. Canton did so despite the fact that the national newspapers controlled by the Party radicals were continuing to defend the production-technique-oriented approach.

Whether organized as industrial knowledge or as chemistry/physics, the science courses seem to have been relatively popular (as was math) compared to subjects such as politics or Chinese literature-and-language.* Until about 1971, the textbook in the latter course contained mostly Mao selections, which were supplemented by occasional readings from the new "model revolutionary plays" and by editorials emanating from whatever campaign was ongoing. Students accepted that Mao study was "important" but they found the repetition tedious. Even more boring to them was the strong accent on political campaigns in the Chinese literature class, which meant newspaper recitations and sloganeering against the evils of Lin Biao . . . or Confucius . . .or Deng Xiaoping. Equally boring was the repetitious praise for the national policies and models of the moment. Sometimes the political messages were so obscure (as in the Anti-Confucius Campaign's attacks against the Zhou Enlai faction) as to be incomprehensible to the students. But that was not crucially

---

* The curricula of several Canton schools are provided in Appendix C.

important to the teachers, who were concerned first with self-protection. When the literature course did turn on rare occasions to a topic about which some of the students were curious—be it a short selection from *Dream of the Red Chamber* or a week of readings from the rollicking adventure tale *The Water Margin* (there was an allegorical political campaign in China denouncing one of its heroes, which provided an opportunity to read it)—interviewees report attentive silence in the classroom. At least some students appreciated the reintroduction in 1972 of stories by Lu Xun, a few traditional poems, and a few lessons on classical Chinese. Respondents report, too, that when they did have the rare teacher (usually in a science or math course) who still had enthusiasm for his courses and a flair for presenting them, students did listen. But they sensed most of their teachers had little desire to teach, and that the knowledge of most of the newly graduated teachers was quite limited.

English was the least liked of all subjects, because it was *patently* of no utility to students and yet would require considerable memorization to master. It was a course, too, which could not be justified to students as ideologically important, unlike politics and literature-and-language. Yet English was taught in almost all Chinese schools. This ran counter to the logic of the other post-Cultural Revolution reforms; but Mao in a recorded 1968 conversation had casually commented that young people should learn the language.[5] It was one of the few concrete utterances by Mao on curriculum content available to educators, and they protected themselves by adhering carefully to the Chairman's word. Without strong middle-level administrative organs to process educational policy, Mao's chance remark became directly transformed into local programs without intervening correctives. The 1971 detente with America gave added thrust to the spread of English instruction,[6] and in Canton and many other cities English classes were made part of the curriculum from the third grade of primary school onward![7] As one teacher relates, there was little success:

A few students were interested in English but most were going to be sent to the countryside and so had serious ideological problems. They felt "What's the use of English?" and some of them misbehaved during classtime. We tried to persuade them on the grounds that later everything in the countryside would be mechanized. We said that they'd have to learn something of the most modern farming techniques then, and that many of these could be borrowed and adapted from English-language journals. Yes, we were of course talking nonsense, and the students knew it.[8]

This particular school was located near a large military hospital whose staff included senior PLA doctors who had joined the revolution before Liberation. They were therefore deemed "revolutionary cadres," with the influence that went with such a designation. The teacher continues:

> Those PLA doctors' kids were very eager in studying English, because they knew that later, some day, they'd have medical research to do, and that it might be facilitated by a knowledge of English. Yes, it is common in China that high-ranking parents can get their children into jobs similar to their own.[9]

Before the Cultural Revolution the middle- and bad-class students had been best academically and among the most interested in their courses. They reportedly continued to find their schoolwork easier to accomplish than the working-class students. But most of them now put little effort into it. The result was that some of the cadres' children were now among the best students.[10] To them studying was not useless.

ANTI-INTELLECTUALISM IN THE SCHOOLS

Before the Cultural Revolution the middle-class students had been motivated to study not just by the prospects of better careers but also by the favorable view of learning which they had acquired from their parents. This concern to do well had been reinforced by their teachers' signs of approval and classmates' admiration. After the Cultural Revolution at least some of these young people initially had continued to place a positive value on studying, despite recognition of its "uselessness." But they soon discovered the new school environment not only made learning difficult but even literally discouraged academic achievement. In fact, under the aegis of the Party radicals, the government's political rhetoric for the first three or four years after the Cultural Revolution so disparaged the importance of academic work that students in secondary school who were too eager to do well at their studies and too willing to outdistance their classmates were apt to find themselves rebuked publicly in student meetings for striving to become "bourgeois experts."[11]

Some of the teachers were again content to go along with this. A teacher from a rural senior high school in northern Guangdong recollects:

> In 1970–71, the textbooks were filled with lots of quotes by Mao and Lin Biao. [These were provincial texts; those published by Canton had cut

back on the Mao quotes earlier.] Then in 1972 the books changed greatly and just had Mao quotes on the front page. The other pages had stuff on knowledge. Some teachers liked the change, but others didn't because the new books meant that if a new movement like the Cultural Revolution came along they might find themselves accused of teaching too much on knowledge, not enough politics. Yes, true, it would be a book by the province, not by themselves, but nonetheless they felt they might be criticized for teaching it, for *following* a revisionist line. On the other side, there was the possibility that if they were still using the older textbooks they might have found themselves accused of not teaching knowledge, of not wanting the poor and lower-middle peasants' children to acquire knowledge. Yet the older teachers were largely wary about the new emphasis in the texts. They had a point, as can be seen in the present (February 1976) campaign in the universities attacking the pursuit of knowledge over politics.[12]

At the same time teachers also continued to shy away from courses involving any real discussion or lectures on politics, so as to avoid any chance of error.[13] Whereas in the 1960s some teachers had been too dictatorial in their style of teaching and intolerant of any disagreement from students, now some had become too hesitant and pliable to teach effectively.[14]

This timidity reflected more the general wariness of the teaching staffs than any actual danger of being hurt politically. Of all my interviewees, not one could recall any incidents after 1969 where any students had used "politics" seriously as a weapon against a teacher. In fact, former students were amused by the question. It had never even entered their classmates' minds, they said; young people were rowdy but politically "simple" and always followed the schools' and teachers' lead on political questions. In their depictions of actual events the former teachers generally concurred—but nevertheless their memories of the Cultural Revolution caused some of them to see their students as *potential* sources of trouble. And such memories were kept alive through the mid-1970s by the continuing intermittent efforts of the radical leadership faction to stir up student assertiveness.

The Party radicals were still perturbed by the possibilities of the Chinese revolution's routinization (which in large part is what they meant by the rubric "revisionism"). As with Mao in the mid-1960s, they wanted an activist student body, but made of stuff different from the docile Lei Feng. In 1973 they launched a media campaign calling for "going-against-the-tide" heroes—heroes willing to oppose various "conservative'' trends. A 12-year-old primary-school pupil became one of the campaign's foremost symbols.

This girl, Huang Shuai, had written remarks critical of her teacher in the diary she kept as part of her homework, taking the teacher to task for an authoritarian manner. In reply the teacher had publicly criticized her in class and had, in the time-tested way of Chinese classrooms, gotten other children to reproach her in small-group meetings. The girl in turn had written to a newspaper asking, ''What serious mistake have I made? Are we children of Mao Zedong's time still supposed to be slaves to the teacher's absolute authority created by the old educational system?'' Her letter and extracts from her diary were blazoned across the front page of the *People's Daily* of December 28, 1973.[15]

The girl again made national news six weeks later. Three young cadres had written her a private letter as a result of the publicity surrounding her first venture into the news. In their letter they had come to the defense of China's teachers. ''Nowadays,'' they wrote, ''in many schools the teachers have all become very cautious gentlemen,'' and went on to say that for students to severely critize their teachers was a ''bad tide.'' Huang Shuai's public reply dominated the front page of *People's Daily*.[16] In it, she labeled the letter-writers as ''bourgeois restorationist forces'' and ''disciples of Confucius.'' It was a scenario almost calculated to alienate most of China's teachers.[17]

During the winter of 1974, in line with Huang Shuai's precedent, newspapers and radio stations reported a flurry of big-character posters and letters by students protesting against the actions of teachers. The publicized diary of one child summed up the radical message: ''Do they want to turn us into sheep? . . . We will act according to Chairman Mao's teachings: servility should never be promoted.''[18] In other cases, the complaints revolved around educational issues: schools being rebuked for having reverted to closed-book examinations so as to better control their students. In particular, *People's Daily* carried a letter from a Canton junior high school student who had been severely criticized at school for having copied his classmates' answers during such an exam:

> I think the teachers have used exams as their secret weapon in controlling the students, and they have used ''marks'' as a weapon to restrict the students who have offended them. That was why I was given a ''zero'' mark. Was this not a clear reflection of the practice of ''maintaining the dignity of teachers''? In effect this is a struggle of political lines.[19]

By 1974, as we observed in chapter 4, a large number of teachers in

Canton had abandoned the open-book tests. They were now being warned by the radicals not to try dismantling the Cultural Revolution's "new-born things."*

ACTIVISM AND PEER-GROUP ORGANIZATIONS

Canton's schools during the mid 1970s had maintained the same complex political systems as in the 1960s. There were still the same networks of mass youth organizations, of class officers, of an elite League branch, of small-groups, activist titles, and labor competition. If anything, in the 1970s more was made of such organizational techniques than ever before. But these organizational structures were not able to remedy the situation in the schools.

This was the case even though activism could still help a young person's future. Though a good activist showing in class was no longer beneficial in the direct sense of aiding a student's chances of entering university and from there a desired career, the students' political records still entered their dossiers, which accompanied them through life. A 1974 graduate who joined the League observes, "I entered because I wanted to have a good personal history, so that later the factory leadership would look favorably upon me."

Exactly as in earlier times, moreover, the activist ideals were promoted from an early age through the textbooks and through the teachers' signs of approval. The various primary-school structures for getting children to "practice" activism remained firmly in place. The Young Pioneers were simply retitled Little Red Soldiers (renamed, according to several teachers, just so as to have a title different from Russia's Young Pioneer organization). Entry now began in the first grade, rather than the third grade, in order to begin molding children's activities all the earlier. Membership was denied only to those children who refused to be obedient.

* After the purge of the radical Shanghai faction (the Gang of Four) in late 1976, the national leadership tried to reaffirm the authority of teachers. Teachers were assured that students would be expected to be obedient. The government signaled this by moving the young girl Huang Shuai back to the center of national media attention. The "Huang Shuai Incident" and the "going-against-the-tide spirit" were denounced with great fanfare in 1977 as Gang of Four plots, and it was claimed in People's Daily that Huang Shuai had in fact been reeducated by the "correct" letter of those three young cadres. The leadership in 1977 wanted a more docile type of activism. Chairman Hua Guofeng was publicly and closely identified with a new Learn From Lei Feng campaign.

From the prior experience of the Young Pioneers, the schools had learned that it was best to have the Little Red Soldiers only in primary school; if continued into junior high, as in earlier times, the organization would be considered "childish" and so lose its popular appeal. Youngsters now instead became eligible for membership in a "teenage" organization—the Red Guards—as soon as they entered junior high.

In the years immediately after the Cultural Revolution, as we earlier saw, this Red Guard association had served as an elite class-line-based corps, taking the place of the discredited Communist Youth League. But as the League revived in 1970 and the class line softened in the schools, the Red Guards assumed a "mass organization" role. By 1974 almost every student of senior high school age who was not a juvenile delinquent was expected to enroll as a member. The authorities' desires to gain increased organizational control over the teenage peer-group environment seem to have caused this shift. But this broadening in the membership ranks became self-defeating. Though my middle-class interviewees had resented the class-line criteria intially used in Red Guard recruitments, they at the same time had envied those let in. Elitist activism requires this distinction between those allowed to belong and those not; for that reason alone, probably, some of the red-class students became willing members. By broadening the membership ranks to include the whole classroom, both the "glory" and the feelings of special membership were vitiated. Interviewees recall a growing disdain for the organization and a reluctance to participate in its activities.

This devaluation of the Red Guards did not necessarily occur in all schools, however. It occurred where the informal peer-group opinion was already to some extent at odds with official norms. One, although notably only one, of the schools in my sample had been able to make Red Guard activism seem attractive even at a period when almost all the students belonged. This was a school whose students lived on campus in an isolated setting, which had permitted teachers to gain unusual control over the student milieu:[21]

> The sole activities of our school's Red Guards consisted of performing extra political study and extra labor after school on occasional afternoons.
> "Q. But what were the privileges of belonging?"
> Oh, those *were* the privileges. Yes, most kids wanted to belong. They wanted to because it was activist: because it placed you in the forefront (*daitou*). It was to "*ai laodong*" (love labor). I myself thought it was better to join in, because I didn't want to be thought backward. Yes, some of the truly backward kids didn't want to participate. They played ball instead.

This instance of classroom activism, with its shades of Tom Sawyer's fence, is the only such case in my interview files. But it contained one element that was shared in the mid-1970s by the other classrooms in my sample. The officially sponsored dichotomy among students was no longer explicitly in terms of "class" but rather of "activism"-versus-"backwardness." The Party radicals had already shifted several times in their conceptualization of "class struggle" and were shifting once more now that events in China were again more settled. They no longer wanted to see "class" in caste terms, since that would help to consolidate and freeze in place the *status quo* in China, and would make further political and social transformation more difficult. Within the leadership circles, they had again begun questioning the official interpretation of "class."[22]

Interestingly, as the official rhetoric of "class" began to die away, social relationships in the classrooms quite readily altered in tune. In 1968–70, friendship groups in the classroom had formed almost entirely on the basis of class background, and a clear formal social ranking system had been established, with revolutionary-cadre children at the top. But all of this changed within the space of a couple of years. My youngest interviewees were surprised when questioned about the significance of class at their senior high schools; it had become impolite to inquire directly into others' class backgrounds. No longer exposed to the rhetoric, no longer vying as in the mid-1960s to secure upward mobility through the schools, and with job assignments no longer related to family origins, students obligingly let awareness of class recede to the low-pitched level of 1962–64.

Class no longer was overwhelmingly important even for entry into the revived League. And once again, as in the sixties, it seems that a somewhat higher proportion of middle-class than working-class youngsters were eager to join. The middle-class youths' alertness to measures of achievement, their readier acceptance of the official values the teachers had taught them in primary school, and their recognition that League membership might help later in life to offset the disadvantages of their nonred origins continued to attract a fair portion of the middle class to the League.

But there was no driving competition to get admitted, unlike the situation in the sixties. For most students the disadvantages now seemed to equal the advantages, and even those youngsters who were well-disposed to the League had reason to pause before handing in an application. Their worry was that in senior high school League members would be in an exposed position if chosen for a village. All students who were not their family's last remaining child had to face that possibility of rustication. And if the call did come, to decline to volunteer—to choose to stay idly at home in the city instead—would open you up to charges of having joined the League for calculating reasons. It was safer to keep a low political profile rather than risk humiliation and loss of self-integrity as graduation time approached.

To be sure, in some classrooms there was still the occasional student who sought membership in the League for idealistically activist reasons. And once inside the League such students reinforced each others' views within their own little League subculture. Interviews reveal a few who even ended up sincerely volunteering for rustication out of a determination to prove and "temper" themselves in the countryside. But while much of the worldview of the sixties generation persisted among this subgroup, interviewees report that such students remained very much an isolated minority. Far more students were ambivalent even about whether to behave or misbehave at school, let alone whether to hold to highly activist ideals.

THE SMALL-GROUPS' BROADENED ROLE

To counteract this ambivalence, the high schools turned to student small-group sessions. These were to provide the formal settings in which the small activist core would grasp the peer-group leadership. Together with any students even modestly willing to conform, they were to bring peer-group pressures to bear against delinquents, to isolate them through formal peer disapproval. This became in the 1970s the major tool to control deviant behavior. A former student observed:

> Small-group criticism or classwide criticisms by fellow students is the only "punishment" at our school. If a student's done wrong, he's to be subjected only to "thought education" by his classmates; it's their responsibility, not the Revolutionary Committee head's [i.e., the principal's] or the teachers'. Even if a kid steals, there's merely peer-group pressure in discussion rather than any formal sanctions against the kid. There's no expulsion from the school whatsoever. After all, if his thinking hasn't been reformed by his schoolmates and he goes out into society he'll just commit bad things there. Such students should remain in school.

Since students were supposed to pay at least some attention to their academic lessons, teachers were even able to use such peer-group techniques to corral the worst offenders into putting at least a modicum of effort into their studies. Recalls a secondary school teacher:

> The kids didn't worry. They knew that if they failed they'd still be promoted. So we sometimes had to use political pressure to force such kids to prepare for their course exams. We'd organize other kids to criticize them. This would be through a session to criticize the ideology of "studying is useless," an idea that we attributed to Liu Shaoqi.* But actually, there were still some kids who completely refused to study, and to that we had to close one of our eyes.

To promote its goals, a small-group was equipped with several props it had lacked before the Cultural Revolution. First, the small-group head was now democratically elected, no longer selected by the teacher. The students knew they were supposed to select someone activist, and in the classes in my sample they did precisely that. Because the choice was their own, the small-group leader was supposed to enjoy an added element of legitimacy. But he or she still was supposed to operate as the representative of official opinion, not as a relaxed "buddy." To prevent the small-group from becoming a friendship group dominated by the peer group's own mores, its membership was purposely reshuffled each semester before it had time to develop an informal group solidarity.

As a second tool, the small-group's formal appraisal of each of its members was provided with a new significance. Every semester each small-group held a special session for which the student wrote a report on what he thought of his own performance during the term. The other members then used this self-appraisal as the basis for their own critique of him: whether he has been trying his best or not, how can he better develop himself, etc. The gist of these remarks were then written up as a brief report by the small-group leader and presented to the teacher,

---

* In a school environment where "Politics takes command," attributing the phrase to Liu Shaoqi put the errant student in a politically indefensible position. Early on, the national mass media began claiming Liu as the author of the phrase "studying is useless," so as to oblige students to publicly repudiate their own way of thinking. After 1971, it was revealed in the press that the author of the phrase was actually none other than Lin Biao, and in 1977 the press discovered, *mirabile dictu*, that the Gang of Four's Zhang Chunqiao had been the originator of that same phrase.

who appended a third report. All three of these appraisals—the student's, the small-group's, and the teacher's—were included in the report card sent home to the parents. Before the Cultural Revolution, the small-group's appraisals had never gone outside the classroom like this. Family pressures were now being sought to persuade students to conform to the "formal" peer-group norms.

More importantly, these same three sets of semester appraisals entered the student's lifetime dossier. A bad set of reports could start off a teenager's job career on a bad footing, while an exceptionally good set provided some of the same benefits as League membership—to a lesser extent, perhaps, but without the discomfort attached to being an official activist.

Notwithstanding these mechanisms, the small-group heads still often encountered great difficulty getting their group members to cooperate. The students' own informal peer-group norms were sometimes too much at odds with the official prescriptions; and not many students seemed strongly concerned about bettering their initial postgraduation standings at their assigned work-units. Small-group sessions very frequently became unmanageable. A former small-group head who graduated in 1973 describes the appraisal sessions he ran:

> The critiques given by the kids depended on friendships and conflicts. It was the girls who criticized each other—mutually. So as group leader, when it came to writing the appraisal, I couldn't take these comments at face value. And the boys didn't want to criticize each other at all, not even to criticize the punk who participated in gang fighting outside of school. Some of the kids just chatted privately during the appraisal sessions, not paying attention. So in the end I just wrote anything, whatever I felt.

The problem was that this mode of correcting deviant behavior through peer pressures presupposes that most of the peer group abide by the proper norms and, for one reason or another, also care that others do likewise. In at least some schools the bulk of the students did adhere adequately to the rules of the game, and helped pull their mates back into conformity with the official system. But at most of the schools in my sample the group influence was the opposite. The strong peer influence at Chinese schools, which had been used so effectively by the authorities in a "pro-social" way before the Cultural Revolution, very often had swung loose and become autonomous in the 1970s. The authorities were not quite sure how to handle this.

As symbols of a new teenage counterculture, many boys illicitly smoked when they got a chance, and a great many in Canton listened to Hong Kong music on their radios. Moreover, the young people's discontent at rustication, their continued disdain for their studies, the dispiritedness of their teachers, the confusing shifts and infighting among the national Party leaders, and the influence of older siblings who had been disillusioned by the Cultural Revolution's outcome had all combined to give at least a touch of political cynicism to teenagers' attitudes. This was true for most of my younger interviewees (legal emigrants accompanying or rejoining older relatives, not self-willed refugees); and they insist that most of their classmates had attitudes similar to their own. Somewhat older informants, who had been high school students before the Cultural Revolution, were dismayed by their younger brothers' and sisters' habits, flippancy, and materialistic interests. They themselves had been puritanical as teenagers in the 1960s, had held devoutly to the views they were taught in school, and as students had tried to improve their own character through stringent "tempering." Several of these older respondents remarked to me that a teenager *should* be idealistic, and that it was a terrible shame that the new generation had not had this experience. They found themselves on the opposite side of a generation gap.

The changes after 1976 in China's national leadership and programs have not erased that generation gap. Years of student discontent and indiscipline have perhaps irrevocably left their mark in personalities and group behavior. Teenagers took avantage of the opening to the West by sporting bellbottom trousers and long hair, to their elders' shock.[24] At the close of the seventies, juvenile deliquency in the schools still posed serious problems.[25] One and a half thousand soldiers had to be stationed in the Peking school system in 1979 to guard against disruptions.[26] Truancy, too, remained high. One high school in 1979 reported 10 percent of its students had been absent for more than three months.[27]

Mao's philosophy had been that you cannot make a revolution without breaking a few eggs. The radical educational changes he favored had dramatically and precipitously smashed the shell of the prior educational structure; and now the new authorities are finding it almost impossible to put Humpty Dumpty together again. The ultimate irony is that Mao and his followers had insisted that education must concentrate on instilling "proletarian" and "revolutionary" virtues; yet the school system's loss of control over so many of its urban students during the decade of "Maoist" schooling will, if anything, help hasten the dying away in China of the revolutionary ethos that Mao had promoted.

CHAPTER TEN

The Fight Over Higher Education

IN THE early part of this century, the German sociologist Max Weber wrote a scathing analysis of academic diplomas and entrance examinations:

> The development of the diploma from universities and business and engineering colleges, and the universal clamor for the creation of educational certificates in all fields, make for the formation of a privileged stratum in bureaus and offices. . . . When we hear from all sides the demand for an introduction of regular curricula and special examinations, the reason behind it is not a suddenly awakened "thirst for education" but a desire for restricting the supply for these positions and their monopolization by the owners of educational certificates. Today, the "examination" is the universal means of this monopolization, and therefore examinations irresistibly advance. As the education prerequisite to the acquisition of the educational certificate requires considerable expense and a period of waiting for full remuneration, this striving means a setback for talent in favor of property.[1]

Mao and his followers felt that precisely such arguments were applicable to China. They believed that the weight given to the academic diplomas of the old regime's educated classes had helped them to perpetuate their advantaged statuses after the victory of socialism in 1949. These so-called "experts" still wanted to retain strict academic "standards," selection examinations, and a lengthy curriculum in order to keep ordinary people from joining their ranks.

The Party radicals were determined in the early 1970s to devalue the university diploma. Decrying what Weber had called the "privileged stratum in bureaus and offices," a Chinese writer observed,

> In the eyes of the capitalist class it is inconceivable for college graduates to become just ordinary workers. "Then what is the use of having colleges?" the bourgeoisie ask. They declare that their purpose in running universities is to turn out higher trained "experts," such as scientists, engineers, lawyers, economists, administrators, and so on. They regard these as the "elite" of society and as superior to the working people.[2]

In order that graduates from universities would not think of themselves as anything but skilled workers, the radicals counted on several reforms: an obligatory period of several years of work between secondary school and higher education; the abolition of entrance exams and introduction of new selection criteria; and a revamped, shortened, "proletarianized" university curriculum. We shall examine these in turn.

THE WORK INTERVAL

This intervening period of work had ironically been an idea of Khrushchev, the arch "revisionist" of Chinese propaganda. He and other Russian leaders had been worried in the 1950s that Russia's high school graduates tended to look down on the manual labor jobs most of them would have to assume. Khrushchev was also unhappy that the young people who got into higher education did not know much about practical work and therefore had little emphathy with the manual workforce. In 1958 the Russian government passed regulations (soon rescinded) stipulating that after the seventh or eighth year of schooling all youngsters should spend time working at a factory or farm, and only after that would they be able to take the entrance exams for a higher—usually vocational—stage of education. In addition, in 1959 Russia adopted a university curriculum where, for the first 2 to 3 years of college, students would participate part-time in labor. Only in the last years of university would they devote themselves entirely to their studies.[3] These Russian initiatives attracted a great deal of attention in China, and the radicals had reworked them over the years into their own package of prescriptions for vocational training and college education.

VOCATIONAL SCHOOLING

In the 1970s, the secondary-level vocational schools no longer operated alongside the regular senior high school system as in the sixties.[4] Instead, if a factory needed manpower skills of a certain kind it was supposed to select several young employees who had already had a few years of work experience. After attending the appropriate technical school, these workers were to return to the factory. An interviewee describes how her younger brother secured his training:

> He graduated from senior high school in 1972 and was assigned to work in a very large photographic processing plant. Our dad's a traditional Chinese doctor and my brother had been put to memorizing remedies at the age of 4 or 5. When coworkers had colds, he'd prescribed remedies that worked, and so it became known that he had a knowledge of Chinese medicine. So when the factory had to choose someone to go to the medical classes, a bit less than two years after he had joined the factory, they figured he had a head start in learning the stuff, and that helped get him selected. They wanted to send as bright a guy as they could, since after graduation he'll be returning and will, after all, be *their* doctor. My brother's class background, while not good, wasn't bad either, and so he at least qualified on those terms. No, there weren't any entrance exams. The unit's Party branch just decided.*
>
> He was sent to attend a *xuexi ban* (study class) run inside a hospital. Young people sent there by villages, factories, and PLA units studied for two years, practicing while they learned. They watched the hospital's regular doctors practicing, and the students even got to prescribe things, which the doctors corrected. The class had exams, but these were treated as unimportant.

This new method for recruiting technical students had certain advantages. The new students, having already worked, knew the needs of their work units, knew exactly what jobs they would be performing when they returned to work, and often had already had practice at somewhat related jobs. They probably possessed a better idea than technical students before the Cultural Revolution as to what in their courses was most useful to study and why precisely they were studying it. The motivation

---

* This has now been changed. Starting in 1978 all applicants to technical and specialist schools had to take the revived national university entrance examinations. More recently, China has returned to the pre-Cultural Revolution system, with a vocational-school track directly after junior high school.

to learn that was so lacking in the high schools was not apparently a problem at these schools.

But there were few facilities provided for this vocational training.[5] This was one reason why students in the 1970s attended "study classes" like that young man in the hospital. In Canton, the major cause for these shortages was the chronic lack of classrooms and teachers for the regular high school system. Since this took priority with the education administrators, in the late 1960s many of the former vocational school campuses had been converted into regular high schools. The radicals' vocational training scheme was crippled from the start.

To make up for this, some of Canton's larger factories revived and expanded their own training programs. Having run half-work/half-study vocational schools before the Cultural Revolution, they already had the facilities to do this. The Party radicals gave strong political encouragement to these factory-run courses. They very much wanted to increase the numbers of blue-collar workers who could claim technical credentials.

Mao himself suggested that these factory training programs be titled universities. They were known as "July 21st" universities (after the date in 1968 when Mao had directed that workers and peasants should receive priority in university education),[6] and the blue-collar workers who participated, even if they only acquired a modest technical training, were to receive a university "diploma" equivalent to the regular university-trained technicians. Looked at another way, the significance of a real university degree was to be purposely devalued.

UNIVERSITY ENROLLMENT PROCEDURES

On the one side the followers of Mao *wanted* to deflate the status of "experts" by devaluing university credentials; and on the other side they felt they safely *could* devalue academic "standards" and credentials without damage to the economy. As observed in earlier chapters, the Party's radical wing had convinced itself that the experts' so-called theoretical knowledge was nothing but a purposeful mystification of common-sense ideas and procedures. A layman could quickly be taught these if, as in the high schools, university courses in the sciences were to downplay theory and stress the tangibly practical.

There was hence little need, thought the radicals, to be worried about the academic "quality" of university entrants. Many of them could be chosen simply for being political enthusiasts, and might include peasant youths with merely junior high school or primary school educations. The entrance procedures were initially devised to permit this.

In this new system, a provincial committee in Guangdong determined every year which factories would be awarded a university position, how many openings were to go to PLA units, and how many were to be allotted to each of the various rural counties. Each summer, following these decisions, the Guangdong provincial enrollments office sent out teams of cadres and professors to each city and county capital. There, the team members were augmented by several district- and county-level cadres and teachers.[7] Applications then passed through a local procedure that was described by an official jingle:

> The applicant applies,
> The masses recommend,
> The leadership approves,
> The college [enrollment office] reviews.

In reality, the "recommendation of the masses" was always *pro forma*, at least in the knowledge and expertise of the people I interviewed. It was the local political leadership who actually decided—and in some cases without the nominee even having to apply.[8]

The urban Party officials (for personal reasons that shall be observed) and the university staffs preferred that the rural areas choose rusticated urban youths rather than peasant youngsters, and to the extent that Party bureaucrats and colleges gained control over the seclection procedures the real local youths tended to lose out. The 1970–71 enrollment figures for Wuhan University in table 10-1[9] suggest the degree to which this could occur (this is the most extreme example that I know of).

Table 10-1. Wuhan University Enrollees, 1970–71, by Type of Recruitment (N = 1,245)

From factories	*36%*
Rusticated urban youths	*34%*
Peasant youths	*4%*
PLA soldiers	*6%*
Others (barefoot doctors, cadres, etc.)	*20%*

In Guangdong, this tendency was never so blatant. There were a number of counties and communes, in fact, where rural cadres were only willing to nominate local youngsters, cutting off the chances of rusticated applicants entirely.

In about 1972, therefore, separate quotas were established for these different "peasant" youths, to assure that each group got its "fair share." The Party moderates in the person of Zhou Enlai were responsible for this national directive. The county-level enrollment committee now devised separate quotas for rusticated youths, for "poor and lower-middle peasant" youths, and for bad-background local youths who had publicly "drawn the line" between themselves and their parents. If a given county was allocated 10 university places, a certain number of the communes would be designated to submit the names of several rusticants, different communes to submit a list of nominees who were local peasant youths, and perhaps every second year one of the communes would be instructed to nominate non-red-background village youths, to fulfill that last small quota.[10]

Despite the objections of the Party radicals, the recruitment system began to distinguish further between local and rusticated youths. The colleges in China are essentially of two types: the major ones are run directly by the national government or provinces, as against junior colleges run by the rural districts (administrative clusters of ten or more counties).[11] These district colleges, which include the former agricultural labor universities, are geared to agro-technical curricula, and their graduates returned to the communes from which they had enrolled. The trick, reportedly, was that when the enrollment committee handed down its quotas, the openings at these local colleges usually went to peasant youths; but when the opening was for a prestigious university, the communes very often were instructed to nominate a rusticated urban youth.

The greatest proportion of the places in the practical sciences and in the engineering schools were reserved for young factory employees with experience on the shop floor,[12] and they normally returned to their work units when their university training was completed.[13] But as if to offset the engineering schools' recruitment policies, the urban youths recruited from the countryside were given the greatest share of the seats in philosophy, the social sciences, mathematics, and the pure sciences. The entrants to these disciplines almost never had to return to the countryside. The universities came to be seen by rusticated youth as the best means to escape from a life of impoverishment and hard labor.

The unintended result was that corruption set in early. In the absence of stringent entrance examinations or other strictly regularized means for selecting the new students, officials whose own children had been assigned to settle in the countryside could begin pulling strings and making use of the Party's old-boy networks to win a university seat for their daughter or son. From interviews with former rusticated youths detailing who had been selected to attend a university from their own communes, it would seem that a substantial percentage of the rusticated youths who got in were from the families of Party officials, and that many of the peasant entrants were closely related to commune or village leaders.

At Peking University, according to separate interviews with six foreign students who were taking courses there during 1974–75, approximately 30–50 percent of the student body was composed of the sons and daughters of Party officials.[14] And even those figures do not tell the full story of the influence-peddling at work; a fair number even of the other students were accepted through family connections and influence. An interviewee cites an example:

> A good family friend, an engineer in a bridge-building unit, has a daughter who, like other pre-Cultural Revolution high school students, was sent to the countryside in 1968. Her dad was best friends with his unit's leaders, and after the daughter was in the village for 2–3 years the dad's work-unit found a way to get her back to the city to join the unit. Soon after, they selected her for a university. She'd been just a first-year student in junior high when the Cultural Revolution erupted. She studied at one of the Shanghai engineering institutes for about three years and has already graduated and returned to her dad's unit.

She was now a "credentialed" engineer, with a lifetime total of only ten years of schooling!

From interviews with former students and teachers from Canton, it seems that most high school students felt there was no use even contemplating a university education. The university enrollments were smaller than before the Cultural Revolution, and with millions of pre-Cultural Revolution high school students also eligible, the odds of any given post-Cultural Revolution graduate being admitted had become very slim indeed. Added to this was the widespread impression that almost all the available places were going to the children of the officials and their friends. Students no longer even calculated the possibilities. "Going to a university," a former Shanghai high school teacher observed, "was out of the question for them, like people don't think about whether it would be nice or not to live on the moon."

Wang Hongwen, the Party's radical new Vice-Chairman from Shanghai, took up the issue of university admissions "through the back door" in a major speech to the 10th Party Congress in August 1973. While the Shanghai radicals* had not wanted university places to go disproportionately to the "bourgeoisie," they equally did not want the universities filled with the offspring of a self-perpetuating "new bourgeoisie" of Party officials. They probably also felt that the "backdoor" recruitment scandals would draw public opinion to their own side in an attack against the bureaucratic class (and incidentally against the Shanghai group's own political enemies).

In January 1974 the radical Shanghai faction obtained a copy of a petition by a student named Zhong Zhimin, the son of a Long March veteran. Zhong was requesting that his university grant him permission to withdraw from school and return to the countryside. The petition provided an effective publicity tool to launch the new campaign. The *People's Daily* put it on its front page of January 18, 1974, followed a fortnight later by a strongly worded "ideological report" by Zhong. The young man's confession is revealing:

> I entered college through the back door. . . . After graduating from junior high school in 1968 [when the Cultural Revolution began he had been a first-year junior high school student], I was sent to mix with the commune members in labor. . . . In the beginning I was reluctant to go, . . . but my parents told me: "You go first and we will have you transferred back later." During a PLA conscription drive [three months after he rusticated] I went to see the political commissar of the county's armed forces department and he willingly promised to help me. My conscription quota belonged to another commune.
>
> After joining the army I was very anxious to go to college to learn a few things and discussed this several times with my parents. It seemed all right for dependents of cadres to receive a little special treatment. When universities were enrolling students in April my father, who is in charge of PLA cadre work in the military region, telephoned the departments concerned. It was quickly decided that I could go to college.
>
> [Sent out to do labor stints while a student] I heard many complaints about "going in by the back door". . . . In May and June 1973 . . . I heard the announcement of Chairman Mao's letter to [the Fujian schoolteacher] and witnessed the strong reaction among the worker masses. . . . I was

---

* When I began analyzing these splits in the leadership the radicals had not yet fallen nor been labeled the Gang of Four. I had dubbed the group the "Shanghai faction," since its most prominent members were natives of Shanghai (e.g., Zhang Chunqiao, Yao Wenyuan, Wang Hongwen, and Mao's wife Jiang Qing) and since their ideological magazine *Study & Criticism* was published in Shanghai.

deeply shocked, ideologically, realizing that I had done something wrong and that I should wage a struggle to oppose this kind of thing. . . . [But my mother said] "The children of other leading comrades haven't withdrawn from school." My brother-in-law told me: "You're ultra-leftist, thinking you're the only one who makes revolution." One of my relatives said: "Withdrawal from school may obstruct from the 'left' the implementation of Chairman Mao's revolutionary line. Since there are so many cases throughout the country of 'going in by the back door,' your actions may cause a disturbance. . . ."

Concerning this question, what do I feel about the cadres' children? When I was a Red Guard of the No. 2 High School in Nanzhang in the early stages of the Cultural Revolution, I recall that I considered the reactionary blood-line theory was correct—that sons of heroes are brave fellows; sons of reactionary fathers are bad eggs. I even wrote a big-character poster supporting this reactionary theory. Now I become worried when I think of this question: How much revolutionary sentiment do the children of some cadres have? How many children of cadres can actually become Marxist-Leninist? . . . If the Party wants to practice Marxism-Leninism, "going in by the back door" must be struck down—this is a question concerning whether one works for one's own interest or in the interests of the common people.[15]

In the wake of Zhong Zhimin's withdrawal from school, a flood of other young people were publicized for following Zhong's example,[16] and mild *mea culpas* were broadcast by some of their parents. Despite this the irregular admissions practices persisted (according to more recent reports) until at least 1977. And when the Gang of Four fell in late 1976, accusations were soon heard on Peking Radio arguing that "the Gang of Four, by saying that 'taking the backdoor' was a betrayal of Marxism, viciously and publicly attacked and humiliated leading comrades . . . who adhered to Chairman Mao's revolutionary line."[17] The "anti-back-door" campaign had struck too raw a nerve to have gone unremembered by some of the victorious bureaucrats.

This particular problem had never been a bone of contention among the Party's top leaders, however. They had all held a common distaste for the "backdoor" corruption.[18] But much of the Party leadership—the Party "moderates"—were considerably disturbed about the academic standards of even the legitimate entrants to the universities. The disagreement concerned, essentially, whether China should use higher schooling more as a redistributive/egalitarian mechanism or more as a development tool.

THE DEBATES BETWEEN "RADICAL" AND "MODERATE" LEADERS

Put simply, the Chinese Revolution had come to power in 1949 on the strength of two popular appeals: a nationalist promise to restore Chinese pride and prosperity through economic development, and a social revolutionary pledge to improve the opportunities available to China's great majority of have-nots. From the early 1950s onward all of the Party leaders supported both goals; but as we have already seen, whenever new policies were determined there was always controversy on where and how to draw the balance between the two goals. The "moderates"— the several groupings within the leadership which presently share power in China—usually have defined the revolution more in terms of its nationalist/development goals; Mao and the radicals, on the other hand, usually placed priority upon the redistributive goals favoring the "proletarian" classes.

It was over higher education, and *particularly* in the 1970s, that these fundamental disagreements surfaced most clearly. The "moderates" had been alarmed by the new policies. As these veteran Party administrators began moving back into positions of power in the early 1970s, they increasingly made their voices heard about the new university admissions qualifications. But the more radical wing of the Party feared that allowing any sort of academic criterion would provide the entering wedge for "moderate" efforts to put academic qualifications back in the forefront. As late as 1975–76, the radicals were publishing editorials, for example, taking to task faculty members of Qinghua University, China's foremost institute of technology, for doubting the abilities of a young peasant activist who had entered Qinghua with three years of primary-school education.[19]

Given students with such inadequate academic backgrounds, the universities and provincial authorities understandably were finding many of the enrollees ill-equipped for even the elementary courses which had been prepared for them.[20] The moderates in Peking backed up these complaints. In 1972, several provinces, including Guangdong,[21] took the initiative to institute a simple written screening exam at the final county-level stage of the enrollment procedures. In April 1973, the State Council decided—at Zhou Enlai's suggestion—to institute similar examinations in all provinces.[22]

Mao Zedong and the Shanghai faction did not have sufficient strength in the state organs to block the new measures. They foresaw, worriedly, that the new exams would be made more stringent each year, with the "old system" stealthily reinstalling itself. They were determined to nullify the new decision by any means available to them. One of the main strengths of the Party radicals was their near-control of the mass media— and Mao decided to put this to use. At a Peking meeting between some of the radicals and Mao's nephew Mao Yuanxin, who was in control of the Liaoning provincial press, it was decided that "Liaoning would provide some [media] materials to be employed against the new exam scheme."[23]

At this opportune moment, a young man named Zhang Tiesheng entered the scene. A junior-high student in Liaoning at the time of the Cultural Revolution, Zhang had been rusticated in 1968. In the summer of 1973 he was nominated to enter a university, but he found himself stymied in the written examination by all the questions in the math and science section. Turning the examination paper over, he wrote an angry complaint. He was too busy with agricultural labor, he argued, to review his books—and added that he detested bookworms who did not labor.[24] Zhang's complaints were publicized nationwide. Along with the 12-year-old girl Huang Shuai and the university student Zhong Zhimin, Zhang Tiesheng became one of the three most famous "going-against-the-tide" heroes.

The media campaign and the backing offered to it by Mao forced the provincial administrations to downplay the examinations they had prepared.[25] Some provinces rescinded them; Guangdong retained an exam but announced it was open-book, with applicants free to discuss the answers among themselves.[26] Some nominees, who had been turned down on the basis of their performance on the summer's closed-book exams, were now let into college on the strength of the political recommendations of their work-unit. A year later, in its 1974 recruitment drive, Guangdong carefully refrained from offering a structured written examination. The college enrollment committees instead tried through less formal means to pass judgment on the candidates' academic level. But for these continued efforts to have professionals judging academic standards, the Guangdong educational authorities found themselves under attack in the left-dominated national press.[27] Guangdong's universities and enrollment committees did not regain their powers to make the final decision on entrants until 1975.

Thwarted in the first instance from selecting students who met what they considered to be minimal academic standards, the college staffs in Guangdong adopted an alternative strategy. They began a special six-month introductory "refresher" course in the autumn of 1973,[28] on the grounds that the new university entrants had "forgotten" many things while out of school. At the end of this half year of high-school-level courses, a set of review tests was administered. Those who were hopelessly behind were either dropped quietly from school or shifted to an undemanding vocational discipline.[29] Most universities eventually adopted Guangdong's "introductory course" scheme. University education, which had begun on the basis of a 2–to–3 year curriculum, was raised through this to 3 1/2 years.

The moderates made one further type of effort to restructure the admissions procedures. They were worried that under the radical enrollment system the nation would not be producing the new generation of scientists necessary for developing sophisticated weaponry and for keeping China abreast of world scientific advances. In 1972, according to interviewees from China and more recently published reports, Zhou Enlai sent instructions that some freshly graduated high school students with a "bent" for research work should be admitted to universities, not just youths who had been out working.[30] The Premier's intent seems to have been dual: first, to make sure that at least some decisions on enrollees remained in the hands of the high schools, as one means of assuring better quality; and second, to avoid the possible loss of talents— such as in the pure sciences—which are said to mature in very early adulthood.

Again the radicals had tried to block the move. The de facto head of the State Council's Scientific and Education Group, Chi Qun—who was one of the major radical spokesmen—refused to set up the necessary administrative machinery.[31] Despite this, some university leaders established informal links with high school administrators and began to funnel small numbers of academically talented students onto campus directly from high school—not just in mathematics and science, but also in art, music, sports (!), and, in one case known to me, history. But since there were political risks to this direct admissions venture, the university administrators protected themselves by selecting principally nominees of irreproachable class background. (Of the four cases of direct admissions on which I have detailed information, all were from revolutionary-cadre families.) Altogether the numbers of such entrants remained comparatively small, and when Zhou Enlai fell seriously ill in late 1975, the radicals moved to abolish the practice entirely. In the December 1975 issue of Red Flag, Zhou's 1972 directive was singled out (though carefully unattributed to Zhou) as a target for attack.

Despite the moderates' efforts, only a small percentage of the skilled manpower which the higher scientific echelons felt they needed was being provided. There seems to have been increasing alarm in the scientific and military establishments that China would be endangering its future if the radical prescriptions in higher education remained in effect much longer.

THE DEBATE OVER UNIVERSITY CURRICULA

The radicals repeatedly observed in the press that before the Cultural Revolution China's universities had too often structured their curricula so as to meet the needs only of the very small proportion of college students who would become pure researchers. The coursework of the students at the regular universities had dealt almost entirely with pure theory, to the extent that the great majority of the graduates, holding no practical skills, could only be allocated to serve as schoolteachers.*

The radicals argued, further, that China did not even have any great need for abstruse or highly sophisticated research. Cases were cited of costly and esoteric research that had been conducted in medicine and the sciences while even common diseases and rudimentary technology problems continued to plague the countryside. What seems to have been a more moderate wing of the radical camp argued that China's best strategy was to stick to intermediate practical research, since for several generations to come China would be able to borrow technologies and scientific advances from the economically more advanced countries.*

The radicals' curriculum reforms now sought to gear even the "purest" university disciplines toward more immediately practical coursework. Medical training, which had formerly been a six-year course, was shortened to three years by teaching not much more than symptoms and prescriptions—and only for the less exotic ailments. In all disciplines, as in medicine, higher education in China would be limited to producing practitioners, not specialists or researchers or advanced scholars. Before

---

* Appendix B of this book describes China's university system before the Cultural Revolution, and indicates the validity of the radicals' criticism.

* This common-sense argument apparently won backing even from many of the Party's "modernizers." They sought after 1971 to buy and adapt advanced technology and scientific know-how from abroad, rather than rely upon China's own efforts to develop them—only to find the import schemes opposed by some of the "Shanghai" radicals.

Mao's death in 1976, programs of graduate studies had been resumed at literally only a handful of the nation's universities.

The modernizers in the leadership became worried that the radicals' curriculum reforms so downplayed theory, and the academic level of the students was so low, that eventually China would no longer possess even the expertise to understand and *adapt* major foreign technical developments. They feared that China would not even have competent technicians or practitioners of applied science.

From all evidence, their concerns were justified. At Qinghua University the mathematics teachers were spending the whole of each freshman year—not just the initial six months—teaching simple arithmetic to entrants who could not add fractions.[32] Within another 2 to 2 1/2 years these students would be graduating in their specialties. It was scant time to master their professional training, made scantier by the fact that the students were supposed to devote 30 percent of their scheduled time to labor and political study.[33] In fact, considering the many political campaigns that punctuated the school years, perhaps even more time than that became occupied by political activities.[34]

The university staffs were disturbed also by the quality and character of the academic portion of the curriculum. Since the universities were in the political limelight more than the secondary schools, there was special pressure from the radicals to let workers and peasants take the rostrums to do some of the teaching. Scientists were worried also that many of the college labs had been closed and replaced by campus-run industrial workshops.[35] Educational leaders began complaining openly that the coursework, rather than abiding by Mao's formula for cognition—practice, theory, practice—had turned into "practice, practice, practice, with no theory."[36] The deputy Party secretary of Canton's Sun Yatsen Medical School took the risk of writing in a national newspaper in 1972 on the folly of teaching only the purely practical. He argued that his faculty had alerted him to the dangers of teaching students to make out prescriptions and perform operations without an adequate understanding of pharmacology and anatomy.[37]

The ineptness of the new university graduates became immediately obvious beyond the campuses when the first graduating class in 1974 took up job postings.[38] Wider support was generated for the moderates' demands that the universities' curricula and enrollment procedures be revamped again. By 1975 they felt ready to push through such changes. They already had taken control of most of the levers of power in China. Education and the mass media were two of the remaining sectors where

the radicals still maintained political dominance, but even here the moderates had made inroads. In January 1975 they had been able to restore
the Ministry of Education and place on of their own partisans, Zhou
Rongxin, at the helm. As Minister, Zhou was blunt about the radical
programs' failings:

> To become an apprentice requires three years to satisfy the requirements;
> going to a university requires three years to graduate. If we do not need
> professors and specialists to lecture and instead invite workers to present
> lectures; if we only talk about practice with no necessity for theory and
> knowledge; well, if so, I see no need for studying at a university. Going
> to work in a factory is better—and it's three years either way![39]

Zhou Rongxin maneuvered to restore the Branch Dictates schema
in educational affairs. But his efforts inevitably met resistance from the
radical camp in Peking and from the reds who still controlled the Party
committees at most of the best-known universities. With the Minister's
channels of command disrupted, the moderates found themselves stale-
mated. As a result, in August 1975 and again in November, half a
dozen members of the Qinghua University Revolutionary Committee—
the moderate minority—addressed letters to Mao, apparently hoping
either that he could be won over to their own perspective or to a neutral
stance.[40] Their letters, reportedly relayed to Mao by Deng Xiaoping,[41]
alleged that the students were "not even capable of reading a book" in
their own specialties when they left university.[42]

Mao acted in the autumn of 1975, but not as the moderates had
hoped. He sent the letters back to Qinghua, ordered that their contents
be made public, and requested the students there to "debate" the subject.
Almost simultaneously, the main radical spokesman in educational affairs, Chi Qun (who had become head of Qinghua University's Revolutionary Committee), released on Qinghua's campus the compiled
speeches of the Education Minister, Zhou Rongxin.[43]

The Qinghua students responded with a prodigious volume of wall-
posters condemning both the Qinghua moderates and the Minister.[44]
These condemnations quickly spread to other campuses. At least some
of the college students had good reasons to participate. They must have
been grateful for an enrollment policy that permitted peasant and worker
children of poor education (and the cadres' children) to gain a good
portion of the university credentials—yet now the moderates were chal-
lenging the validity of these credentials. Such students knew, moreover,

that they would be placed under great pressure if more emphasis were placed on academic performance. They preferred a curriculum they could handle, like the one they were undertaking—with relatively low academic demands, involving a great deal of physical labor, and with success determined by active participation in the students' Youth League and Party branches rather than by academic performance. According to several foreigners who were teaching at Chinese universities at the time, the best of their students were lackluster in the new campaign. But the less capable students became willing and emotionally-involved allies of Mao and the Shanghai-based leadership in their drive to topple Zhou Rongxin.

There was an exquisite irony here. A decade earlier, when the Cultural Revolution began, Zhou Rongxin was Secretary General of the State Council. He apparently had sensed that the Cultural Revolution might turn toward attacks against the Party-led bureaucracy. Perhaps hoping to forestall this, he had been one of the earliest and most vociferous supporters of the initial good-class Red Guards.[45] He had even given support to their demands that status, upward mobility, and access to higher education be determined entirely by class-line standards. By the winter of 1966–67 the largely middle-class Rebel Red Guards had joined with the Party radicals to topple him and other Party administrators. Now, nine years later, Zhou Rongxin found himself advocating the contrary— that academic criteria count more heavily in determining enrollments and upward mobility. And the radicals on this occasion were allying with red-class students to oust him from office a second time. History was repeating itself, but much as in Marx's adage: the first time as tragedy and the second time as farce.

On cue, the new university student protests were picked up by the national media controlled by the Shanghai faction. These attacks reached their crescendo in early January 1976, in the week before Zhou Enlai died.[46] The timing seems to have been anything but coincidental. When Mao had returned those letters to Qinghua University in November 1975, Zhou Enlai was already on his death bed. His condition had left the moderates without a powerful standard-bearer. It had also presented Mao with a final opportunity to try to determine the leadership succession.

In retrospect, it seems Mao had selected the issue of higher education as his opening move in the renewed succession struggle. The university students' attacks on Zhou Rongxin were merely the prelude to efforts to bring down Zhou Rongxin's "backstage boss." By early February 1976, Deng Xiaoping was under attack on the campuses and in the mass media, among other things for having been behind the demands for sweeping changes in education and scientific research.[47]

But the ailing Mao and the Shanghai radicals behind whom he was throwing his weight did not hold sufficient power at the center of the Party to force Deng into exile. It was already becoming obvious that the moderate faction would control China after Mao's death. Not until the massive Tiananmen Square riots of April 1976—in which huge unorganized crowds of Zhou/Deng adherents battled Peking's police—was a shaken Politburo majority finally persuaded to delay the political showdown between the two factions by dismissing Deng Xiaoping from his posts.

While the radicals had turned to the university campuses for support, at the Tiananmen riots large numbers of younger students reportedly participated in the protests against the radicals. And in the provincial capital of Yunnan, where serious rioting erupted two days after the Tiananmen incident, the disturbance's epicenter was the city's largest high school.[48] Some of these teenagers probably were simply delinquents attracted by the excitement of a confrontation. But some of the participants probably were responding to the feeling in urban China that the radical faction was far more committed to the disliked rustication policies than the followers of Zhou Enlai. It was also known that the moderates wanted to put increased economic resources into urban industry, which would generate greater numbers of factory jobs for the urban youths. The radical press complained a month after the Tiananmen Incident that

> Deng Xiaoping and those who whipped up this gust of wind went so far [in the summer of 1975] as to openly attack the great movement to rusticate educated youth, and opposed this revolution. They pulled the wool over the eyes of the educated youth by saying . . . there was no need for them to go to the countryside or to integrate themselves with the workers and peasants if they would follow them to make a "new earth-shaking long march" around "the four modernizations."[49]

Interviews that I conducted during 1975 and 1976 suggested that the Party radicals had lost most of their urban bases of support—and education and rustication were two of the key issues. Eight years earlier, at the close of the Cultural Revolution, the radicals' arguments on access to higher education must have seemed attractive to the masses of people who were not favored by the pre-Cultural Revolution recruitment systems—the millions who were of red working-class backgrounds. But politically the radicals had lost ground heavily by ignoring the urban desires for economic development and urban jobs; and working-class sympathies in education had been alienated by the obvious (and stubbornly uncorrected) failings of the radicals' egalitarian efforts.[50]

The radicals had even less hope of turning to their erstwhile Cultural Revolution allies, the Rebel Red Guards. In fact, in Guangdong these groups' remnant networks had become aligned solidly against the Shanghai leaders. They had good reasons. The Rebels after the Cultural Revolution had seen their own prospects quashed by the rustication program of 1968 and the new college enrollment criteria; the radicals' opposition to "bourgeois expertise" had eroded the status and security of their parents; and having developed ideologies in the Cultural Revolution of mass democracy, they now saw dangers of Party despotism in the radicals' advocacy of "Politics in Command." By the spring of 1974 a number of the former leaders of Canton's Rebel Red Guards were meeting with Guangdong's old-guard Party leaders to negotiate a temporary strategic alliance. Under the guise of criticizing Lin Biao and Confucius, the former Rebels agreed to mount a wall-poster publicity offensive in Canton against the Shanghai faction.[51]

Two years later, the radicals had fallen. The new configuration of Party heads could not have been entirely to the liking of the former Rebels. But on issues such as education and economic development the Rebels' own views and interests were now politically vindicated: academic merit counting heavily in university selections; the "class line" overturned; the political dedication of "experts" recognized. The irony is that these new policies are practically carbon-copies of the program of pre-Cultural Revolution days. Chinese politics has traversed a complete circle. The young people who as Red Guards had helped topple the educational and economic administrators of the 1960s were now the same young people, as shall be seen, who have benefited most from the revival of the old order of things. It has been the final joke in the saga of the Cultural Revolution student movements.

EPILOGUE

The Return
of the Old Order,
1977–1980

WITH MAO'S death in 1976 and the overthrow of the Shanghai faction, the Chinese widely publicized the proposition that China had squandered a decade in education and technical know-how that quickly had to be made up; and to do so they looked backward in time.

In the autumn of 1977 it was announced that an educational edifice not far different from what was described in the first chapters of this volume would be reassembled brick by brick. In a series of decrees, the competitive school ladder was restored; entrance examinations were reintroduced for both junior and senior high school;[1] and selection examinations once again counted most heavily in determining university admissions.[2]

But the new school system was not quite a replica of pre-Cultural Revolution education. Instead, with the momentum of a pendulum swinging back past its original resting place, the programs of 1977–80 were more elitist and more "talent" oriented than any that existed in the fifties and sixties. Because the authorities were so preoccupied with modernizing China's stagnating economy, they made no efforts to sustain a balance between the "quality" education they wanted and the revolution's putative egalitarian objectives. And because their concerns in 1976–77 were so intensely focused upon the radical educational abuses of the early seventies, they showed little concern to provide safeguards against the recurrence of a "diploma disease." Far more than in the 1960s, the academic competitiveness of students and their preoccupation with examinations was tolerated and even encouraged.

The new leadership believed that an important lesson had been learned during the radical era: that abandoning the sixties' system of academic selectivity had, at one and the same time, harmed the quality of college education and sapped the incentives of students in the lower levels of schooling. A stress on selective examinations, they surmised, would help put things right again from top to bottom. Thus, contrary to the preachings of educators in the sixties, the educational authorities now *wanted* the higher-education entrance examinations to influence the attitudes of students and teachers. "The system of standardized college entrance examinations," boasted a 1980 newspaper report, ". . .has spurred better teaching in the high schools . . .and has motivated large numbers of young people to be 'study activists.'"[3] The educational pyramid was restructured on the basis of these selective entrance exams.

ELITE VS. MASS EDUCATION

Since the new leaders' immediate concern was to rebuild China's shrunken corps of high-level specialists, one of the first priorities was to reconstitute in full the system of "key-point" schooling. In the autumn of 1977, twenty high schools in Canton and its suburbs were designated as key points (including the very same schools that had been key points before the Cultural Revolution), and 47 primary schools were granted the same special status.[4] These schools soon began to suck funding away from the rest of the school system.

Initially, the education authorities had not thought that they would have to make any painful choices between elite and mass schooling. In the national press in 1977, they were pushing hard and exuberantly for much higher expenditures for *all* types of education. The prospects for this seemed good, since many of the top national political leaders were in open agreement on the desperate need for a better educated populace.

But almost from the start, Party bureaucrats at the provincial and municipal levels sidetracked the planned expenditures.[5] They were under strong pressures to modernize industry and expand agricultural production in their regions, and their budgets were already strained. Speakers at a Guangdong education conference futilely complained that these

Party bureaucrats disregarded education as a "soft mission" compared to the tangible needs for more chemical fertilizer plants and the like.[6]

Faced with a straitened budget, the educators placed rural education, as always, lowest on their priority list, even though it was obvious that the rural school system did not yet provide adequate training even in how to read and write. (The *People's Daily* noted in 1980 that because of the shortcomings of rural education, only 60 percent of China's children graduated from a primary school and only 30 percent reached a fifth-grade academic standard.[7]) But the schools would have to hobble along as best they could on their own local resources.[8] The newspapers, in fact, were turning once more to promoting the half-work/half-study system as a financial prop for rural schooling.

Most of the urban schools, too, would have to accept sacrifices in behalf of the college-preparatory "mission" of the key-point schools. The neighborhood high schools were stripped of their best teachers and their best administrators to allow the key-point system to rebuild a quality staff. Already understaffed, the ordinary high schools scraped through by absorbing former primary-school principals and teachers (which placed some of the primary schools in even deeper trouble).[9] Only the key points, moreover, received the funds to improve school facilities. While these elite schools were able to reduce very sharply their programs of student labor in order to let their students concentrate almost entirely on studying, some of the neighborhood schools, to bring in a needed supplementary income, were obliged to retain and occasionally even expand their school-run factories and workshops.[10]

The school system's acute financial problems fixed the education authorities' attention upon the lopsided nature of the new education structure. They had inherited from the radicals an urban system of universal education through senior high school, and they had proceeded to convert this wholesale into a college-preparatory track. Editorials began arguing that this patently did not make sense, financially *and* otherwise.

The structure of secondary education is too uniform, with serious consequences. In the Cultural Revolution, Lin Biao and the Gang of Four wantonly trod upon the principle of "walking on two legs with multiple forms of schools," and the cities' specialist, technical, and various other sorts of vocational secondary schools were almost all closed. Those which were left almost all were full-day high schools. Moreover, the regular-track senior high schools' development exceeded the national economy's ability to provide the proper material conditions, and qualified teachers, facilities, and finances were in severely short supply. The quality of education is [accordingly] extremely low. The students at school all read from a single bible—the regular-track secondary school curriculum. When they graduate they all take one road—taking the exams for the universities. Actually only about 2 to 3 percent are able to go on to a university. The great majority will go into industrial and agricultural production. But they do not have any skills or any knowledge of a profession.[11]

In Canton two solutions were attempted. First, in 1980 Canton started a vocational curriculum at several of its neighborhood senior high schools for final-year students who were not expecting to take the university entrance exams.[12] Second and more significantly, Canton reconverted some of the senior high schools back into specialist and technical schools and reopened technical-worker schools near various large factories. As in the sixties, these latter schools began enrolling junior high school graduates and thus reduced the number of students who fruitlessly obtained senior high school certificates. Also like the sixties, all of these vocational schools came partially under the management of the relevant industrial bureaus and factories and became conduits to jobs in those units.[13] Hence once more like the sixties, there was a strong and immediate competition to gain admission to these various vocational programs.[14]

But the administrators of Canton's school system had not shifted their own priorities. They still were concerned almost entirely with university pass rates and key-point schooling. For them, the new vocational system served as a way to perform a financial sleight-of-hand, in order to conserve money for the elite schools. They did so by dumping financial responsibility for the vocational schools into the laps of the city's industrial and commercial organs. The outcome was predictable. Despite its popularity among young people, the revived vocational scheme became the various bureaus' unwanted stepchild. Canton's major newspaper editorialized:

> Canton's 33 vocational schools . . . have not been provided with adequate space . . . and some of these schools have to run "guerrilla" classes permanently. The education bureau . . . takes care of the teaching . . . but considers these schools as under the jurisdiction of the various industrial etc. departments, and so does not care. The industrial bureaus on the other hand concentrate on production and so show little concern. . . . The reality is that a number of different departments are and yet are not managing the schools, each pushing the responsibilities onto the others.[15]

STREAMING STUDENTS

The education system also became stratified in a further manner, almost unknown to pre-Cultural Revolution schooling. On the rationale that the previous decade's turmoil had created wide gaps among young people in their levels of learning, the children were now channeled into fast, medium, and slow classes at many of the regular-track neighborhood schools.[16] One intention was to allow the better-than-average students to study unimpeded by their slower, less orderly schoolmates.

But streaming students also had adverse consequences. In order to hold onto their funding by obtaining better records on the higher-level entrance exams,

> many schools have turned their "fast progress" classes into "higher examination classes" and have assigned to these most of the teachers with a higher professional level . . . while neglecting students of "medium progress" and "slow progress" classes, who comprise the majority of the students.[17]

A Canton primary school teacher, interviewed in 1980, says, "We discovered the tracking system wasn't good for the kids. Those in the fast track got pushed too hard and some couldn't keep up. And the pupils in the slow track just plain felt inferior." The system had cast the latter pupils into the role of unwanted misfits, isolated at the bottom. This was even more the case in the high schools. By 1980 there were angry reports in the national press about high schools where the children in slow classes were told they could stay away from school and still be promoted, and of some particularly overcrowded schools which did not even bother to assign classroooms to the slow classes.[18]

Canton's school system had become divided into two distinct worlds: in facilities, teachers, *and* student behavior. In the revived key-point high schools and some of the "fast progress" classes, students were competitively racing to make up for lost time. They were studying hard and even angling to obtain the activist credentials of League membership. But in the ordinary as well as the slow classes at the neighborhood high schools, students had few expectations of getting ahead through their academic performance. Most of them remained rowdy and indifferent to their studies. Due to the lingering influences of the past decade, they were, reportedly, far more disorderly than had been the students of similar schools in the sixties.

COMPETITIVE PRESSURES AND ROTE LEARNING

In the key-points and "fast" classes, the students became preoccupied with exam prepping, again more so than the students of the sixties. For one thing, in the contest to climb higher on the school ladder, examination results now counted more than in the mid-sixties, and a good "activist" record somewhat less, in line with the new stress on modernization and expertise. For another, though few of these students would ever do well enough academically to get into a university, educational attainments promised to be helpful to them even in the competition for lesser careers. Some of the factories in other provinces and cities, in order to obtain better educated personnel and reduce "back doorism," had begun using examinations in the selection of new workers;[19] and rumors circulated that similar measures might be introduced soon at some of Canton's enterprises.[20] Even the road upward into "political" careers looked likely to be strewn with examinations. The Party Central Committee's Organization Department announced in 1980 that, henceforth, new white-collar Party cadres would be selected from among the graduates of universities and technical schools "instead of from among workers and peasants with a little education."[21]

The exam prepping in the "fast progress" classrooms and at the key-point schools soon exceeded the authorities' intentions. Teachers ignored the course syllabi handed down from the education department in order to aim their teaching exclusively toward the examinable materials of each subject. Some schools arbitrarily added class hours to the curriculum and piled on extra homework in the evenings.[22] "Diploma disease" symptoms were far more acute than in the sixties: after-school private tutoring; school-sponsored weekend "cramming" sessions; ambitious students exhausting themselves. A Canton primary school teacher reports that his school was conducting "exam review" classes every evening of the school year for anxious fifth-grade students preparing for the junior-high entrance exams. A visitor to Canton's #7 high school was told that each teacher was giving a quiz at the end of every lesson throughout the semester.[23] Whereas before the Cultural Revolution the poorer high schools and students had been the most prone to stress tests and memorization, now the major culprits could be found in the better schools and among the more competent students.

In the newspapers of 1980, educators pinned most of the blame for the inordinate "cramming," tests, and memorization upon these schools' and students' all-consuming concern for passing examinations. But as contributing factors, writers noted also the dearth of adequately trained teachers and the poor education the students had obtained during the prior decade. Needing to bring themselves up to the examinations' standards in the course of only one or two school years, they were turning anxiously and frantically to the memorization of facts and formulas to paper over their various academic deficiencies in time for the exams.

MUTING THE CLASS LINE

We have examined, chapter by chapter, two major themes regarding Chinese education: how the structure of the schooling influenced children's study habits; and how the contest to be upwardly mobile pitched the interests of different classes of young people into conflict.

The leadership's demands for modernization in the late 1970s opened an entirely new chapter in this latter contest. In favoring "expertise," Party policy tilted against using "class" to judge people. When recruiting for the universities, in particular, family origins no longer were to count as of any great influence.

The new Party policy on class allowed even young people from bad-class homes to climb the academic ladder. The newspapers pointed to the artificiality of class distinctions three decades after Liberation: for instance, that "Decendants of landlords and rich peasants are now in their third or fourth generation, and most of them were born after Liberation. Facts show that most of them love our socialist motherland and support the Communist Party."[24]

Separately, the "rightist" label which had given a bad-class status to 400,000 families (largely those of intellectuals who had been too outspoken in the 1957 Hundred Flowers movement) was entirely expunged, and the Party admitted a "mistake" had been made in creating the label in the first place.[25] Most of the former rightists' children now again held a middle-class status. The pool of non-red-class young people who could hope to compete successfully for a place in higher education had been expanded considerably.

As an even more dramatic departure from past practices, the middle-class professionals were designated part of the laboring masses—"mental laborers." By this stroke of the Party pen, the "class line" in education was robbed of most of the remainder of its meaning. For the new Party line proclaimed that since "intellectuals are part of the working people

. . . their children should be treated on an equal footing with those of workers and peasants"![26] The gates had been opened for them to flood the universities.

The intelligentsia's children of this younger generation enjoyed a considerable headstart academically. It was not that they had bothered to study much at school during the radical era. Scarcely any students had. But that, ironically, was precisely their advantage. As a Chinese publication observed in 1978, when

> the role of school education was drastically weakened . . . [due to] the Gang's sabotage of educational undertakings, . . . family education and self-study by young people began to assume a role of increased prominence. There are a greater number of college students from intellectual families than from worker and peasant families because the former have [had a better home] environment for learning.[27]

But these students were not even the largest single contingent to enter the universities in 1978. Their elder brothers and sisters held that privilege.

UNIVERSITY ENROLLMENTS AND THE ISSUE OF CLASS

In late 1977, in the first recruitments under the new system, it was stipulated that the young people who had been in the final or next-to-last years of senior high school in 1966 were to be exempted from a rule which set the maximum age-limit for candidates at 25 years.[28] The reason for this exemption was clear. These were, after all, the last groups of young people who had received a quality high school education. Though a dozen years out of school, this older generation did embarrassingly better on the university entrance examinations than the 1977 high school graduates, and they were very heavily represented in the universities' intakes.[29] At Guangdong's premier school, Sun Yatsen University, only 17 percent of the freshman class came directly from high school.[30]

In succeeding years, as these older candidates gradually were eliminated from the contest, the percentage of university enrollees selected directly from the senior high schools grew. By 1980 they comprised the majority of the university entrants. But the program of recruiting a part of the freshman class from among youths already engaged in work seems likely to survive, for the Chinese news media has continued to stress the value of a work experience. Thus, as of 1980 the medical and pharmaceutical colleges reserved some of their places for young barefoot doctors; the agricultural colleges recruited primarily from among educated young peasants who had returned to agricultural labor and rusticated urban youths; and teachers colleges set aside places for rural *minban* teachers.[31] Of all the "new-born things" of the 1968-76 school system, only this program of intervening work seems scheduled to last—and only for a small minority of college entrants.

For the great majority of the university seats, the prospects of the intelligentsia's children were improved yet again in mid-1978 through a new set of regulations. These stipulated that class origins and political activism could not even be taken into account unless the applicant first scored above a minimum cut-off point on the entrance examinations.* Since the working-class candidates' chances were further reduced by this exam-score barrier, the government sought to retain their good-will by publicizing the new rules as a tool to prevent "back door deals" by the privileged and powerful.[32] "The important thing," a university administrator explained to a foreign visitor, "is that everyone [now] has an equal chance [through the entrance examinations], an equal opportunity to try. Then if someone doesn't succeed, he'll say, 'that's all right; it was my own fault.'"[33]

But not all of the good-class candidates were willing to buy that line, not when an "equal opportunity" denied them the results they thought they deserved. In particular, many Party officials were not happy about what the new policies did to their own children's chances. A Canton radio broadcast in 1978 accused cadres whose children had failed to get into a university of "babbling, 'Stress was placed on intellectuals and the good-class peasants [sic] were rejected' and '*Selection of the "best" means that in the face of exam marks everyone is unjustly equal regardless of class origins.*'"[34]

A few senior Party officials were censured and removed from office as public examples in 1978, for having rigged examination results in their children's favor.[35] But the legal workings of the examination system were

---

* The cut-off point was set quite high for the national key-point universities and somewhat lower for the provincial universities. This system of cut-offs strongly resembled a 1962 scheme, imposed when "expertise" was being sought (and the class line downplayed) after the Great Leap Forward's collapse. On this earlier system see Appendix B.

soon bent modestly to mollify lower-level Party cadres and to accommodate the interests of the powerful. Scoring above a minimum cut-off point was still necessary to enter the final pool of eligible university candidates, but the cut-off point was set low enough to create a pool several times larger than the numbers of university seats available. Coming from highly literate urban homes, a fair number of the Party officials' children could expect to score above that cut-off point on the exams; and then a university entrance board could use its discretion to favor them.[36] Two foreigners who taught English in 1978 and 1979 at Canton's Sun Yatsen University noted that a disproportionate number of cadre children were getting admitted—reportedly through such "connections."[37] Certainly, many Chinese thought so. In the autumn of 1979, disappointed university candidates staged angry demonstrations in Peking, charging that they had done well enough on the examinations to be admitted but had been thwarted by the favoritism shown the cadres' children.[38]

GROWING TENSIONS?

In the years to come, as the education offered in the lower schools improves, this competition to enter higher education can be expected to become progressively more frustrating. Just as the mid-1960s witnessed a dangerous log jam of students in the senior high schools, so too a crisis of unfulfilled expectations can be expected to build in the 1980s among today's students.

In that earlier crisis, the issue of academic excellence versus redistributive goals had been turned into a potent political controversy, with different mass constituencies ranged on each side. Although the radicals' drastic prescriptions now stand discredited, that old central issue of whose children will be permitted to pursue the coveted careers in China—and on what grounds—has never been dispelled. As we have just seen, voices on both sides were still being heard in the late 1970s.

Since the "modernizers" had the stronger voices in the councils of power after Mao's death, "expertise" was being stressed in the late 1970s more than at any point in the previous two decades. But the government repeatedly had to justify that tilt through promises that rapid economic advances will eventually result. The promise is that more urban jobs will be opened up, resulting both in higher living standards and in greater opportunities for the working-class children's advancement in the *next* generation.[39] If the Four Modernizations do not make quick or significant progress, the patience of the more ambitious of the working-class families may become frayed, and growing numbers of voices—and a leadership faction—may well begin chorusing demands for a renewal of redistributive enrollment policies. The arguments over educational priorities which have wracked China these past two decades may not be laid safely to rest for some time to come.

In multiple ways, China finds itself back at square one, back at the issues and problems that we examined in the first chapters. Twenty years have passed; but little has been solved. China faces the same sets of dilemmas, retracing a familiar road. If anything, the problems are greater. The quality of the teachers and the standards of the students are lower; the "diploma disease" symptoms are far greater; the ideological convictions of the students are greatly diminished; and the competition to enter a university may soon become every bit as acute as in the mid-Sixties. Chinese education has come full circle in two decades, only to have lost ground.

APPENDIX A

The Debates Over "Talent"

THE QUESTION of natural "talents" and "intelligence" among children is not normally a matter for public discourse in China. The Party does not consider it a topic simply of scholarly interest, but rather one with strong political/ideological implications. As such, the Party leaders and Party theoreticians have usually decided through internal Party discussions the proper public line to which all non-Party educators must adhere.

Only once during the first half decade of the 1960s did a genuine debate on "talents" and pedagogic principles appear in the Canton press. The year was 1961, when the failure of the Great Leap Forward and the ensuing economic troubles had encouraged the government to seek out the expertise of the nation's "bourgeois" specialists and intellectuals. During this brief period of "blooming and contending," several non-Party educators placed an article in Canton's evening newspaper proposing that inborn human traits almost entirely determined children's abilities to learn. Pedagogy thus ought to be placed outside the "class-based" realm of politics, the Party's sphere. The authors were claiming for themselves the right to teach the brighter children more quickly, to "teach according to ability" (*yin cai shi jiao*).

The counter-argument to this, which came close to the official Party perspective of the time, was presented in the same newspaper. It conceded there were differences in inborn human traits, but argued that "the principles of pedagogy must satisfy above all the needs and policy of a definite class in a specific society and hence has a definite class nature." What this counter argument implied was that if, say, a brighter or specially talented child were to be treated differently from his or her peers, it was only because it served the purposes of the state and the proletarian revolution to do so.[1]

The Party leadership always was aware that even this second position possessed political dangers. Lu Dingyi, for example, worried aloud in 1960 that even though differences in academic ability do exist, to let those differences enter into classroom teaching would have the effect of favoring the children of the intelligentsia over those of the working classes. "The bourgeois educational principle of 'teaching according to ability,'" Lu Dingyi noted, "holds that 'everything is decided by mother nature' and that the children of the laborers are in an inferior category."[2]

In the early to mid-sixties, thus, the Party line was an uneasy compromise between two educational goals: budding academic abilities were to be "cultivated" through the key-point system; but in any given classroom, teachers were to teach all children in the same manner and at the same pace, while showing special concern and care for the working-class children among them.

Within the Party, increasingly, the debate turned to the different conceptions of "talent" held separately by Mao Zedong and the educational ministries. Mao stood almost diametrically opposed to the view that inborn differences in ability and intelligence objectively exist. In the quotes and passages we have from him, he at times argued that intelligence, like other social phenomena, is class-based. It arose, said Mao, from social experience—through struggles in life—and the masses therefore literally tended to be more intelligent and capable than the established and hence flabby-minded elite of a nation and their pampered offspring:[3] proletarian intelligence was superior to nonproletarian intelligence. If we may expand upon his argument, if middle-class youngsters showed a greater aptitude at school, it would in no way be because any of them were inherently more talented but rather because the intelligence that the schools were judging was in line with the type of intelligence the middle-class youths had learned at home. There are seeming parallels here with the liberal Western view that differences in performance between different groups of children derive from their different home environments. But the Maoist perspective diverged fundamentally from this liberal view. Whereas, for instance, Western educators would say that the poorer school performance of working-class or ethnic-minority youngsters is traceable to "disadvantaged homes," the Maoist would stand this argument on its head; such working-class homes are in fact "advantaged." It is the school system which needs to be rectified—to be "proletarianized."

The Maoists felt a "proletarianization" of education would enhance children's talents in two different respects. First, they believed that while a "bourgeois"-oriented learning process tied to book knowledge was favorable to the acculturated talents of middle-class children, true learning and thinking capacity came from experience. This was one of the senses in which proletarian intelligence was superior—because it grew from tangible contact with reality and struggle with the environment.[4] The Chinese left felt the learning experience hence should be a class-based dialectical process that constantly related classroom "theory" with proletarian "practice" (as in the half-and-half schools). Among other things, it was felt that in such an education, linked to "reality," the abilities of proletarian children could be brought better into play: that it would be in tune with their culturally "advantaged" background.

Second, the Chinese left, including Mao, felt that reshaping the student body's attitudes in a moralistic "proletarian" direction would make subsequent learning easier for the children, for their attitudes toward learning would be improved. Let alone at school, they would even become motivated in later years to continue trying on-the-job to improve their knowledge and skills. It was in the light of all this that the efforts to instill proper viewpoints were to take precedence in schools after the Cultural Revolution. (Unfortunately, as seen in chapter 9, the left's notions on learning were never successfully tested, inasmuch as the post-Cultural Revolution schools failed in practice to instill the hoped-for attitudes. Students showed no desire to learn, let alone any greater capabilities to do so.)

There was an additional dimension to the left's efforts to ensure that learning was motivated by the proper political feelings. They felt that attitudes *shape* talent. Their thinking was traditional in this respect. They shared the views of the Confucianists, who had believed that man was malleable and the product of his environment and that the true mastery of skills and understanding derived not so much from innate qualities as from the proper viewpoint and moral fortitude.[5] This being so, an employee could not possibly be expected to divorce his overall attitudes and goals from his daily professional work.

Such a view was to contribute to the dismissal or downgrading of many of the "bourgeois" technicians after the Cultural Revolution. By the same token it was argued that youths who had acquired the proper worldview and motivation rightly had to be granted preference when making selections for vocational training or higher education, over youths who academically good but whose "talents" were *qualitatively* unsound.

The policies which prevailed in the mid-1960s did not subscribe to these perspectives. But they did share the fear that "talents" might end up serving the wrong ends. All sides within the Party accordingly had agreed that vigorous measures should be taken to promote "redness" in the schools. But the left wing of the Party showed during and after the Cultural Revolution that it doubted the efficacy of such efforts so long as these were embedded in an educational system which put "grades in command" and which rewarded, through admissions to higher education, those students who were "talented" in their bookwork.

Once the moderates came back into command after 1976, precisely that earlier educational program was revived. The official perspective on talent has been reformulated to match this, with Mao's views repudiated. The official rhetoric now declares:

> Differences in intellect exist objectively and they by and large result from different environments, practice, and education, and are *also* connected with adeptness in learning. . . . Far from opposing "reaching the pinnacles of knowledge," we treasure and show respect for talents. We use various means to discover talents and give them training so that they will become proficient in building socialism.[6]

The view has come full circle, back to the more conservative aspects of the official perspectives of the early 1960s.

APPENDIX B

The Upper Reaches of the Pre-Cultural Revolution Ladder: Into and Out of the Universities

THE UNIVERSITY system erected after Mao's death is almost a carbon copy of the university structure of the 1960s. The schools of higher education have been divided into different categories by the government using almost exactly the same administrative criteria; the student enrollment procedures are strikingly similar to the pre-Cultural Revolution decade; and the shape of the curricula and the contents of courses also closely resemble those of a decade and a half ago. An examination of the pre-Cultural Revolution system accordingly provides us with a window through which we can glimpse how the present system operates. We may surmise, for example, that students in the late 1970s and early 1980s have developed strategies for getting ahead in the system very similar to what will be recounted here about universities in the sixties.

ADMINISTRATIVE JURISDICTION OVER HIGHER EDUCATION

The schools of higher education fell administratively into four different categories before the Cultural Revolution. In descending rank order, these were as follows:

(1) The "key-point" institutions were financed and controlled directly by the national government. These national "key points" included such famous schools as Peking University and Qinghua University. In Guangdong, Sun Yatsen University and the Sun Yatsen Medical School belonged to this category. Their graduates could be allocated to any geographic area in the country (though in actual practice most of the graduates of Sun Yatsen University appear to have stayed in Guangdong).

(2) Second were the schools of higher learning that were controlled by the regions (the South-Central Region comprised five provinces including Guangdong). The funds for these schools came from the national government via regional headquarters. Such schools normally drew their entrants from within the region and allocated graduates in accordance with quotas devised by regional organs.[1]

(3) Provincially controlled and funded institutions included almost all the "lesser" schools of higher education. The level of control and a school's "quality" were in fact linked. If the reputation of a college increased sufficiently, the next higher level could request jurisdiction over it; say, the Region appropriating one of Guangdong's provincial schools, or the Education Ministry in Peking taking direct control of a regional school that had attained a national reputation. (This seems again part of a broader administrative pattern in China; it applies too to Chinese factories.) In general it was possible to estimate the quality of a university or institute by ascertaining which level of government administered it.

(4) Some of the lesser and more localized "vocational" tertiary schools came under Special District or municipal governments. (Guangdong Province is divided into eight such Special Districts, averaging about 5 to 7 million people apiece). In particular, these Districts (*Zhuan qu*) ran a number of Agricultural Labor Universities, which employed a half-work/half-study curriculum to train rural youths to become local agricultural technicians. Yet again, the administrative level that financed their educations got to retain their skills within its own boundaries. Indeed, beginning in 1962, the Labor Universities observed a "from the commune, to the commune" policy, dictating that all their students were to be assigned to postings within the same local rural areas from which they had come.

In the decentralization of higher education during the early seventies, the key-point institutions lost their special national status and came under provincial control. E.g., Guangdong took over financial responsibility for Sun Yatsen University. After Mao's death, the former administrative struc-

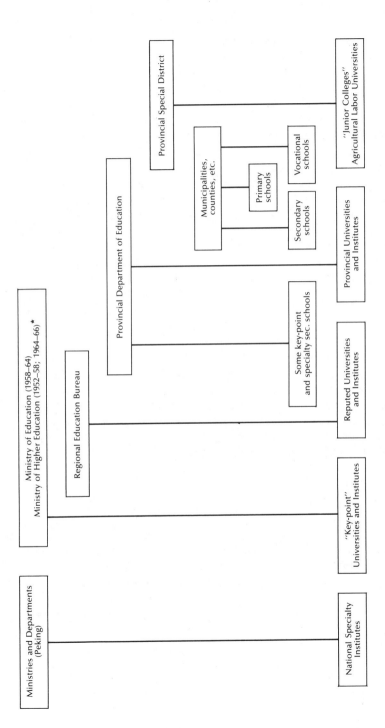

Figure B-1 Structure of Control and Financing in the Pre-Cultural Revolution Education System, Revived in 1977–78

*The Ministry of Higher Education was eliminated in 1958 and its functions transferred to the Ministry of Education. In 1964 it regained a separate Ministerial identity. After the Cultural Revolution there was no education ministry at all until early 1975. Since then, both mass and higher educational affairs have been under the auspices of a single Ministry of Education.

ture was reinstalled—specifically to make sure that extra government money and special resources and attention were concentrated in re-building the quality of the nation's premier institutions. Sun Yatsen University, Sun Yatsen Medical School, the South China Engineering Institute and an offshoot formed from one of its departments (the Guang-dong Chemical Engineering Institute) are now nationally financed "key points."

China's schools were (and are) also divided into different categories in a second way. In 1952 China had revamped its higher education system to bring it into line with the Russian model. Rather than having the *universities* (*daxue*) handle all of the disciplines, certain important specialities were cleaved off and formed into independent tertiary *insti-tutes* (*xueyuan*), as in Russia. In Canton, for instance, the four faculties of engineering, agriculture, medicine and teacher-training were removed from Sun Yatsen University and became large and entirely separate schools in their own right. Over the years, as China's development re-quired new and different types of specialized professional training, further institutes usually were inaugurated rather than having the new disciplines included within the universities' structure. For example, foreign language institutes were founded to train China's interpreters and diplomats, aer-onautical institutes to bolster her military strength, and institutes of for-estry to prepare specialists for China's afforestation program. The de-partments which were left to Sun Yatsen University were primarily those which prepared students for "intellectual" vocations and higher research: the liberal arts, the social sciences, and the pure sciences.

THE COLLEGE APPLICATION PROCESS

Since the early 1950s, a well-thought-out strategy was always required in filling out a college application form. Each candidate individually had to gauge the chances of being accepted by each type and quality of institution. His or her future depended upon a correct estimation.

In the application form a candidate was allowed to list one or two dozen choices.[2] For each of these, the candidates applied not just to a given university but also to a given department.* For example, an out-

---

* In mid-1978, under this revived system, the rule was that applicants could list five uni-versities and two departments at each university, providing ten choices (*FBIS*, June 19, 1978, p. E16).

standing student might put down as first choice the Industrial Chemistry Department at Peking's Qinghua University, China's premier science and technology institute. If the application was rejected for that particular department, his or her candidacy was next appraised by the school and department listed as second preference. Though it was permissible to list a second department at Qinghua, say, Industrial Engineering, it was rash to do so. It was near certain that the department would already be filled from among the very highly qualified applicants who had listed it as their first choice. Wise candidates therefore picked as their second choice a department at a different and less prestigious school where their own qualifications would likely be better than their competitors'. For the same reason, each successive department and school which they listed had to be progressively less desirable; as their sixth or seventh choice they might write down, for example, one of the least popular disciplines at a local, poorly reputed technical college.[3]

The applicants had to be careful, too, to select departments and schools whose admissions criteria accentuated their own strong points as a candidate and took lesser account of their weak points. Even brilliant students, for example, would have been foolhardy to apply to the Peking Aeronautical Institute or any other school or department concerned intimately with military affairs unless they could claim sterling "class" and "activist" credentials. For the same reason, youths of worker or revolutionary-cadre family background boosted their own chances by applying precisely to these disciplines and institutes, rather than competing against an army of bright, middle-class youths fighting to enter a discipline that took class background less into account.

In July each year the college applicants gathered at their locally designated testing centers to take the nationally standardized higher education entrance examinations. In the fifties the Education Ministry had divided all the various academic disciplines into three broad categories, and the applicants in each category took a different set of examinations. Accordingly, a student's application opportunities were always restricted to the group of disciplines which fell within that one examination set. As of 1960 these three sets[4] were as shown below:

SET A:	SET B:	SET C:
The Hard Sciences and Technology	The Natural Sciences	The Social Sciences and Liberal Arts
(For candidates in Chemistry, Physics,	(For candidates in Medicine, Biology,	(For candidates in Literature, Political

Architecture, and Engineering)	Agriculture, Pharmacy, and Psychology)	Science, History, Law, Finance, Economics, Arts and Foreign Languages)
Exams:	Exams:	Exams:
Politics	Politics	Politics
Chinese literature & language	Chinese literature & language	Chinese literature & language (with a
Mathematics	Biology	second exam
Physics	Physics	section not offered
Chemistry	Chemistry	to applicants in sets
English or Russian	English or Russian	A and B)
	Mathematics ("for	Chinese history
	reference only,"	English or Russian
	not included in the	
	cumulative exam	
	score)	

The Politics examination section normally served more as a barometer of political trends in the Party than as a serious examination. In 1963, a year in which "ideology" was taking a back seat to expertise in national educational policies, the Ministry of Education did not even bother to administer a Politics section. Contrarily, as ideology took stage center in subsequent years with the commencement of the Socialist Education Campaign, the examination not only reemerged on the examination syllabus but was even rhetorically touted as premier in importance. But my own readings of the sample examination outlines for 1957 and 1960[5] reveal the politics sections both years were extremely simple, requiring little more of a graduating student than that he should have paid attention to the political line presented by the national media of those years and that he should have read the booklet's sample questions carefully.[6]

As Party policies changed, so too did the science examination requirements. In 1964, the year that the class line became evident in education policies, examination sets A and B—the Physical Sciences and the Natural Sciences—were combined into a single Sciences category, by dropping Biology as a required subject.[7] In the following year even the Physics section was eliminated.[8] Only Chemistry remained as a core subject. These decisions entailed an easing off in secondary-school science education; and the reason probably had to do with the growing concern to let more good-background youths get into the schools of higher education. The small-town and rural high schools and some of the urban neighborhood schools (i.e., the types of schools where the worker and poor-peasant students were concentrated) may well have been hard put to provide adequate training in three science subjects. Now they could concentrate all their best science teachers on the Chemistry course.

The foreign language section also reflected changing trends in political policy. Until 1955, a foreign language examination was demanded of all applicants. For several years thereafter it was not specifically required, but was reintroduced in 1959 and retained as education again became more formalized in the wake of the Great Leap's failure. But this time around, students who had not had sufficient foreign language training were to be exempted from the language requirement. This meant another concession to students from rural areas and small-town school systems. In 1964 and 1965 the regulations eased further, this time also exempting demobilized soldiers, school teachers, minority peoples, and all youths who had engaged in factory or farm labor for at least two years.[9] The national government, it seems, was trying to minimize the difficulties that fading memories had previously imposed upon applicants who already held down jobs. Indirectly, the radicals' premise that incoming college students should have prior work experience was being felt for the first time in regular admissions procedures.

Exam Set A, 1965–66: *The Sciences & Technology*	*Exam Set B, 1965–66:* *The Social Sciences & Liberal* *Arts*
Politics	Politics
Chinese literature and language	Chinese literature & language (2
Mathematics	sections)
Chemistry	Chinese history
English or Russian	English or Russian
(required only of urban high	(required only of urban high
school students)	school students)

(These same two exam sets were offered again in 1979–80. The only distinction was the addition, in 1979–80, of geography and mathematics in Set B and physics again in Set A. The trends of the mid-sixties were now operating almost exactly in reverse order. In 1980 China again required the foreign language exam section, but it was to count for only 30 points, as against 100 points for each of the other exam sections. In 1981, in a

further shift back toward stiffer examination requirements [and thus going against the interests of the students from small-town and rural schools] the government reverted to the 1960s system of three exam sets: students in the natural sciences, medicine, and agriculture would have to take a biology section in addition to the other science examination sections.)

Throughout the early and mid-sixties, students from the impoverished and educationally backward inland provinces held a separate advantage in competing for a place at one of the nationally run universities. China's education authorities, recognizing that youths from the nation's major coastal urban centers would otherwise numerically dominate the university scene, established quotas by regions of origin.[10] *(Again, this holds true too for the new educational structure as of 1978–80.)*

THE SELECTION SCRAMBLE

The actual procedure for selecting the successful candidates was of a complexity that often bordered on the chaotic. The Guangdong Committee for University Student Enrollments established headquarters in a large Canton hall. Each university sent its own corps of enrollment officers, with the enrollment emissaries from the national universities flying in by plane. Each university manned separate sets of desks, and all the first-choice applications from Guangdong province would be dumped into that university's in-tray. As a convenient index of an applicant's all-round academic quality, the university's admissions personnel would peruse the cumulative numerical total of the student's examination scores. Satisfied from the initial glance that the candidate might be up to the mark, the admissions officer honed in on the particular examination section(s) most closely related to the discipline for which the candidate was applying. In addition, each candidate's file contained a dossier sent from his secondary school. As well as official materials on his family origins, this dossier included reports on his political activities and attitudes written by his homeroom teacher and his classroom's Communist Youth League branch—that is, by certain of his classmates!*

Having chosen the applications which it wanted, the university would pass on the remainder to the desks of the various second-choice schools that had been listed by the unsuccessful candidates. The officers

---

* The ramifications of this on classroom tensions are observed in chapter 5.

of these second-choice universities would riffle through the bundles, and if one of these files seemed obviously better than an application they had tentatively accepted from their own first-choice batch, they might de-select such a student, put the new applicant into their file of acceptees, and send on the de-selected application to the desk listed as *its* second choice; and so forth. The reason why it was so important for a student to devise his list of applications with such special care was that he would not be selected at his second-choice school at the expense of a prior candidate if he himself were only marginally better. The trick was to land your own application in a pile of acceptees before someone who was of about equal standing to yourself.

Confusion and snap judgments seem to have been the order of the day in these large halls filled with many dozens of desks and hundreds of scurrying file clerks. As the files circulated among the desks, an application might even end up in the acceptance pile of a department and school which the candidate had neither applied to nor perhaps even heard of. It might happen that a personnel officer at one of the candidate's chosen schools considered his or her file appropriate for some academic field or school that had difficulty filling its rosters with good applicants, and would simply assign the application to that less popular desk. Or the application might simply be sighted and carried off by a hard-up admissions officer on the look-out for likely enrollees among the rotating files. (*Almost exactly the same system was put back into use in the late 1970s.*)

This bewildering application system was permitted by the state partly because it did secure qualified entrants for the least popular disciplines and schools—normally those which implied assignments to the coun-tryside or border wastelands.[11] In fact, all candidates were requested to sign a pledge at the bottom of their application form promising to enter any school or department which accepted them. In the 1950s, however, youths who discovered that a livestock veterinary institute had enrolled them rather than the prestigious departments of biology to which they had applied might repudiate their pledges and retake the examination the following year, confident that the shortages of senior high school graduates would allow them to secure a more desirable place the second time around. By the 1960s, though, youths were wise not to risk spurning even a career as a rural animal doctor, since their only ultimate alternative might be to become an ordinary peasant.[12]

In applying to major in this or that discipline, hence, candidates weighted their choices not only in terms of what subject of study actually appealed to them, but also on the basis of what departments they could most readily enter and where the graduates of these different disciplines were likely to be allocated to work. This is illustrated well by a middle-class interviewee whose personal dreams since childhood had been to write literature:

> I decided to apply to become an engineer, though math and science weren't my strong suit. After all, only a *few* kids made it into university in Lit. My dad was an engineer and said if you're an engineer it didn't matter who the emperor was, you'd still have work. I applied to study sugar chemistry on my dad's advice, the idea being that in all of China only Guangdong grew sugar and so I'd be assigned to a city in Guangdong, near home.

Many applicants, using similar reasoning, applied to a provincially run school as their first choice even if they felt that they had a good chance of being accepted at a regional or national university. For them, the prospect of being assigned a job in their home province was more important than the chance of a higher-level career.

Many other applicants, though, did aim for a desired discipline or school, no matter what their chances and no matter what the prospects of subsequent assignments. The most striking example of this latter orientation is provided by Medicine, one of the most difficult of all disciplines to get admitted to. Mao complained publicly that China's medical programs prior to the Cultural Revolution were almost exclusively favoring the cities, but his charge was not altogether valid. Though the rural medical system did remain inadequate, from the early 1960s onward ever greater proportions of the medical schools' graduates were being assigned to the countryside. As early as 1961 a majority of the new doctors in Guangdong (largely graduates of Canton's national key-point Sun Yatsen Medical School) were being sent to rural posts;[13] and by 1965 fully 90 percent of Canton's medical graduates were being dispatched outward to rural lives.[14] Medicine nonetheless retained undiminished popularity among college applicants. The reason, it seems, was that the youths aspiring to a university education quite often were motivated by a complex mix of both personal drive and idealism. In school they had been instilled with the notion that it was important to "serve" the nation and the revolution; and they had been raised by their parents to regard the medical profession as providing the greatest contribution of all vocations. In a rural medical career, their two sets of aspirations—

valuable service and skilled professional career—could be made to co-incide. Yet, at the same time, these youths were trying to avoid being enrolled to train as agricultural technicians or rural school-teachers, which were widely considered two of the most "lowly" professions.

In somewhat similar fashion, several of my middle-class interviewees have justified their teenage desires to enter a "prestigious" university department on the rationale that by seeking out the more highly skilled professions they were being true to the national good. Their secondary schools, in pushing the notion of diligently "studying for the revolution," had lent an official vocabulary and a sense of legitimacy to these students' own views. Their sentiment was not one, however, of disdain for physical labor, and if they failed their university entrance exams they probably would have taken up most sorts of manual work without any feeling of shame. In fact, a number of them did end up working as peasant laborers and initially took to their new lives with a certain willingness and good will. I mention this because a traditionally educated Chinese, contrarily, would have been appalled at the prospect of physical exertion and indeed would have cited the innate superiority of mental over manual endeavor as one of the primary reasons for choosing one line of work over another. The justifications for seeking the jobs requiring a high-level education had changed considerably, and the candidates to university held sincerely to these justifications.

Yet they were still pursuing many of the same professional aspirations as the pre-Liberation generations. The notion of "service," it appears, was being stretched by Canton's young intelligentsia to encompass whatever careers they personally valued.

THE "CLASS LINE" IN ADMISSIONS TO HIGHER EDUCATION

The class-line concern over "who" received a university education had first been forcefully manifested in the radical Great Leap Forward of 1958. But during that radical period of the late fifties, any moves to reject the academically superior non-red-origin applicants would have meant severely lowering the quality of the universities' student bodies. The education officialdom had been willing, hence, to accede to a radical Great Leap program of *mass* university enrollments. The enlarged student numbers enabled them to boast that the percentage of college students from working-class homes had risen sharply, while the colleges at the same time retained the same numbers of non-red-origin students as in past years. A great many of the new students of worker-peasant origins found themselves crowded onto new jerrybuilt campuses—some hardly deserving to be titled centers of learning[15]—while the older and better institutions continued to train academically gifted non-red students. But this mechanism was not entirely viable politically. In the radical atmosphere of the late fifties and very early sixties, the finest schools and even the most abstruse disciplines were soon obliged to show that they too had raised the proportions of good-class students in their student bodies. In 1960, in fact, such an obligation was even contained implicitly in the national enrollment regulations.[16]

The universities and institutes were accordingly worried to find the average academic standards of their student bodies slipping. The college administrators were concerned since they still were held responsible for producing China's new generation of high-level expertise. An official Cultural Revolution publication was later to complain: "As a result of the anti-Rightist Tendencies Movement of 1959, the number of children of workers and peasants in the 1960 enrollments [at Peking University] was comparatively high. However, they [the Peking University Party leadership] spoke loudly about the 'stupidity' of the new students: 'The quality of the 1960 class is of a low level.' "[17] But by 1961, as the Leap collapsed into economic chaos and widespread hunger, the radicals were hard put to argue that "politics" and "class struggle" could so readily take the place of expertise, and the universities and institutes were able to cut back once more on class-line admissions.

In the national enrollment regulations for 1962, in fact, rules were laid down to assure that examination scores firmly took precedence.[18] Candidates were divided up into sections according to their cumulative exam scores; and not until applicants in the high-score sections had been selected were those in the low-score sections even allowed to be appraised.* Under these new priorities, there quickly arose increased competition between the universities to claim high-scoring entrants as a measure of their own prestige. When an interviewee arrived in 1962 at People's University in Peking, he was greeted with an opening speech by the university president which proudly centered on the record-high scores that the new class had achieved.[19] At Peking University, enrollments in the geophysics department (compiled from a Chinese journal)[20]

---

* This system of exam-score floors was reestablished in 1978.

Table B-1. Admissions to Peking University's Geophysics Department

Inherited "Class" Category of Entrants	1960	1961	1962	1963
"Revolutionar cadre"	20%	10%	13%	—
Good-background working-class	41%	30%	27%	18%
"Middle-class"	31%	48%	37%	—
Bad-background	8%	12%	23%	—

suggest how the new priorities bolstered admissions from the non-red classes—in particular the "bad" classes. Following suit, to keep up their university admissions records the "good" secondary schools in 1962 began to admit more bad-class youths of good academic caliber.

By 1963, the national policies were again turning, and applicants no longer were divided into high and low sections in accordance with their cumulative university entrance exam scores. The continued annual shifts leftward in admissions criteria up to the Cultural Revolution were never dramatic: academic ability still always stood first. But with the competition to enter higher education becoming increasingly keener as the numbers of candidates mounted, even marginal changes in the standards for entrance could put an aspiring non-red-class student's chances considerably at risk—and the students soon came to realise this.

The schools of higher learning, for their part, do not seem to have resisted these shifts in national policy. One reason, probably, is that as the ranks of senior high school students grew in the 1960s, the universities obtained a wider selection of competent students from whom to choose, and the potential "sacrifice" entailed by enrolling a given proportion of good-class-background youths consequently lessened. It was, in short, no longer so difficult to maintain their standards while giving greater play to the "class line."

This affected different schools to differing degrees. The class line seems, for example, to have been more strongly implemented at the prestigious regular universities than even at the best of the civilian engineering schools. The reasons were clear. The theoretical sciences, social sciences, and liberal arts which the universities handled were considered in China to be highly sensitive politically. There was an official fear of independent intellectual activity, influenced even more by Chinese history than by Leninism. Traditionally, China's intelligentsia—its literati—have always been associated with the political realm in an official or semiofficial capacity. China's works of history and philosophy traditionally were employed to stake out political positions and to prop-agate moral (ideological) lessons. The Communist Party leadership, raised within this intellectual perspective, paid close attention to assuring that the various strains of intellectual thought always remained strictly in accord with official ideology. There was the feeling in the Party that youths of red-class origins could more readily be trusted in this capacity, and as larger numbers of qualified red-class youths became available in the 1960s they were recruited in growing numbers into such "intellec-tual" work.

The chances in such disciplines of the non-red class students were shrunken yet further by the fact that Sun Yatsen University was reducing its enrollments at a pace more rapid than most of Guangdong's other colleges. Between 1963 and 1966 the size of its student body fell by almost 20%.[21] The educational authorities had determined that Guang-dong's need for pure scientists, social scientists, and scholars was less than for new engineers and agricultural technicians.

Middle-class youths who persisted in trying to enter the regular university disciplines—under these multiple handicaps of increased nu-merical competition, few university places, and a strengthening "class line"—labored under an almost total misappraisal of their own prospects. As shall be seen below, this was particularly so in view of the fact that even if they succeeded in their dreams and got into a university depart-ment, the policies for allocating university graduates to job postings were likely to deny them entry to the careers they wanted.

THE JOB ASSIGNMENTS OF GRADUATES

All the schools of higher learning allocated their graduates directly to work posts. The graduates did not look for jobs on their own. But in these assignments there existed a clear distinction between the institutes on the one hand (which had trained their students for practical pursuits in in-dustry, agriculture, and the government) as against the comprehensive universities on the other (whose graduates were strong on theory but possessed few immediately applicable skills).

The institutes received quotas each year detailing the particular work units which needed new personnel. For example, the State Planning Commission would inform an engineering school run directly by the central government that three graduating students were needed at such-

and-such a factory in Peking, five others were to be assigned to an industrial bureau in Inner Mongolia, etc. The school itself, once it received the list of job assignments from above, had to determine which of its students should be assigned to what particular postings. The professor who headed an academic department held the formal responsibility of assigning his discipline's students, under the overall guidance of the school's Party Committee. But helping out closely in his decision-making would be the academic department's "political counsellors" (fudao-yuan), a special category of college instructors who had been selected for their records of political activism and who took charge of students' political study. The personal desires of graduates, except in hardship cases, do not seem to have been taken very much into account; national needs were to be put in first place.

The academic department used a mixed bag of criteria to decide who ended up with what jobs. Generally, both political histories and class origins counted noticeably in determining who went to postings which could in any way be construed as involving "national security."[22] But academic competence counted most when the remainder of the assignments were considered. The more adept students went to the more intellectually taxing jobs. But one's record of political activism always did count for something; even if academically outstanding, any student assigned to a research unit or to a post requiring real decision-making or as a teacher at a school of higher education—that is, those obtaining the best big-city assignments—had to have a good political showing. Hence, a career-minded college student competed not just to do well in his or her studies but also to turn in an up-to-the-mark record in political activities: during sessions of labor, in politics classes, in small-group meetings, in everyday comments and behavior. As in the high schools, rising tensions among the student body and opportunistic play-acting became attached to this "activist" competitiveness.

COLLEGE RECORDS AND
ON-THE-JOB PROSPECTS

A college always sent to a graduate's new work-unit a resumé on the student, devised during his or her final year of college. It included a self-appraising essay by the student and a second private appraisal by the school leadership, compiled with the assistance of the classroom Party and League branches. In addition, the graduates themselves brought to their work-post the diploma, which listed each of the courses they had passed.

The political appraisal in the dossier probably held greater significance for the newly employing unit than did the diploma's listing of coursework. With the former document, the unit at least knew whether the graduate was worthy of political trust. But the diploma told the new employer only that certain courses had been accomplished, not that the new graduate was actually able to handle a specialist job competently.

Normally the assumption was that he or she would have to be judged on-the-job. A new engineer assigned in 1964 to an office for the design of glass-making machinery recalls that new post-graduates like herself were put on a one-year traineeship. During this they did not hold individual responsibility for the reliability of their output. By the end of the year the office had learned the capabilities of each of them and assigned them to projects accordingly.

Once in a work unit, it was rarely ever a question of being kicked out, however. If a new engineer was found not to be up to par, he or she thereafter simply would be allocated easier tasks or teamed with a more competent colleague. Technically incompetent red graduates had an advantage here, in that they could be transferred into a "political" supervisory position in the same technical department. Thus a record of political activism at college, transmitted to the work unit by way of the dossier, could prove beneficial to graduates long after they began work. This fact probably did have a backwash effect in the colleges, promoting additional attention by students to their political activities.

POSTGRADUATE STUDIES

The situation at the regular universities *vis à vis* postgraduate allocation differed considerably from the institutes. Students at the institutes at least knew that after graduation almost all of them would be assigned within the careers they were training for. But only some of the university departments, such as the foreign languages department or economics department, had provided their students with skills of immediate use to the economy or polity. And even here, say in foreign languages, the learning was less narrowly practical (for example, less geared toward simultaneous translating) than in the specialty language institutes. Having been "academically" trained, most of the university students who missed the hurdle into postgraduate studies would be assigned instead to teach at a secondary school.

There were three separate routes by which to acquire postgraduate training:

(1) Graduates could be recruited into government research institutes as junior employees, where they worked under the supervision of senior scholars. This applied principally in the sciences. After the Cultural Revolution, this all-too-narrow path became the only remaining avenue to effectively train new high-level expertise.

(2) Some of the graduating students would be picked to become college teaching assistants (*zhujiao*). They collectively taught most of the freshman university courses, but were granted sufficient spare time to continue to train themselves. These teaching assistants were designated to become the next generation of university faculty. In the selection of teaching assistants, the final decision always rested with the school's Party branch, but the professors had influence in choosing students they liked. Since the vocation principally involved lecturing, the professors looked for students who were not only bright but also articulate and apt to teach well. Because of the politically sensitive aura attached to intellectual activity in China, they in addition had to be politically sound— and perferably though not necessarily of respectable class background. (Since these younger faculty members usually held histories of political behavior quite different from the older professors, there arose strains and conflicts that later were to spill over into Cultural Revolution charges against the elder faculty.)

(3) Graduate studentships at the universities led to posts later as high-level researchers. Under the individual tutoring of university professors these graduate students (*yanjiu sheng*) engaged in on-campus study and research in their specialty for 3–4 years, submitting a research thesis to graduate. Stiff formal examinations were taken to gain a place in these graduate-studies programs, but in the final decisions, made by each university's Party Committee, the candidate's political history and family background counted perhaps even more heavily than in the selection of teaching assistants. It was, after all, felt that even more than with the profession of university-level teaching, the full-time researcher was in a pivotal intellectual and technical—and hence "political"— position.

Enrollments in such graduate studies were rather minute in numbers, so it was a foolish student who set his hopes on winning a place. Only some 20 entrants were accepted in all of Guangdong Province in 1963 and only 65 entrants in 1964.[23] (These figures included, moreover, not just the universities but also the advanced training offered by three of Guangdong's institutes, in engineering, agriculture, and medicine.) Those permitted to take the entrance examinations were preselected by their schools or organizations, but even so less than 10% of these favored applicants were admitted,[24] and nine-tenths of these lucky ones were League or Party members.[25] The prospects of any given ordinary university student entering graduate studies were, hence, infinitesimal. Since class background was taken into at least some account, the chances of middle-class and especially bad-class students were dimmer yet.

All told, it seems from interviews that only about a fourth or a fifth of the students at the comprehensive universities in Guangdong were able even to enter the careers which their disciplines centered on—either through gaining a teaching assistantship, or graduate studies, or direct assignment to lesser discipline-related jobs. Many of China's finest students instead found themselves allocated to become high school teachers (quite unlike the West, where it is often the academically average students who are routed into such jobs). Though China's secondary school system benefited, which was perhaps all to the good, the point significant to us was that these students had not been aiming for careers as schoolteachers and in fact rated the profession rather low. More than one interviewee cited the Chinese proverb "Teachers are like candles, which light up the darkness but burn themselves out in the process"—in short, a tiring job that brings little to the occupant himself. The teachers colleges were accordingly among the least popular of the various institutes of higher education; yet the comprehensive universities, for most of their student bodies, turned out to be little other than high-class teachers colleges.

But to have applied from secondary school to an institute meant that a student learned only the particular skills needed in a specific practical career—say, to become a chemical engineer. With such a training he or she was not equipped to make the leap to become a research scientist. For all practical purposes, only a regular university graduate in the sciences could achieve that. In the eyes of many college candidates, thus, Sun Yatsen University remained the most desirable school in all of south China. It remained more popular with applicants from high school than did the technical institutes whose graduates were assured of good jobs as top-flight engineers and technicians. As a former student at South China Engineering Institute notes:

The kids who ended up at Sun Yatsen University were better than those at South China Engineering. In fact, even those from Sun Yatsen who ended up as school teachers were often better in their studies than the best graduates from South China Engineering. . . . Sun Yatsen was popular simply because these young people wanted to try to be the lucky ones who got the jobs as professors and scientists.

In short, Canton's most able junior high school students were preferring to enroll in a senior high school rather than a specialist or technical school, even though they would likely have to become peasants if they failed to jump the next hurdle into university; and these teenagers then compounded the danger of ending up with what they considered to be an undesirable job by applying to a comprehensive university rather than an institute. As we observed when examining the lower ends of the academic ladder in chapters 1 and 2, they were intent on a course of very unrealistic risk-taking.

APPENDIX C

The Course Curricula and Daily Schedules of High Schools Before and After the Cultural Revolution

THE CURRICULA

THE GUANGDONG school curriculum of the sixties was a general-education program that was meant to be well-rounded, with no specialization by students until they reached the university. It resembled, in fact, the pre-Liberation school curriculum that had been copied from America by the Guomindang.

In the regular-track secondary schools, all students took the same complete set of compulsory courses. In Canton this curriculum was approximately as shown in table C-1 (inexact because culled from the memories of interviewees).

Several former students and teachers from China, who either through teaching jobs or relatives have become acquainted with the math and science programs of Hong Kong and Macau, recall the math and sciences in Canton's pre-Cultural Revolution secondary schools as superior—in

Table C-1.

1st Year Junior High	Classes* Per Week	3rd Year Senior High	Classes* Per Week
Chinese lit & language	5	Chinese lit & language	6
Algebra & Geometry	5–6	Analytic geometry	6
Foreign language	5	Foreign language	3–4
(English or Russian)		History	2
Geography	2	Physics	3
Natural science (Botany)	2	Chemistry	3
Politics	2	Politics	2
Chinese history	2	Compositions	2
Music (singing)	1	Sports	2
Drawing	1	Labor †	2
Sports	2		
Labor †	2		

SOURCE: Memories of two interviewees
* Length of each class, 40 minutes.
† Plus some two weeks of full-time rural labor during harvests.

the amount covered, in the depth of treatment, and in the teaching styles used. By the time youths graduated from a Canton senior high school, they could usually handle mathematics up through elementary calculus rather competently, going by the judgments of two former senior high school math teachers. All graduates had also passed courses in chemistry, physics, and biology. But the education did not center on math and science. These accounted for only a bit more than a third of class time. If technicians were to be trained, the Party educators wanted to be sure that they would be acquainted with the Marxist conception of China's history, with China's socialist literature, its political theory, and its geography. The education authorities did not want to produce merely narrow experts, because to do so would be to negate the importance of ideology and nationalism.

The *post*-Cultural Revolution curriculum generally reduced the number of history and geography courses, while boosting the hours spent on afternoon political studies. It initially also converted the science courses into "industry-agriculture-military" coursework. But as can be seen in table C-2, the proportion of time devoted to the various broad sectors of study remained rather similar to the curricula of the pre-Cultural Revolution schools.

Table C-2.

JUNIOR HIGH, CANTON, 1970–71	Classes* per week	SENIOR HIGH 2, CANTON, 1970–71	Classes* per week
Chinese lit and language	6	Chinese lit and language	6
Algebra	4	Math	5
English	2	English	2
Ind–agri–military	7	Agricultural knowledge	2–3
Politics	3	Industrial knowledge	3
Sports	4	Natural science	2
		Military	2
		Politics	2
		Labor class	2

JUNIOR HIGH 2, YUNNAN, 1971–72		SENIOR HIGH 2, CANTON, 1971–72	
Chinese lit and language	6–7	Chinese lit and language	6
Geometry	4–5	Math	6
English	n.a.	English	3
"Science" (called so that year)	3–4	Physics	3
		Chemistry	3
Ind–agri–military	4	Agricultural machinery	2
Geography	"just a bit"	Culture (arts & singing)	1
		Military exercise	2–3
Politics	5–6	School factory	one
Sports	2		afternoon

("But this is just how it looked on paper. It was really sort of chaotic. Classes were always disrupted.")

SENIOR HIGH 2, FUJIAN, 1972–73		SENIOR HIGH 2, SHANGHAI, 1972–73	
Chinese lit and language	6	Chinese lit and language	6
Math	6	Composition	1
English	4	Algebra	4–5
Physics	5	English	3
Natural science/geography	3	Physics	3
Politics	4	Politics	

SOURCE: Memories of six interviewees
* Length of each class, 40 minutes.

Table C-3. After Mao's Death

JUNIOR HIGH 2, PEKING, 1978–79		SENIOR HIGH 2, PEKING, 1978–79	
	Classes per week		Classes per week
Chinese lit and language	5	Chinese lit and language	4
Math	6	Math	5
English	4	English	3
Physics	2	Physics	4
Chinese history	2	Chemistry	4
Music	1	Biology	2
Politics	2	World history	2½
Sports	2	Politics	2
		Sports	2

SOURCE: A school visited by Professor R. P. Dore.

DAILY SCHEDULES

Below are the daily activities of students at two boarding schools. The first is the schedule for the junior-high division of Girl's High, Canton, as of 1965–66. The second daily schedule is for a post-Cultural Revolution school, c. 1971–72.

Daily Schedule, 1965–66

6:00	Awoke.
6:30	To the exercise field. Until 7:00 they did jogging and played sports.
7:00	Whole school exercised to music, then returned to the dorm to clean up.
7:30	Breakfast in dining hall.
8:10	First Class.
	In the morning they had four 40-minute classes, with 10-minute breaks between the first and second and between the third and fourth, and a 20-minute relaxation break between the second and third. The last class ended at 12:20.
12:20–1:00	Lunch.
1:00–2:30	Sleep.
2:40–3:20	Fifth class. This was an academic class, normally an unimportant one (i.e., a course nonexaminable on the higher-school entrance examinations).

3:30–4:10 Self study period (homework).
4:10–6:30 Free activities. Mostly sports for one to two hours: basketball, relays, etc. During this period of time, class officers held their meetings, as did the League branches and the various other student organizations.
One day every week, during this period, students had 2 hours of labor class. That day, they did not have their afternoon sports. The labor normally involved work in a vegetable garden.
6:30 Dinner.
8:00–8:40 Homework in classroom.
8:50–9:30 Self-study period. During this, if students finished their homework, they could read what they liked, but had to stay in the classroom. (From the above, one can see that students who lived at school probably had more opportunity for homework and reading than those who lived at home.)
9:30 Private chores and getting ready for bed.
10:00 Lights out.

As can be observed, there was scant time for independent or spontaneous activities. The students' schedule at a key-point boarding school was regulated from above from dawn to bedtime.

What follows is the reported schedule for Canton High School No. 87, which had established its campus at a former commune school in a rural market village. The new school consisted only of a senior-high division.

Daily Schedule, 1971–72
6:30 Arose. 30 minutes of "military training," which consisted of exercise including a run around the rim of a large field. The "training" was followed by a short assembly for school announcements.
7:30 Breakfast: steamed or baked bread or rice gruel or regular rice.
8:00–8:40 First class.
8:50–9:30 Second class.
9:30 Exercises while listening to music broadcast over the radio.
9:45–10:25 Third class.
10:35–11:15 Fourth class; followed by a relaxation period of ½ hour.
11:45 Lunch and a nap till 2:00.
2:00 Two hours of politics study or large politics assemblies.
4:00 Labor: planting vegetables, tending pigs, helping construct the school buildings. Also the time of day when the school's sports teams practiced.

6:00	Dinner.
8:00	Self-study of homework assignments, or relaxation.
9:30	Lights out.

Both before and after the Cultural Revolution, schools operated on a full-day schedule for five weekdays and a half day on Saturday. The Saturday schedule included a classroom assembly and discussion period. Saturday afternoon and Sunday were vacation periods, during which students at the boarding schools usually returned home.

Sources and Abbreviations Used in Notes

Listed below are the Chinese sources and English translation series that are cited most frequently in the Notes.

CHINESE LANGUAGE NEWS MEDIA AND PERIODICALS

Canton Radio—American and British intelligence services monitor Canton broadcasts. These are published for the general public *only* in English, in three separate series that are discussed in my bibliographic listing of English-language materials: the U.S. government's *Foreign Broadcast Information Service* and the British authorities' two series, *BBC Far East Broadcasts* (*BBC-FE*) and *News from the Chinese Provincial Radio Stations* (*NCPRS*).

Da Gong Bao (大公报)—the official newspaper of Hong Kong's Communist Party branch. It contains frequent reports on Guangdong.

Guangming Ribao (光明日报)—published in Peking, one of the two national dailies in China.

Guangzhou Ribao (广州日报) [Canton Daily]—one of the three newspapers published in Canton prior to the Cultural Revolution. It suspended publication in 1959 and started up again in mid-1965. Its presses were shut down once more during the Cultural Revolution and it never reopened.

Hong Qi (红旗) [Red Flag]—published in Peking, the official magazine of the Central Committee of the Chinese Communist Party.

Ming Bao (明报)—a conservative Hong Kong newspaper, but with the anomalous circumstance that it was founded with a loan from China. It remains an occasional conduit through which Chinese officials unofficially release information to the West. It is a particularly valuable source for Chinese documents of the mid-1970s.

Nanfang Ribao (南方日报) [Southern Daily]—the Communist Party's "official" Guangdong provincial newspaper, published in Canton.

Renmin Ribao (人民日报) [People's Daily]—the official newspaper of the Chinese Communist Party, published in Peking.

Wen Hui Bao (文汇报) (Hong Kong)—a Communist daily newspaper, which publishes a fair amount of official news on Guangdong.

Wen Hui Bao (文汇报) (Shanghai)—Shanghai's major newspaper.

Xing Dao Ribao (星岛日报)—a conservative Hong Kong newspaper generally hostile to the Chinese government. It carries substantial news on Guangdong, often gathered by monitoring Guangdong provincial radio reports. Use was made of this newspaper to obtain paraphrases of otherwise unobtainable official provincial reports.

Yangcheng Wanbao (羊城晚报) [Goat City Evening News]—a Canton daily, excellent as a source for short factual articles on municipal affairs, including education. It stopped publishing during the Cultural Revolution and did not resume publication until 1980.

Zhongguo Qingnian Bao (中国青年报) [China Youth News]—published in Peking, this is the news-daily for teenagers run by the Communist Youth League.

Zhongguo Qingnian Yuekan (中国青年月刊) [China Youth Monthly]—a national magazine edited by the Communist Youth League, with a mass circulation among secondary-school students.

Zhongguo Xinwen (中国新闻)—a Chinese government news service located in Canton, which compiles news reports for Chinese-language newspapers abroad. Since most overseas Chinese trace their ancestry to Guangdong and Fujian, this news service frequently carries articles on these two provinces.

ENGLISH-LANGUAGE TRANSLATION SERIES

CR   *China Reconstructs*—an English-language monthly published in Peking.

CE   *Chinese Education*—an American quarterly journal composed mainly of Chinese translations.

CB   *Current Background*—collections of articles from the Chinese press, each issue organized around a single subject. Formerly published at infrequent intervals by the U.S. Consulate in Hong Kong. Available in many university libraries. *CB*'s articles were indexed quarterly by topic, in coordination with the *SCMM* and *SCMP* series.

FBIS   *Foreign Broadcast Information Service: China Daily Reports*—published each weekday by the U.S. government; a wide selection of Chinese provincial radio broadcasts, obtained at great cost and for inscrutable reasons by America's intelligence community.

BBC-FE   *Far East Broadcasts Service*—provincial Chinese broadcasts translated and published five times weekly by Britain's BBC China monitors. (The BBC and America's CIA have shared their monitoring duties [!] and so the translations that turn up in this series occasionally are identical to those used in *FBIS*).

JPRS   *Joint Publications Research Service*—published in Washington D.C. by the U.S. government. This series includes a vast number of translations from China's national newspapers and magazines. Unfortunately, until recently the translations frequently were slipshod, with one serious error after another. Whenever possible, readers of Chinese should avoid the pre-1978 *JPRS* series and go directly instead to the original Chinese-language materials.

NCNA   *New China News Agency* (London release)—a weekly news bulletin published by the Chinese Embassy in Britain, using news releases telexed from China.

NCPRS   *News from the Chinese Provincial Radio Stations*—monitored and mimeographed in Hong Kong by the British government. Now defunct.

PR   *Peking Review*—published weekly in English in Peking by the Chinese government. In 1979, the journal's title was changed to *Beijing Review*.

SCMM   *Selections from China Mainland Magazines*—formerly published in Hong Kong by the U.S. Consulate. (With the onset of detente between America and China the series title was changed to *Selections from People's Republic of China Magazines*.) Now defunct.

SCMP   *Survey of China Mainland Press*—formerly published five times a week by the U.S. Consulate in Hong Kong. A quite accurately translated series, it is available in most major libraries in Europe and North America. (The series title was altered in the mid 1970s to *Survey of the People's Republic of China's Press [SPRCP]*.)

SCMP Suppl.   *Survey of the Chinese Mainland Press Supplementary Series*—comprised of assorted local Chinese newspaper materials gathered irregularly by the U.S. government over the years, this series was not available to the general public until the mid-1970s. Xeroxed back-issues of the series for the years 1960 onward have now been placed in the stacks of the School of Oriental and African Studies library in London, the Universities Service Center in Hong Kong, and half a dozen research libraries in the United States.

TKP   *Ta Kung Pao Weekly*—a weekly magazine published in English by the newspaper of the Hong Kong Communist Party.

URS   *Union Research Service*—a translation series published regularly by Hong Kong's Union Research Institute, using the URI's own collection of Chinese materials and its own monitoring of Chinese provincial radio stations.

SECONDARY (CHINA-WATCHING) SOURCES IN ENGLISH

China Background—brief reports based partly on interview transcripts, formerly published in mimeographed form by the U.S. Consulate in Hong Kong.

China News Analysis— published in Hong Kong, this is a politically conservative, information-packed biweekly.

China News Summary—until the mid-1970s published weekly in mimeographed form by the British government's China-watchers in Hong Kong. In December 1976 the series title was changed to *China Record*.

China Notes—formerly published sporadically by the British government's China-watchers in Hong Kong.

China Topics—published irregularly in London by British government China specialists.

Current Scene—previously published by the U.S. Consulate in Hong Kong (USIS).

Notes

My documentary work using Chinese language materials was conducted primarily at Hong Kong's Union Research Institute (URI). This is the most comprehensive repository outside the People's Republic of post-Liberation Chinese materials. A great many of the articles from Canton newspapers cited in my chapter notes are available only through microfilm reels of the URI's news article holdings. These sets of reels are owned by a number of Western research libraries.

In the following chapter notes, except when citing my sources for statistics, I have tried to include only the Chinese articles that I consider of greater than normal value to other researchers. For example, if a certain campaign generated a dozen or more essays on the same theme, I have selected for citation only a few particularly informative pieces. In this sense, the following pages of notes constitute a selected bibliography.

For the added convenience of researchers, whenever possible my notes indicate whether an English-language translation of the article is available. This is so even when I myself made use of the original Chinese-language version. Accordingly, my own brief quotes from articles may at times differ in wording from the published translations that I cite.

INTRODUCTION

1. The project's first publication—and one of the best available comparative analyses of modern education—is Ronald P. Dore's *The Diploma Disease: Education, Qualification and Development* (London: Allen and Unwin, 1976; and Berkeley: University of California Press, 1976).

2. See, e.g., Mark Blaug, "Economics of Education in Developing Countries: Current Trends and New Priorities," *Third World Quarterly* 1, no. 1 (January 1979), p. 73. Two empirical studies are Mark Blaug, Richard Layard, and Maureen Woodhall, *The Causes of Graduate Unemployment in India* (London: Penguin Press, 1969); and David Abernathy, *The Political Dilemma of Popular Education: An African Case* (Stanford: Stanford University Press, 1969).

3. Gunnar Myrdal laments, "Teaching in South Asian schools at all levels tends to discourage independent thinking and the growth of that inquisitive and experimental bent of mind that is so essential for development. It is directed toward enabling students to pass examinations and obtain degrees and, possibly, admittance to the next level of schools." Gunnar Myrdal, *Asian Drama: An Inquiry into the Poverty of Nations*, vol. *III* (New York: Pantheon Books, 1968), p. 1647; see also pp. 1807–8.

4. George Z. F. Bereday, "School Systems and the Enrolment Crisis: A Comparative Overview," *Comparative Education Review* 12, no. 2 (June 1968), p. 131.

CHAPTER ONE. UP THE SCHOOL LADDER

1. If the father of a school applicant was too young to have been self-supporting immediately prior to the Liberation, the father and in turn his children bear the family class category that has been affixed to the grandfather. In borderline or complex cases, great problems arose in affixing accurate class statuses, such as with migrants and transients or persons who had held a wide variety of jobs during the years in question. In many such individual cases, class statuses continue to be readjusted whenever new information surfaces.

To precisely settle class backgrounds is so complicated a matter and so central to a person's status and life-chances that the investigation and judging of class backgrounds has occupied in modern China a role similar in importance to the profession of law in the West. People's University in Peking even established a separate academic department specially devoted to teaching the criteria and methods for settling class-status cases. University students who were of sufficiently good class backgrounds and political behavior could "major" in this subject and make it their life's career.

2. Mao Zedong, "Analysis of the Classes in Chinese Society" (1926), in *Selected Works of Mao Tse-tung*, Volume I (Peking: Foreign Languages Press, 1965), pp. 13–19.

3. *Nanfang Ribao* [Southern Daily], October 15, 1959, p. 6. In 1957 the rate of primary school entrance in Canton had been 84.6 percent (*ibid.*).

4. The son of a former capitalist recalls that, for this same reason, in the mid-1950s he had had to attend a private primary school set up by a "Chamber of Commerce" of former businessmen. Because the government had been unable to provide a state-sponsored schooling for all the urban seven-year-olds seeking access, "at that time we children of capitalist-class background weren't allowed to attend the ordinary schools."

5. These entrance tests, recalls a former primary-school teacher, broadly were meant to ascertain both how bright and how well prepared for school a child was. A school's enrollment committee would discuss several daily utensils with the child, or ask the child to identify a picture of Chairman Mao, or see whether the child recognized simple numbers, etc.

6. As late as the end of 1964, after the depression had already lifted, it was reported that "in the densely populated workers' district in the western part of the city [a city in Anhui Province], it was discovered that a number of school-aged workers' children failed to attend school either because of part-time labor or housework such as taking care of younger children or cooking." *Guangming Ribao*, December 16, 1964, in *Translations of Political and Sociological Information on Communist China*, no. 24 (*JPRS* 28315), p. 19. That there were also such children in Canton can be seen in the establishment in 1965 of urban half-work/half-study primary schools, inspired by the rural campaign discussed in chapter 3. These urban pupils were organized to work in small factories and streetside workshops during the day, with classes in the evenings. Canton contained 19 of these half-and-half schools. But this suggests, if anything, that by 1965 few of the children in Canton needed to engage in remunerative work. Only 2,000 children attended such schools in all the city, less than half of one percent of Canton's primary school population. *Da Gong Bao* (Hong Kong), December 14, 1965.

7. Earlier, in the Great Leap Forward, irregular neighborhood classes had been set up to reach children who could not otherwise attend school. But in the subsequent years of economic depression government organs throughout China were trying to regrasp control of China's floundering affairs by restoring bureaucratic controls. In 1962 the Canton city government therefore promulgated these regulations, so as to create out of the impoverished neighborhood classes a.more coherent (and self-financed) structure of education to stand along side the state-run schools. (The regulations were published in *Yangcheng Wanbao* (Canton), September 9, 1962, and again September 19, 1962; they have been translated into English in *SCMP Suppl.* no. 100, pp. 17–19, and *SCMP Suppl.* no. 108, pp. 23–25).

8. The tuition fees of these irregular primary schools were, by regulation, permitted to range between 6 and 10 *yuan* per semester. (*Yangcheng Wanbao*, September 19, 1962, p. 1), which compared to the regular system's fees of 3–4 *yuan*. The entire salaries of the *minban* schools' staffs came out of these. The city provided only a bit of funding to improve the schools' facilities: the sums of the 1963–64 school year came to less than a thousand *yuan* (US $600) per school. (*Yangcheng Wanbao*, July 19, 1964, p. 1). Pupils sometimes were advised to provide their own desks and chairs.

9. *Nanfang Ribao*, August 23, 1962, p. 3. The *minbans* specifically were permitted to give short shrift to any primary school courses which did not appear on the junior-high entrance examinations. On the Canton government's approach to parents about *minban* education, see *Yangcheng Wanbao*, September 11, 1962, p. 1, and September 19, 1962, p. 1.

10. *Yangcheng Wanbao*, October 5, 1962, p. 1, and *Yangcheng Wanbao*, July 19, 1964, p. 1. Altogether, by 1963–64 Canton had 400,000+ primary school pupils, which meant that no less than one fifth of Canton's populace was in primary school! (See *Yangcheng Wanbao*, July 12, 1964, p. 1; *Nanfang Ribao*, July 16, 1964; and *Nanfang Ribao*, July 19, 1964, p. 3.)

11. In 1960–61, 24,000 new students entered junior high school (*Yangcheng Wanbao*, September 1, 1960); in 1964–65 more than 35,000 entered (*Wen Hui Bao* [H.K.], April 2, 1965).

12. *Yangcheng Wanbao*, May 5, 1964, p. 1. These new school facilities were a very considerable expense for Canton. It was calculated in 1965 to cost about 500 *yuan* for each new student-place provided—equivalent to a year of a worker's factory wages. (Canton Radio, December 21, 1965, in *NCPRS*).

13. The educational organization of Canton (and apparently of most big Chinese cities) was and is constituted as follows: Canton has an Education Department (*Jiaoyu Ju*) which is divided into two sections: the No. 1 Education Bureau (*Jiaoyu Bu*) which handles secondary schools; and the No. 2 Education Bureau, which handles the primary schools. The No. 2 Bureau, because of the great numbers of primary schools, divides responsibility for administering the primary schools among five District Bureaus. (The secondary schools all remained directly under their citywide bureau.) The primary school district bureaus supervised the teaching staffs and held the teachers' dossiers (*dang-an*). The district level hence held greater control over the teachers than did the school principals. If a teacher was inadequate in his or her teaching, the district level had the responsibility to find means of improving the teacher's performance. The districts also held all responsibilities for hiring, transferring, and firing teachers, and paid teachers their salaries. The district bureaus also supervised the primary-level *minbans*, though these hired and paid their teachers independently. High-school *minbans* came under the supervision of the No. 1 Education Bureau, again at the citywide level.

14. In Canton's pyramid of schools, ordinary neighborhood schools were to provide the same type of demonstration effect for the *minban* schools: "The *minbans* and their neighborhood's state-run primary schools have links. They send teachers to these[neighborhood] schools to hear classes and to prepare and to research their own lecture notes." (*Yangcheng Wanbao*, July 19, 1964, p. 1.)

15. This function of providing a model for other units to emulate has roots in traditional Chinese modes of thought. It was felt traditionally that a commendable idea, technique, or moral virtue should be concretized in a real example which others could take as the standard for their own actions. The resulting "key-point" system is found today not just in educational affairs but also in most sectors of China's economy. Every commune has its key-point production brigade, every county its key-point communes, every province its key-point counties.

16. These matriculation examinations apparently were devised at provincial level and may well have been uniform throughout Guangdong Province. But only pupils from within Canton were eligible to compete for a place in the city schools. At the senior high school level, a token number of peasant youths were admitted to several of the best schools. (These few schools were provincially financed). But due to the peasant students' poorer academic background they usually were placed in separate classrooms. The city's own education funds were entirely reserved for the city's own constituency.

17. *Renmin Ribao* [People's Daily], May 18, 1965.

18. The difficulties which even the brightest working-class youths faced in trying to compete academically could be observed clearly at the Guangdong Experimental School. Set up to prove the viability of a shortened school curriculum (see chapter 3), the school accepted talented primary school graduates into its junior-high classes purely on the basis of their scholastic aptitudes; in this one special school, class background counted for nothing. In these circumstances, as seen in the adjacent table, the children of the middle-class "intelligentsia" numerically predominated. But these admissions criteria also meant that each individual "red-class" entrant was of an academic calibre equivalent to the middle-class entrants.

Three years after entering this experimental accelerated 5-year high school program, the youngsters had to take a set of achievement exams. These weeded out and sent back to the regular high school system all of the students who had fallen too far behind academically. Through interviews, I have secured information for two of the four classrooms

The "Class" Composition of the Guangdong Experimental School (2 classrooms)

	Students in First-year Jr. High, 1961	Students with Successful Exam Results, 1964
"Revolutionary cadre"	11	4
Proletarian	13	6
Non-intelligentsia middle-class	5	4
Intelligentsia middle-class	56	47
Bad-class	15	12

of the entering class of 1961. The data on who was or was not weeded out (though presumably inexact) strongly suggest that few of the red-class youths could keep apace academically, even though they were of high aptitude and even though their schoolwork was initially on a par with the children from intelligentsia homes.

19. These sets of circumstances seem true of almost all countries. On the very similar situation in Russia, for example, see Walter D. Connor, *Socialism, Politics and Equality: Hierarchy and Change in Eastern Europe and the USSR* (New York: Columbia University Press, 1979), p. 191 and 211.

20. Table 1.1 was compiled from interviews conducted by Edwin Lee and myself.

21. This quote comes from an interview transcript of Stanley Rosen, who graciously let me read and make use of many hundreds of pages of his interview findings. Prof. Rosen's doctoral thesis (forthcoming as a book) dealt with Red Guard politics in Canton.

22. The overall results would not have been appreciably altered if the questionnaire responses that were culled had been included. Their data are largely in line with the 74 that were used. With two of the classrooms that were used, moreover, there was an opportunity to crosscheck. Independent responses were received from two sets of former classmates, and in both cases the correspondence between their remembrances was quite close.

23. *Xiaobing* [Little Soldiers] (Canton), September 11, 1967, p. 2. This was an East-is-Red ("loyalist") faction Red Guard newspaper.

24. Such a proposal had, though, been made in 1964 by a high education official and, oddly enough, at that juncture had received Mao Zedong's personal blessings! Their discussion is contained in a volume of Mao's "private" talks and writings, published for intra-Party study in 1969 and entitled *Mao Zedong Sixiang Wansui* [Long Live the Thought of Mao Zedong], p. 464. A U.S. government translation appears in *Miscellany of Mao Tse-tung Thought (1949–1968), JPRS* 61269-2 (February 20, 1974), p. 335.

25. One of the clearest examples of these Cultural Revolution charges is found in *People's Daily*, December 17, 1967; in *SCMP* no. 4100, p. 9.

26. There were actually two sets of examinations for which to prepare—the school's own graduation examinations (which were held twice to give those who flunked a second chance), followed by the senior high school entrance examinations. Generally, the worst and the best students in a neighborhood school are reported to have shown the greatest concern: the worst students worried about the graduation examinations for fear they would not get their degree; while the high achievers were tense about the later city-run selection

examinations, since they were eager to make it into the next higher level of education. The middle group of students exhibited rather less concern.

For those students hoping to enter senior high school, four exam sections had to be taken at a designated examination hall: a combined algebra/geometry section; one in Chinese composition and literature; a foreign language section (some students taking English, others Russian); and a Politics exam section. Interviewees were convinced the mathematics and Chinese portions counted most, and that poor showings in either would preclude entry to senior high school. The politics section was officially important, but the answers were stereotyped and could be near-memorized beforehand by any conscientious student. Candidates had felt assured that they and the other students could not do poorly, and that the examination therefore did not count much in determining who got into senior high school.

27. The small minority of unattached junior high schools which did have aspirations seem from reports to have taken the exams most seriously, and sometimes even constructed dubious strategies to improve their results. An interviewee who attended one such school recalls that his classroom's student class head, who was from a very poor family and had had to work daily after school, was not permitted to graduate because she had done poorly in her graduation exams on the math and Chinese portions, the two subjects most important on the subsequent senior-high entrance exams. The school, apparently concluding that this girl would not make it past the senior-high entrance exams, was eliminating her from the *graduating* class. This tactic would boost the percentage of the now smaller graduating class which would win admission to a senior high school.

The very same ruse was commonly practiced by both primary schools and junior high schools in rural Guangdong, where the competition to get past primary school, let alone into a senior high school, remained keen, and where the prestige of a market town school was built upon its pass rate. *Nanfang Ribao* (June 11, 1964, p. 3) accordingly complained in 1964 that "if we do not pay sufficient attention, some of these [rural and small-town] schools, in order one-sidedly to pursue a high rate of admissions to higher schools, will lack feeling for students with bad grades, or will seize on various means to leave more students back so as to raise the rate of admissions to higher education."

28. These schools' tuition fees per semester were supposed to amount to 12–18 *yuan* for the senior high level, fixed by municipal statute. (*Yangcheng Wanbao*, September 19, 1962; in *SCMP Suppl.* no. 100, p. 16.) Interviewees suggest the fees were in fact higher. These schools' selection procedures opened after the regular state-run schools had already announced their decisions, so as to enable parents whose children had been rejected due to either the "class-line" or poor exam showings to have time to sign up at a *minban*.

29. The academic track senior high schools had 12–15,000 students in 1965–66; all told, the vocational programs had some 10–11,000. (I am indebted to Stanley Rosen for these figures.)

30. The teachers training program was the least in demand of the various vocational school routes. Most youths, it seems, deemed the primary-school teacher's lot considerably less desirable than an industrial worker's. In their minds, the worker's status was boosted by the central place which Marxist ideology and rhetoric gave to the industrial proletariat; and the primary-school teacher's pay, being no better than the pay in the state-owned factories, held no compensating attractions. Young men in particular held the vocation of primary-school teaching in distaste, in part because it had acquired the lowly image of "women's work." The teachers' schools accordingly attracted mostly teenage girls, usually from impoverished and/or large families that could ill afford to enroll them in any other

types of school. To attract such girls, the teacher training schools were entirely free of charge, the only free full-time secondary schools in Guangdong. Even with this enticement, however, there were never sufficient applicants to staff Canton's expanding elementary school system. The city resorted to hiring some of the untrained, unemployed graduates of the regular senior high schools who, as did two of my interviewees, took on the job only as a last resort. (The picture was altogether different in the countryside, where almost all posts which did not involve field labor were sought after, and where educated young men competed to be chosen as village school teachers.)

31. Of the two types of manual-job vocational schools the preferred variety were the "technical schools" (*jishu xuexiao*). These provided specialist training for specified industries; e.g., the Guangdong River Transport School trained ship pilots, enginecroom maintenance engineers and the bookkeepers *et al.* needed to help staff the river transport bureaucracy. Such schools were run by the pertinent provincial or municipal industrial bureaus, in collaboration with the provincial or city education department. As if to indicate to applicants that these schools were not part of the regular ladder of the educational system, they did not utilize the provincial secondary-school entrance examinations, but instead used a separate set written by the Canton municipal secondary school bureau.

The less preferred form of industrial vocational schools, the "technical-worker schools" (*jigong xuexiao*), were normally geared toward less highly skilled industrial jobs. These technical-worker schools usually were managed by large factories (not directly by industrial bureaus), though again in cooperation with the municipal education department. Such schools had been popular during the upsurge of mass education of the Great Leap Forward because they answered the twin desires of many working-class parents: to see their children receive further education while improving their chances for a factory job. But since these schools' intakes were geared to the specific manpower needs of their particular industry, if the local economy soured the entrants ran the risk of being dismissed from the program halfway through their studies. They were doubly vulnerable because their school's survival depended upon the profitability of the factory or industry responsible for managing it. Thus, during the terrible depression of 1961–62, almost every one of these technical workers schools simply had closed down and their students put under pressure to sign up for a 3-year stint laboring in the countryside. By 1963 fewer than half a dozen of the schools remained in operation in Canton. But as the economy revived, so too did most of the schools; and several brand-new ones were established in 1964–66. The facilities often were rudimentary in the extreme: simply the offices and storehouses and spare shopfloor space of their industrial sponsors. Mostly they were run as half-work/half-study programs, which not only enabled them to integrate their training with practice on the shopfloor, but also allowed the factories to recoup part of the education costs by using the youths' labor free on a half-time basis. The length of study ran variously from one to three years. (Of the many news articles that were published describing the facilities, courses, and student bodies of Guangdong's urban half-work/half-study vocational schools, the three most informative are *Yangcheng Wanbao*, September 10, 1964, p. 1; *Nanfang Ribao*, October 8, 1964, p. 3; and *Nanfang Ribao*, September 24, 1964, p. 3.)

32. Guangdong and Canton separately operated a number of these specialist schools. The provincially financed ones drew students from throughout Guangdong—and were especially popular with small-town youths of good academic quality and good or reasonable class background as an escape hatch into the "big city." One of these provincial specialist schools is described at some length in G. Bennett and R. Montaperto, *Red Guard: The Political Biography of Dai Hsiao-ai* (New York: Doubleday, 1971) and Martin Whyte,

Small Groups and Political Rituals in China (Berkeley: University of California Press, 1974), chapter 6.

CHAPTER TWO. THE SENIOR HIGH BULGE AND DWINDLING CAREER OPENINGS

1. In 1954, for example, China's universities had 94,000 openings as against 71,000 graduating secondary-school students. See *URS*, vol. 36, no. 12, August 14, 1964, p. 189. Also John P. Emerson: "Manpower Training and Utilization of Specialized Cadres" in John W. Lewis, ed., *The City in Communist China* (Stanford: Stanford University Press, 1971), p. 199.

2. In 1957 the universities enrolled 107,000 candidates, but 90,000 other new graduates had to be rejected. *People's Daily*, April 25, 1957; cited in *URS*, as in footnote 1.

3. *People's Daily*, June 4, 1960; in *SCMP* no. 2285, p. 17. The newspaper instructed employers to deny jobs to all new senior-high graduates, in order to force even the reluctant among them to sign up for the university entrance examinations.

4. *Da Gong Bao* (H.K.), September 9, 1959, p. 3; *Yangcheng Wanbao*, September 3, 1962, p. 1; *Zhongguo Xinwen*, September 6, 1962.

5. The Canton news media did not usually give university enrollment totals for the years after 1961, so I have had to piece together this information from two sources. *Zhongguo Xinwen* of January 20, 1964, reports that Guangdong's universities had 120 percent more full-time students than in 1957; *Zhongguo Xinwen* of January 23, 1966, reports the numbers of university students were 100 percent more than 1957. The one schoolyear after 1961 for which we do have an enrollment figure is 1964–65, when *Zhongguo Xinwen* (August 19, 1964) reports 36,000, down from the extravagant 46,000 enrollment of 1960–61 (*Wen Hui Bao* [H.K.], September 7, 1960).

6. This figure is from a Reuters interview with Canton officials (*Hong Kong Standard*, October 18, 1965).

7. Ezra Vogel, *Canton Under Communism* (Cambridge, Mass.: Harvard University Press, 1969), p. 369. By 1965, the problems posed by large families must have been apparent to much of the populace. Yet the birth rate still registered 25 per thousand that year (*Hong Kong Standard*, October 18, 1965). This was equivalent to the pre-Liberation rate, but by now the infant and child mortality rates had dropped to negligible proportions.

8. Christopher Howe, *Wage Patterns and Wage Policy in Modern China* (Cambridge: Cambridge University Press, 1973); John Emerson, "Manpower Training," p. 188. Between 1952 and 1957 the urban population grew by an estimated 5–6 percent a year. (John Emerson, "Manpower Absorption in the Non-Agricultural Branches of the Economy of Communist China, 1953–58," *China Quarterly* [July 1961].)

9. The senior high schools were empowered to select a few of their graduates to attend one-year teacher training courses, to help alleviate the teacher shortages caused by the rapid expansion of junior-high education. The Canton schools also began to select entrants to one-year courses for training as bookkeepers and for specialized industrial posts such as laboratory aides at chemical factories, which required a senior-high graduate's knowledge of chemistry. But these various job possibilities were so limited in number that many graduating students who had not been able to line up their own job prospects preferred to

keep their schools from knowing this. They knew it would be the school's duty to try to persuade them to volunteer for the countryside.

10. *SCMM* no. 653 (1969), p. 22.

11. Newspapers sometimes carried distressed letters-to-the-editor from school graduates caught in the service trades. Good examples are in *Nanfang Ribao*, July 23, 1964, p. 2, and *Da Gong Bao* (Peking), August 7, 1965. After the Cultural Revolution, *Renmin Ribao* (January 6, 1972, p. 2) admitted there was still the common feeling that "Work in the service trades is low-grade work." The views of interviewees are summed up well by a 1972 high school graduate, describing the new system in which graduating students were assigned directly to jobs:

A friend was allocated from school to a little eating place. Refused to take that job, of course. It's a question of face. Yes, that type of service trade is better than becoming a peasant, but it's much much worse than being a worker. Being a steel worker is really good. But of course, there are workers and there are workers. So if someone says he's a worker, you ask what type. The same even in the trades. If you're at one of the big department stores, it's comparatively prestigious, but if at some small place, it's bad work, a loss of face. Most disliked of all jobs is to be a street cleaner. You have to sweep the streets before everyone's eyes, and at night collect their shit. Yes, it's better to become a peasant in the countryside.

12. Cited in "Youth to the Countryside—and Back Again," *Current Scene*, vol. 5, no. 16, October 1, 1967, p. 5. This message, in precisely the same wording, reappeared, e.g., in *Zhongguo Qingnian Bao* [*China Youth News*], January 7, 1965, and *Jingji Yanjiu* [*Economic Research*], November 1965 (in *SCMM* no. 507, p. 17).

13. Interview by Anita Chan; this particular student attended a school in Guangxi Province.

14. In all, 56 of these half-work/half-study vocational schools were established in Canton in 1964 (*Yangcheng Wanbao*, January 24, 1965, p. 1). Though half of these were so poorly run and so much a nuisance to the factories operating them (Canton Radio, December 11, 1964, in *NCPRS*) that they were closed again the following year, the ones which survived grew rapidly in size. Consequently the total numbers of students undertaking the largely two-year curricula continued to increase up to the Cultural Revolution. *Zhongguo Xinwen*, August 18, 1965; Canton Radio, September 23, 1965 (*NCPRS*); *Yangcheng Wanbao*, August 31, 1965.

15. *Yangcheng Wanbao*, August 31, 1965.

16. Most of these 600 youths flocked back into Canton during the Cultural Revolution and formed their own vociferous Red Guard group, trying to have themselves restored to urban postings. Some of the many broadsides and essays which they composed to support their cause reached Hong Kong. A selection of these materials is in *URS*, vol. 50, no. 3; also see *SCMP* no. 4118 and *Zhongbao Zhoukan*, July 11, 1969, p. 1. Interestingly, it seems from these that the family origins of these 600 bad-class youths were predominantly "non-intellectual": their fathers were either "bad elements" from the lumpen-proletariat or former small overseas merchants. From this it would appear that the more intellectual and/or moneyed bad-class families had not yet been so willing to give up their hopes of succeeding in the other more formal educational routes.

17. An official report from China cited in *Xing Dao Ribao* (Hong Kong), August 6, 1965.

18. *Red Flag*, February 1, 1976, in *SCMM* no. 859, p. 33.

19. These regulations are described in China Background (U.S. Govt.), no. 17/68.

20. To persuade the mounting numbers of unemployed teenagers to volunteer for the countryside, and to keep them off the streets and out of trouble in the meantime, Canton's districts inaugurated "youth labor reserve courses" in April 1965. In these the unemployed youngsters were offered part-time paid labor and in return had to participate part-time in politics classes, largely given over to discussing the merits of rural immigration. The crush of young people entering the "courses" suggests the desperation of the unemployment situation. By the end of 1965 the "labor reserve course" enrollments had risen to 12,000, almost equivalent to the number of school graduates that previous spring. Xing Dao Ribao, July 19, 1965, citing Yangcheng Wanbao; also Canton Radio, December 16, 1965 (NCPRS).

21. E.g., a bad-class interviewee was told that if she settled in a village she would be permitted to reregister from there for the next year's university entrance exams. She was also told that in her second-time-around exam effort she would be helped by the political good mark of having volunteered for the countryside.

22. Interview by Anita Chan.

23. China Topics, February 26, 1968, Appendix A; and "Sources of Labor Discontent in China: The Worker-Peasant System," Current Scene, March 15, 1968, p. 19.

24. Hai Feng, A Brief Account of the Cultural Revolution in Guangdong (in Chinese) (Hong Kong: Union Research Institute, 1971), p. 287. I am indebted to Stanley Rosen for bringing this to my attention.

25. Zhinong Hongqi [Aid-Agriculture Red Flag], a rebel-faction newspaper edited by rusticated youths who had returned to Canton, January 1968. Translated into English in SCMP no. 4125 and China Topics, May 27, 1968.

26. Quoted in a second article from the January 1968 issue of Zhinong Hongqi; in English in JPRS 45447, May 17, 1968.

28. Zhinong Hongqi, as in footnote 25.

29. Geming Qingnian [Revolutionary Youth], a Red Guard newspaper from Hunan, November 1967; in English, in SCMP no. 4102 and China Topics, February 26, 1968, Appendix D.

30. Two excellent discussions of the urban teenagers' views of rustication are Gordon White, "The Politics of Hsia-hsiang Youth," China Quarterly 59 (July/September 1974), and John Gardner, "Educated Youth and Urban-Rural Inequalities," in John W. Lewis, ed., The City in Communist China, (Stanford: Stanford University Press, 1971).

31. Yangcheng Wanbao, September 19, 1962; in SCMP Suppl. no. 105.

33. Canton Radio, November 19, 1964 (NCPRS).

34. Ibid.

35. This figure was compiled from Canton Radio (NCPRS, November 19, 1964) and Yangcheng Wanbao, June 19, 1969, p. 1.

36. Canton Radio, December 4, 1965 (NCPRS) and Nanfang Ribao, January 5, 1966, p. 3. Nationwide, the rustication campaign's statistics were similar to those recorded for Guangdong Province: increasing gradually after the depression. In all, between 1962 and 1966 inclusive, about a million urban youths went to settle in the countryside. (Wen Hui Bao [H. K.], September 26, 1966). Of these, a bit more than 200,000 went in 1962 (Yangcheng Wanbao, July 22, 1962, p. 1). In 1964, in contrast, fully 320,000 went (Renmin Ribao, May 5, 1965), and in the first eight months of 1965 they were joined by a further quarter million (NCNA, September 23, 1965). In short, the rustication program was gathering momentum. In fact, compared to the 1.2 million of 1956–66 (Peking Review, January 9,

1976, p. 11), 14 million urban youths were sent down in the giant rustication drives of 1968–1976.

Western academic studies of China's pre-Cultural Revolution rustication policies normally cite the astronomical figure of 40 million urban youths settling in the countryside during those earlier years. This error comes from a Chinese figure which includes all the rural youths who returned to their home villages after graduation from school, including graduates of rural primary schools returning from their commune market towns.

37. Frederick Wakeman, *The Fall of Imperial China* (New York: The Free Press, 1975), pp. 22–23.

38. In Czechoslovakia, since the Communists' advent to power, the wage gap between the higher professions and blue-collar workers has been narrowed to the point where there no longer are any meaningful financial reasons to compete for higher education. Working-class parents have been content for their children to obtain factory jobs; middle-class parents have continued to prod their children to study and to compete. The ironic net result: social mobility between the different strata of society has declined. Ernest Gellner, *Contemporary Thought and Politics*, (London: Routledge and Kegan Paul, 1974), p. 167; Walter Connor, *Socialism, Politics, and Equality: Hierarchy and Change in Eastern Europe and the USSR* (New York: Columbia University Press, 1979), p. 195; R. P. Dore, *The Diploma Disease*, p. 194. On the Russian experience see Murray Yanowitch and Norton Dodge, "Social Class and Education: Soviet Findings and Reactions," *Comparative Education Review* 12, no. 3 (October 1968), pp. 253–54.

CHAPTER THREE. FLAWED REFORMS: RURAL AND URBAN ALTERNATIVES TO THE REGULAR LADDER

1. *Renmin Ribao* [People's Daily], May 18, 1965. In relatively prosperous Jilin Province, it was estimated that fully 50–60 percent of the peasant children were not in school and that these unschooled children were "mostly from the [class categories of] poor and lower-middle peasant families, and therefore the universalization of primary school education is substantially a question of [our] educational work's class line." *Jilin Jiaoyu* [Jilin Education], July 15, 1965, p. 15.

2. *Xin Hua She*, September 24, 1962; in *SCMP* 2828, p. 13.

3. *Xingdao Ribao* (Hong Kong), October 12, 1963, p. 4, citing an article in *Huaqiao Xiangbao* [Overseas Chinese Rural Journal], a Guangdong publication. By these figures, twenty-one primary-school children could have been educated for the cost of one university student.

4. *Zhongguo Xinwen*, May 31, 1964.

5. Don Adams and Robert M. Bjork, *Education in Developing Areas* (New York: David McKay, 1969), pp. 129–30.

6. Jonathan Unger, "Collective Incentives in the Chinese Countryside: Lessons from Chen Village," *World Development* 6, no. 5 (May 1978).

7. The radicals who came to power after the Cultural Revolution revamped rural education in ways that pushed even more of the burden onto the localities. The government "transferred downward" even the old state-founded village schools, which now were all placed under village control. The government agreed, though, to continue to pay the salaries

of the pre-Cultural Revolution teachers of such schools (even if they were shifted to other village schools). This policy apparently derives from the state's promise to teachers in the 1950s and 1960s that if schooling were decentralized their salaries would not be allowed to fall. Such villages must provide the pay, however, of all newly recruited teachers—at a village-set wage well below what those older state-paid teachers were assured.

8. On the 1940s see Mark Selden, *The Yenan Way in Revolutionary China* (Cambridge, Mass.: Harvard University Press, 1971), pp. 270–74. For the 1950s government policies, see the Introduction to Ronald Montaperto, ed., *China's Schools in Flux* (White Plains, New York: M. E. Sharpe, 1979).

9. Two very good secondary sources on these half-and-half schools are Julia Kwong, "The Educational Experiment of the Great Leap Forward, 1958–59: Its Inherent Contradictions," *Comparative Education Review* 23, no. 3 (October 1979), p. 443–55; and Robert Barendsen, "The Agricultural Middle School in Communist China," in Roderick Mac-Farquhar, ed., *China Under Mao* (Cambridge, Mass.: MIT Press, 1966).

10. *People's Daily*, April 9, 1960, in *CB* no. 623, p. 11. The impact of the Leap's economic collapse had not yet hit home; only two months before, *Zhongguo Xinwen* (February 6, 1960) had reported only two-thirds as many half-and-half agricultural high schools—20,000+, with 2,190,000 students and 60,000+ teachers.

11. Five-sixths of the agricultural half-and-half schools had folded by 1962, and the system's enrollments were only a ninth of what they had been in the Great Leap Forward. Nationally, attendance at primary schools dropped from 80 percent of all school-aged children in 1958 to 56 percent in 1962, due largely to the collapse of most of the "irregular" rural primary classes. *SCMM*, no. 836, p. 15. By early 1964, 78 percent of all the rural primary schools were of the type run and financed directly by the government (*Zhongguo Xinwen*, May 31, 1964).

12. See, e.g., *Nanfang Ribao*, December 7, 1964, p. 2, and *Renmin Ribao*, June 9, 1966, p. 1.

13. E.g., *Nanfang Ribao*, August 24, 1962, p. 3, which also recommended that students be better prepared through "political education" for their inevitable return to village jobs. In addition the report criticized some of the rural schools, saying that "their success at getting students into the next higher level of education is the only thing these schools are concerned about, with the consequence that the education in these schools is somewhat abstracted from reality."

14. E.g., a newspaper report on a Guangdong provincial education conference in 1964 concluded that "If we insist on following the educational policy of 'walking on one leg,' if we only want full-time schools run by the state and stress conformity, we will ban the children of the broad masses of poor-and-lower-middle peasants from admission to schools, which is in contravention to our class line" (*Nanfang Ribao*, June 19, 1964; in *SCMP* 3259).

15. This directive, entitled "Two Types of Systems of Education and Two Types of Systems of Labor," receives mention in *Nanfang Ribao*, February 22, 1965, p. 2, again in unofficial Cultural Revolution materials, and yet again (approvingly) in *Nanfang Ribao*, May 18, 1980 (*FBIS*, May 21, 1980, p. P1).

16. Xinhui County, Guangdong:

Regular county senior high	120 *yuan* per year
Regular rural junior high	76 *yuan*
Half-and-half agricultural high school	6.8 *yuan*

The first and third figures are from *Mao Zedong Sixiang Wansui* [Long Live the Thought of Mao Zedong], n.p., 1969. Xinhui County's half-and-half school may provide rather skewed figures, since the school was exceptionally well run and became the much-praised and much-visited model for all of China. The figure of 76 *yuan* is from a recommended article on the county's schools in *China Reconstructs* (September 1965).

17. Canton Radio, January 5, 1966, in *NCPRS*.

18. *Guangming Ribao*, October 15, 1964.

19. This estimate is derived by combining two sources: *NCNA*, February 19, 1966, notes that Guangdong's countryside contained 80+ percent of the province's populace, and Canton Radio, October 20, 1965 (*NCPRS*), observed that because of the new irregular schooling, the percentage of school-aged children in Guangdong attending primary school had risen the past year from 69 to 80 percent. Since all of the province's urban children attended primary school, we may deduce that at least 25 percent of the rural children, by these figures, did not.

20. The findings of Parish and Whyte are similar here to my own. (William Parish and Martin Whyte, *Village and Family in Contemporary China* [Chicago and London, University of Chicago Press, 1978], p. 78.)

21. One extreme example of this was a village cited in *Red Flag* where, on the eve of the Cultural Revolution, only 3 of the 40 children at the village primary school were girls. When the *Red Flag* correspondent visited the village in 1970, parents were still saying: "Our daughters will be members of other families sooner or later. What is the purpose of sending them to school?" *Hong Qi*, no. 8 (July 1970).

22. Radio Canton, October 6, 1964 (*NCPRS*).

23. *Yangcheng Wanbao*, June 29, 1965, p. 1.

24. The state, keeping down the flow of education funds to the rural sector, maintained only 81 such full-time agricultural senior high schools as of 1964. The schools had only 17,000 new enrollees that year, for a rural constituency comprising a sixth of mankind (*Zhongguo Xinwen*, March 27, 1964). With growing official support for agricultural technical schooling, the numbers had risen to 160 schools by the summer of 1965 (*Guangming Ribao*, Aug. 8, 1965).

With so few schools and with technical skills in the rural districts scarce, graduates were assured a relatively good rural post and status. Thus the competition to enter was keen. As with the half-and-half schools, the policy was followed of giving priority to the former exploited classes, and to the political activists among them. In 1964 the state proudly calculated that in *this* set of schools more than 99 percent of the student body was of poor or lower-middle peasant parentage and that, moreover, fully 42 percent of them were League or Party members, the cream of political activists (*Zhongguo Xinwen*, March 27, 1964). A spell of prior full-time labor was required of all prospective entrants—again, a post-Cultural Revolution policy with pre-Cultural Revolution roots. The popularity of these agricultural-technical schools was such that even though all applicants first had to be carefully screened and nominated by brigade and commune Party committees, the schools were flooded with candidates on examination day. In Guangdong one school could enroll only 90 new students in 1963 and only 140 in 1964, but each time the communes sent more than a thousand preselected applicants (*Guangming Ribao*, March 26, 1964, p. 1). The competition remained fierce even though the schools had adopted the policy since 1962 of "from the communes, to the communes," which meant that the students had to return to a job in the local unit which had vetted them. Since these technically trained youths were to help expand the agricultural extension services, assigning them back to their own communes meant, advantageously, that a trusted young local person—not an outsider—would be on hand to convince the peasantry to try out new agricultural techniques.

25. *Zhongguo Xinwen,* August 22, 1965; *Peking Review,* January 7, 1966. This switch to half-and-half schooling was decided at a conference of the Ministry of Agriculture attended by both Mao and Liu Shaoqi (*Renmin Ribao,* August 24, 1965). Nationally, more than half of the agricultural universities had adopted the half-and-half program by the end of 1965.

26. *Wen Hui Bao* (H.K.), January 4, 1966.

27. E.g., *Nanfang Ribao* [Southern Daily], December 28, 1964, p. 2, and *Nanfang Ribao,* January 21, 1965, p. 2.

28. E.g., a *Southern Daily* report of July 7, 1965, observed that "some rural people hold up these schools to ridicule, saying that they are 'low-class' and 'irregular,' 'could not guarantee the quality of teaching,' and 'would soon be suspended'" (*SCMP* 3522, p. 10).

29. The national press complained about such lower-level education officials, that:

They contend that schools can be opened only in places with good educational conditions and that it is impossible to extend education in a poor mountain valley. . . . They only want to operate regular full-day schools which they consider "up to standard." They do not want to operate simplified schools which they consider as "not being in fine shape," inefficient, and having lowered the "quality" of teaching and upsetting the school system. (*Renmin Ribao,* June 2, 1964.)

30. *New China News Agency* (English-language), June 10, 1964.

31. See, for example, *Ba-san-yi* ("August 31"), December 1967, a Canton Red Guard newspaper, in *SCMP* 4118, p. 9; also *URS,* vol. 50, pp. 250–54.

32. *SCMM* no. 836, p. 18.

33. In the winter of late 1965, the radicals had pressed to have the whole system of urban schooling converted to half-and-half, but the "moderates" had managed to deflect the proposal through a gradualist compromise, under which it would require 15 years to effect the conversion. The conference decision is discussed in *Da Gong Bao* (H.K.), December 6, 1965, and in Donald Munro, "Maxims and Realities in China's Educational Policy: The Half-Work, Half-Study Model," *Asian Survey* (April 1967), p. 257. An accusation on Liu's delaying tactics at this conference is contained in *SCMP* 4118 (see footnote 31 above).

34. Fang Zheng, "Reform Work in the Chinese Communist Education System," *Zuguo Yuekan* (Hong Kong), 1965, no. 11; in English in *Chinese Education,* vol. 3, no. 2 (Winter 1970–71), pp. 228–38. This essay does a good job of covering the various debates since the 1920s over the length of schooling in China.

35. Good summaries of these Russian reforms are contained in Nigel Grant, *Soviet Education* (Baltimore and London: Penguin Books, 1964), pp. 98–102; John T. Zepper, "Recent and Contemporary Soviet Educational Thought," *School and Society,* vol. 100 (January 1972), pp. 19–21; and Ina Schlesinger, "Soviet Educational Change," *ibid.,* pp. 43–47.

36. A pecularity of the Chinese system is this close connection at the top between the organs responsible for the transmission of ideology and those responsible for education. The link continued into more recent times; e.g., Lu Dingyi's responsibilities over Party propaganda were transferred after the Cultural Revolution into the hands of Yao Wenyuan and Zhang Chunqiao, who also played decisive roles in educational affairs. The reason for this linkage, I would presume, has to do with the importance the Chinese place upon the

ideological/moral training provided by the schools, with the men responsible for propagating ideology accordingly responsible overall for educational affairs.

37. Lu Dingyi's views on this are expressed in his speech to the Second National People's Congress of 1960. (*Renmin Ribao,* April 10, 1960; in English the speech has been translated in *Current Background* no. 623, and *Union Research Service,* vol. 19, p. 216.

38. Lu Dingyi had been instrumental in getting the half-and-half drive started in 1958 (Julia Kwong: *Chinese Education in Transition* [Montreal: McGill-Queens University Press, 1979], p. 91). But speaking during the Great Leap in support of an accelerated 10-year curriculum, Lu Dingyi had declared that in the long term "I am in favor of changing all secondary schools to a full-day system; we must not [permanently] develop half-work/half-study." (Cited in *Jiaoyu Geming* [Educational Revolution], May 6, 1967, translated in Peter Seybolt, ed., *Revolutionary Education in China* [White Plains, New York: IASP Press, 1973], p. 35.) For the "conservative" official views of the Education Minister, Yang Xiufeng, see his speech of April 1959, in Stewart Fraser, compiler, *Chinese Communist Education: Records of the First Decade* (Nashville: Vanderbilt University Press, 1965), pp. 304–5.

39. For Yang Xiufeng's speech see *Renmin Ribao,* April 9, 1960; translations appear in the sources in note 37. A good discussion of these speeches is Robert Barendsen's "Planned Reforms in the Primary and Secondary School System in Communist China," *Information on Education Around the World,* no. 45, U.S. Department of H.E.W., August 1960.

40. *Da Gong Bao* (H.K.), September 3, 1960, p. 1.

41. From former students at Provincial Experimental, I have been able to obtain data for 2 of the 4 classes of the grade that would have graduated in 1966 had not the Cultural Revolution intervened. In one of these classes, only 36 out of 52 students were permitted in 1964 to go on for the two years of the experimental school's senior high, and in the other class only 38 out of 50 were able to continue. (On this, see note 18 of chapter 1.)

42. Information on the programs at four of these schools comes from former participants. I have relied upon the interview transcripts of Stanley Rosen as well as my own.

43. *Renmin Ribao* [People's Daily], June 19, 1966, p. 2.

CHAPTER FOUR. MEMORIZATION AND TESTS

1. Again, the most cogently argued of these studies is Ronald Dore, *The Diploma Disease: Education, Qualification, and Development* (London: George Allen and Unwin; Berkeley: University of California Press, 1976).

2. "The 1963 Temporary Work Regulations for Schools" (translated by S. Shirk), *China Quarterly,* no. 55 (July 1973), p. 543. Three and a half thousand characters is nearly twice the number that the average Japanese adult is expected to recognize.

3. I. Miyazaki, *China's Examination Hell: The Civil Service Examinations of Imperial China* (London: Weatherhill, 1976).

4. Jonathan Unger, ed. and trans., "Post-Cultural Revolution Primary School Education: Selected Texts," *Chinese Education,* vol. 10, no. 2 (Summer 1977), p. 86.

5. Such an idea may well be valid, perhaps as a case of self-fulfilling expectations. A young woman from Canton who volunteered for the countryside before the Cultural Revolution recalls that "in the village, when facing difficult duties, appropriate Mao quotes that I had memorized in the village would come to mind, and they'd provide me with the direction and the willpower to overcome those difficulties. It really worked."

6. This can be seen even through a comparison of first grade reading primers. A foreign

visitor to a Chinese primary school in 1964–65 was informed that the pupils learned 337 characters their first term of primary school (C. H. G. Oldham, "Science and Education in China," *Bulletin of the Atomic Scientists* [June 1966], p. 43; also in Ruth Adams, ed., *Contemporary China* [New York: Vintage, 1966], p. 287). This can be compared with the primer used in 1975–76 in the first grade primary school classes of Guangdong. The first-semester primer contains 257 characters, only three-fourths as many as the 1964–65 version.

7. Richard W. Wilson, *Learning to Be Chinese: The Political Socialization of Children in Taiwan* (Cambridge, Mass. and London: MIT Press, 1970), p. 39.

8. This estimate is derived from interviews with former teachers. After the Cultural Revolution many of China's primary schools tried to abolish this prior system of failing the slowest learners, but such children's difficulties obliged the schools to restore the practice after a few years. See, e.g., *China Reconstructs* (June 1973), p. 11.

9. In this grading, the schools were of a mixed mind as to whether they wanted to encourage or discourage the students' orientation toward grades. In 1958 the schools had switched away from a grading system based on 100 percent. Instead, China adopted the format used in Russia, where grades are from 1 to 5, with a "3" the passing mark. The argument favoring this switch was that the Russian system was less competitive, since the distinctions in grades could not be nearly as fine as under the percentage system. But as the dispute with the Soviet Union heated up during the 1960s, the schools reverted to the 100 percent system, on the excuse that the 5-grade system was revisionist(!).

10. See, e.g., *Nanfang Ribao*, June 19, 1964, in *SCMP* no. 3259.

11. *1960 Gaodeng Xuexiao Zhaosheng Kaoshi Dagang* [Outline of the 1960 Entrance Examinations for Higher-Level Schools], Peking: The People's Educational Publishers.

12. *Nanfang Ribao*, April 7, 1964, p. 2.

13. Actually, the poorer schools' practices probably helped their students' chances on the selection examinations. Since their students might not be able to handle conceptualizations as well as the students at the key points, they had reason to offset this by filling their examination papers with a wealth of fact. But all the available evidence suggests that the teachers at these poorer schools were scarcely thinking of the higher-school examinations when they subjected their students to classroom tests.

14. This quote is compiled from two adjoining editorials in *Wen Hui Bao* (Shanghai), April 4, 1964, p. 4.

15. Two of the best articles of this genre are *Guangming Ribao*, November 30, 1964, and *Guangming Ribao*, January 30, 1965. The list here is drawn largely from these pieces.

16. *Jiangxi Ribao*, July 3, 1965; in *SCMP Suppl.* no. 145, p. 20.

17. *Jiaoyu Geming Cankao Ziliao* [Education Revolution Reference Materials], no. 5, May 10, 1974; *URS* 76, pp. 134–35. This is a journal edited by the Guangdong Teachers College.

18. David Crook, "School Examinations in China," *Eastern Horizon* 14, no. 4 (1975), pp. 22–26.

19. An interview published in *Wen Hui Bao* (Hong Kong), November 10, 1977, p. 1.

CHAPTER FIVE. STUDENT IDEALS AND COMPETITION: THE GATHERING STORM

1. Frank Swetz, *Mathematics Education in China* (Cambridge, Mass.: MIT Press, 1974), pp. 276–77.

2. Selections from the 1960s primers are included in C. Ridley, R. Godwin, and D.

Doolin, *The Making of a Model Citizen in Communist China* (Stanford: Hoover Institute Press, 1971). Analyses of the primers' political contents are also contained in Roberta Martin, "The Socialization of Children in China and Taiwan: An Analysis of Elementary School Textbooks," *China Quarterly*, no. 62 (June 1975), pp. 242–62. (For a longer version, see Dr. Martin's 1972 Master's thesis, East Asian Institute Library, Columbia University.) See also Richard Solomon, "Educational Themes in China's Changing Culture," *China Quarterly*, no. 22 (1965), pp. 154–70; and John W. Lewis, "Party Cadres in Communist China," in James S. Coleman, ed., *Education and Political Development* (Princeton: Princeton University Press, 1965), pp. 408–36.

3. This poem is translated in its entirety in Jonathan Unger, "Post-Cultural Revolution Primary School Education: Selected Texts," *Chinese Education*, vol. 10, no. 2 (Summer 1977), pp. 4–102. The political themes of pre- and post-Cultural Revolution reading primers are surprisingly similar, and my analyses of the reading lessons of the 1960s apply almost equally well to the 1970s.

4. This was, of course, expected in adult relations also, especially among political officials. On this see Ezra Vogel, "From Friendship to Comradeship: The Change in Personal Relations in Communist China," *China Quarterly*, no. 21 (January 1965), pp. 46–60.

5. An historical parallel exists here. The traditional Chinese gentleman similarly was supposed to employ introspection, self-will, and force of habit to become "upright."

6. See Mao's "On the Correct Handling of Contradictions Among the People" speech of 1957, in *Selected Works of Mao Tsetung*, vol. 5 (Peking: Foreign Language Press, 1977).

7. Interview by Anita Chan.

8. Many of the capitalists were still considered national bourgeoisie, not necessarily enemies, so such stories concentrated on the landlord class.

9. I have selected this particular story not only because its message is especially explicit, but also because the book is widely available in English. Accordingly, readers will be able to look up the tale themselves. Entitled *Monkey Subdues the White-Bone Demon,* it was published by Peking's Foreign Languages Press in 1964 and republished by the same press in 1973 and 1975. The decision to republish is one of the many indications that this theme of class struggle and hidden enemies was still taught to China's children after the Cultural Revolution.

Interestingly, the school-learning of Taiwanese children contains a similar theme of outcaste and concealed enemies, as reported by an American scholar who studied Taipei schools: "Most of all, . . . hatred and fear are directed towards those members of society who are purposely disloyal to the group. . . . These objects of hostility are a class of internal traitors, those who repudiate the leader and his followers and organize a competitive loyalty structure. Such people have not merely violated group norms but have sought to change or destroy the group itself. They are thus especially detestable. This is never more true than when their actions are secret and covert." (Richard Wilson, *Learning to Be Chinese: The Political Socialization of Children in Taiwan* [Cambridge, Mass.: MIT Press, 1970], p. 122.)

10. In these small-group criticisms, the child's misbehavior often was contrasted to the teachings of Chairman Mao. This was often an effective technique. Since the children had been taught legitimacy flowed from Mao, a former teacher notes, "Many naughty kids did feel that if there was a conflict between Mao's thought and their own behavior, then they themselves somehow had to be in error."

11. This was for China a new form of teacher/student relationship. Moreover, my interviews suggest it was more true of the late 1950s and 1960s than of the early and mid-1950s; and more true, too, of city primary schools than those in the countryside.

12. In the early grades of primary school the teacher had simply recommended to the children whom they should elect. But by the last years of elementary school, as seen here, the pupils were taking these elections (held every school term) more into their own hands. Though the teacher hinted at her own preferences the students sometimes were putting into office their own favorites instead.

The elections in these last couple of years of primary school and the first couple of junior high were usually the freest in the entire system of schooling through university. The reason was that as influence over the selections slipped away from the teacher it thereafter moved gradually into the hands of the student leadership organs; by the end of junior high school, the seven class cadres were meeting as a committee before the elections to draw up a recommended slate.

13. In the heightened political competitiveness of an activist classroom small-group sessions were sometimes dominated by these exchanges of criticism. Non-League activists often were the most vociferous participants in this. The acrimony arose from the small groups' responsibility for designating labor models, "3-good student" awards, etc., all of which went into a student's permanent political record. In some of the boarding schools, each dormitory-room of students constituted its own small group; and in the case of one of my interviewees the small group's appraisal sessions became so competitive and the dorm-mates so suspicious of each other that they had to seek all of their friendships entirely outside their dorm room.

This fierce competitiveness was not common, however, in most junior-high classrooms and in the poorer and less activist senior high schools, where more students had given up hopes of university. In such schools, the informal mores which regulated friendships and which held classrooms socially together laid down that the criticisms in small groups be skin-deep. Most small-group sessions in China, as in these schools, normally center on each member criticizing *himself,* and other members will then usually commend the speaker's progress or mildly chide him for speaking too modestly about his recent performance. Such a small group session preserves the solidarity of the peer group. The authorities did not discourage this type of session, since the end-effect was that the peer group reaffirmed the propriety of conforming to the officially approved norms. But at the same time, the leadership was not averse to seeing small groups engage in these harsher mutual criticism sessions. It was perhaps felt that such sessions helped break down the informal peer-group loyalties that came in the way of the officially prescribed "comradeship" and loyalty to the greater cause. The mutually supportive sessions and the mutually criticizing ones were, as it were, the two poles of officially acceptable small-group behavior.

For another interpretation of student small groups, see Martin K. Whyte, *Small Groups and Political Rituals in China* (Berkeley: University of California Press, 1974).

14. This system of cooperation was partly institutionalized; from junior high school through university, one excellent student in each course was selected by the subject's teacher to become Course Representative (*ke daibiao*), to help any students who were embarrassed to ask ordinary classmates for coaching. Interestingly, the bad-class-origin students were permitted to hold such posts.

15. The Party Secretary at Attached Middle, Guangdong's leading high school, cautioned League members, "If a member's grades aren't good and he's failing exams, even if he enters the League he can't be effective there. . . . To study diligently is the struggle-mission of the League." *Xiaobing* [Little Soldier, a Canton Red Guard newspaper], September 11, 1967. Also see Tao Zhu's remarks as quoted in the November 9, 1967, issue of the same newspaper.

16. As one example, such children reportedly were told, "You are the children of old revolutionaries; therefore you are the best proletarian successors [i.e. future leaders]." *Jiaoxue Pipan* [Pedagogical Critique], August 20, 1967, in English in *Chinese Society and Anthropology*, vol. 2, no. 1–2 (Fall/Winter, 1969–70), p. 35. The article is a criticism of Canton's army-run August 1st School.

17. Interview by Anita Chan.

18. One such group of "activist" bad-class youths later started their own Red Guard group in Peking and put out a newsletter defensively asserting their political devotion:

> Thanks to the sarcastic taunting of . . . writers and the ceaseless prompting of those comrades of "good intention" in past years, youths of bad family background are always on guard against their families, and the great majority [sic] of them want to draw the line between themselves and their families. They are often subconsciously opposed to what their fathers say. We should have faith in their ability to drag out their fathers when the latter sharpen their knives. We have faith in them because they have also been cultivated for 17 years by the Party like you. (*SCMP Suppl.* no. 183)

19. The predicament of these bad-class students is sensitively portrayed in David Raddock, *Political Behavior of Adolescents in China: The Cultural Revolution in Kwangchow* [Canton] (Tucson: University of Arizona Press, 1977). Almost every one of Raddock's interviewees was of distinctly bad-class background.

20. A Deputy Minister of Education explained to a meeting of teachers in 1962: "One can stress grasping redness for one period, and stress grasping expertise for another period: for different periods one can have different emphases." Quoted in *Jiaoxue Pipan* [Pedagogical Critique], August 20, 1967, translated in *Chinese Sociology and Anthropology*, vol. 2, no. 1–2 (Fall/Winter, 1969–70), p. 60.

21. *Zhongguo Qingnian Bao* [China Youth News], September 6, 1961, p. 1, in *URS*, vol. 25, p. 309.

22. From an interview transcript by Stanley Rosen.

23. *People's Daily*, January 31, 1965; in *SCMP* 3395.

24. In 1965 a large number of essays and readers' letters in *China Youth Monthly* reiterated this point. On this, see James Townshend, "Revolutionizing Chinese Youth: A Study of Chung-kuo Ching-nien (China Youth Monthly)," in A. Doak Barnett, ed., *Chinese Communist Politics in Action* (Seattle: University of Washington Press, 1969). In one very well publicized incident during this period Chen Yi and Zhou Enlai flew to Xinjiang to congratulate young people of bad-class origins who had dedicated themselves to reclaiming the western wastelands. In Chinese news reports of the event the Premier and Foreign Minister indicated that such youths did not entirely have to repudiate their parents to win political respectability. Zhou capped the visit by informing them and China, in words which became something of a national slogan, that "people born of families of the exploiting classes . . . should be judged by their behavior and stand. *A person cannot choose his family but he certainly can choose his own future.*" (*Zhongguo Qingnian Bao*, August 10, 1965, in *SCMP* 3523.)

25. *The Diary of Wang Chieh* (Peking: Foreign Language Press, 1967). For Wang Jie's comments on his class background see especially p. 59 and pp. 81–82.

26. This sales figure is given in "A Young Fighter, Wang Chieh," *China Reconstructs*, May 1966, pp. 10–13.

CHAPTER SIX. THE CULTURAL REVOLUTION

1. The May 16th directive is translated in *Current Background* (U.S. Govt.), no. 852, May 6, 1968.

2. *Nanfang Ribao,* June 19, 1966; also on Canton Radio, in *NCPRS,* June 19, 1966, and *FBIS,* June 22, 1966, p. DDD 3.

3. *Renmin Ribao* editorial, June 18, 1966; in *Peking Review,* June 24, 1966, p. 17. In the universities, Party administrators who were more "expert" than "red" or who in earlier years had handed over some of their own decision-making powers or shown too much kindness to the targeted professors began to come under attack during this period. For a fascinating piece on the downfall of the President of San Yatsen Medical School, the first major Party educator in Canton to be toppled, see Canton Radio, July 2, 1966, in *NCPRS,* pp. 36–40.

4. For the text of the petition see *Peking Review,* June 24, 1966.

5. From an interview transcript by Stanley Rosen.

6. *Renmin Ribao,* June 18, 1966.

7. The Guangdong proclamation declared "an abolition of the existing method of [entrance] examinations for senior high schools and the introduction of the method of recommendation and selection. . . . In this, it will be necessary to give prominence to proletarian politics and to implement the Party's class line, guaranteeing that priority go to the children of workers, poor- and lower-middle peasants, revolutionary cadres, revolutionary armymen and revolutionary martyrs, and the children of other laboring people." Canton Radio, July 7, 1966, in *NCPRS.*

8. More than a year later, in the autumn of 1967, good-class Loyalist Red Guard groups revived the issue in their tabloids, with the backing of the local Party and army authorities. The motives seem to have been three-fold: to move discussion back toward an issue on which Mao supported a stronger class line; to woo Rebel working-class students into the Loyalist fold by appealing to their earlier grievances against the "bourgeois" stress on academic coursework and entrance examinations; and to help quiet the attacks on Party organs by shifting the Cultural Revolution's ideological *raison d'etre* away from the struggle against "capitalist roaders." (On these 1967 Red Guard writings see, e.g., Hong Yung Lee, *The Politics of the Chinese Cultural Revolution* (Berkeley: University of California Press, 1978), pp. 306–8. For greater detail, see Stanley Rosen, *The Origin and Development of the Red Guard Movements* (Ph.D. diss., UCLA, 1979), chapter 7; forthcoming as a book.

9. References to the Monkey story were frequent and explicit in Red Guard big-character posters, as in the clichéd oath to use a "heaven-shattering golden cudgel" similar to the Monkey's to defeat Chairman Mao's enemies. *People's Daily* gave to its June 20, 1966, editorial in support of student posters the title "Revolutionary Big-Character Posters Are 'Magic Mirrors' that Show Up All Monsters," referring to the mirror which Monkey used to reveal the true faces of demons. (*Peking Review,* June 24, 1966, p. 23.)

10. The Peking order withdrawing the workteams is contained in *Current Background* no. 852, p. 8.

11. *Ibid.,* p. 11.

12. Interview by Anita Chan.

13. This pattern of the persecuted having ambivalent feelings and sometimes participating in their own persecution through these self-doubts is seen also in this quote from a capitalist-family respondent interviewed by Anita Chan: "They struggled against the bad-origin people, lined them up to be struggled against. There were no beatings but it was very fierce. In the junior-high sections there were beatings. Very solemn. Some even

admitted they were anti-Party, antisocialism. See how severe it was? The mental strain was acute."

14. In a similar fashion, Mao had de-emphasized "classes" and "class struggle" in his "Contradictions Among the People" speech of 1957. It was during a period when he hoped to launch a rectification campaign against the Party—and he would soon turn for this to the bourgeois intelligentsia in the Hundred Flowers movement of 1957. On this, see Richard Kraus, *The Evolving Concept of Class in Post-Liberation China* (Ph.D. diss., Columbia University, 1974), pp. 123–28; forthcoming as a book.

15. This speech by Lin Biao is quoted in the Red Guard newspaper *Wenge Tongxun* [Revolution Bulletin], no. 6, translated in *JPRS* 44574. An excellent discussion of the bloodline theory and of the radical leadership's rejection of it is Gordon White, *The Politics of Class and Class Origin: The Case of the Cultural Revolution*, Contemporary China Paper no. 9, Contemporary China Centre, Australian National University, 1976. See pp. 38–43.

16. This was reported in a wall poster sighted by a Japanese journalist. *The "Diary" of the Cultural Revolution* (Tokyo: Asahi Shimbun Books, 1967), p. 20. See also Tan Lifu's new "self-confession" on this in *People's Daily*, May 17, 1978, p. 3; also Peking Radio, May 21, 1978 (in *BBC-FE/5820/BII/2*).

17. A discussion and translation of the documents is Klaus Mehnert, *Peking and the New Left, At Home and Abroad*, Research Monograph no. 4 (Berkeley: Center for Chinese Studies, 1974).

18. Interview by Anita Chan.

19. Hong Yung Lee, *Politics*, pp. 312–22.

20. E.g., Tao Zhu, the Party Secretary of the South-Central Region Bureau, had joined the Cultural Revolution leadership in Peking and in the process had turned against the Guangdong provincial-level party. So too did the regional Party apparatus that he headed, and so accordingly in Canton's schools did some of the sons and daughters of that level of Party leadership.

21. Stanley Rosen has pointed out to me that often the formal Rebel leadership posts were given to Rebel members of red-class origins, while behind the scenes the actual decision-making powers remained in the hands of these leaders of middle-class origins.

22. As table 6.2 shows, the only partial exception to the bad-class youths' preference for the Rebels was provided by the students of Overseas Merchant background. Before the Cultural Revolution some of them had labeled themselves children of Overseas Chinese Laborers. During the periods of 1967 when both factions were in need of manpower the Loyalist Red Guards were willing to give them the benefit of the doubt.

23. This clearly seems to have been the case at a university in Yunnan and two universities in Peking, as revealed in interviews with two former university students and a former instructor. For a slight variation on this scenario at a third Peking university, see David and Nancy Milton, *The Wind Will Not Subside: Years in Revolutionary China, 1964–1969* (New York: Pantheon Books, 1976), p. 208. The struggles between the "careerist" students from "upper-class Fujian families" who were good at their studies versus "the less privileged, more politically conscious" students at Amoy University is described in B. Michael Frolic, *Mao's People* (Cambridge: Harvard University Press, 1980), pp. 71–79. My own interviews only detected class as a central issue at Canton's Jinan University, which was financed by overseas Chinese and which accommodated large numbers of their children. These overseas Chinese students rebelled in the Cultural Revolution against the suspect "*Overseas Merchant*" status with which they had been saddled.

24. In Peking, contrarily, the secondary school students were not allowed to participate

in the college students' factions; and since they remained divorced from the other social groupings the "class line" issue continued to occupy prominent attention in their debates and writings for a considerably longer period in the Cultural Revolution. (I am thankful to Stanley Rosen for this information.)

25. The interesting developments in the Red Guard movements of 1967 and 1968 are analyzed in Hong Yung Lee, *Politics*; Stanley Rosen (Ph.D. diss.); and Anita Chan, *Children of Mao: A Study of Politically Active Chinese Youths* (forthcoming book).

26. *Nanfang Ribao,* March 7, 1968; in *SCMP* 4144, p. 9.

27. Inasmuch as two years had passed since classes had been "temporarily" suspended at the Cultural Revolution's start, three years' worth of children would enter the first grade of primary school in the autumn of 1968. To make way for them, the 4th, 5th and 6th grades of Canton's pre-Cultural Revolution elementary schools were declared primary school graduates and transferred into the junior highs. In turn the secondary school students were almost all dubbed high school graduates, though some had had only a single year of junior high.

28. *Nanfang Ribao,* January 18, 1969, in *SCMP Suppl.* no. 246, p. 18; also Canton Radio, January 19, 1969, in *FBIS,* January 24, 1969, p. D12. They were joined by more than 17,000 unemployed "street youths." The figure of 108,000 Canton high school students in the 1965–66 school year comes from Canton Radio, *FBIS,* January 18, 1974, p. D6.

29. Canton Radio, December 10, 1969, cited in *China Topics* (U.K. Govt.), YB540, January 26, 1970, p. 7.

CHAPTER SEVEN. BACK TO SCHOOL, 1968–70

1. E.g., the newspapers after the Cultural Revolution frequently carried statements of the following kind: "To say that students can be more learned than workers and that the bourgeois technical experts are the teachers of the workers, and should therefore have a more important status than the workers and peasants, is to reverse the course of history" (*Renmin Ribao,* June 15, 1971). The press became filled with tales of semiliterate "red" workers devising simple machinery superior to the overly sophisticated ones which discredited technicians had proposed.

2. Mao's own disdain for abstruse learning was articulated clearly in the summer of 1968:

> I said that we should continue to run universities and mentioned the natural sciences and technical subjects, but I did not say that all the liberal arts disciplines should be closed down. However, if the liberal arts are unable to show anything worth mentioning they should be closed. As far as I can see, the basic courses in junior and senior high school and the last two years of primary school are about the same as those offered by universities. One should go to school for six years, at most ten years. The courses given in senior high school repeat those in junior high school, and those courses given in college repeat those given in senior high school. All basic courses are repetitious. As to specialized courses, even the teachers don't understand. (*Mao Zedong Sixiang Wansui,* 1969, p. 693; also in *JPRS* 61269, pp. 474–75)

3. This was repeatedly and explicitly stated. E.g., The great teacher Chairman Mao pointed out:

In all its works, the school should aim at transforming the student's ideology. Whether we should give first place to transforming the student's ideology or give first place to developing him intellectually . . . is a basic distinction between proletarian and bourgeois education. (Radio Heilongjiang, November 27, 1971, in *FBIS*, December 2, 1971, p. G1)

4. On this, see Donald Munro, *The Concept of Man in Contemporary China* (Ann Arbor: University of Michigan Press, 1977).

5. This terminology, which was used widely in the news media after the Cultural Revolution, more recently has been repudiated in the Chinese press as an error of the "Gang of Four." As the national newspaper *Guangming Ribao* (July 1, 1977, p. 2) has recalled critically: "Whoever wanted to do scientific technical work was given the label 'white expert.' Whoever was an expert necessarily became a 'bourgeois' 'reactionary authority.' In order to be a 'proletarian' one had to be an 'uncultured laborer.'" This latter phrase comes from a statement Zhang Chunqiao reputedly made: "I would rather have an uncultured [i.e., uneducated] worker than a cultural exploiter or spiritual aristocrat" (*Guangming Ribao*, December 12, 1976).

6. This wording is contained in Mao's May 7 directive of 1966.

7. The phrase *tiaotiao* suggests a straight line and thus in the bureaucratic context a chain-of-command.

8. Canton Radio, *NCPRS*, July 2, 1966, pp. 36–40.

9. This was part of a Zhou Enlai/Deng Xiaoping counterthrust in 1975 to shift the administrative framework back toward the "experts" in order to restore academic standards in the universities. When Deng Xiaoping was ousted the following year, the most persistent and cogently argued attack against him in the radical-controlled news media was that he had been trying to restore the "branch dictates" structure to China. These accusations against him most frequently referred to industry, where there had occurred the same shift of powers away from the "experts" into the hands of local "red" committees.

10. *China News Summary* no. 555 (U.K. Govt.), February 19, 1975, p. 1.

11. See, e.g., Franz Schurmann's analysis of the Great Leap's decentralization, in *Ideology and Organization in Communist China* (Berkeley: University of California Press, 1966), pp. 195–210. For a discussion of the earlier decentralization efforts in education see Donald Munro, "Egalitarian Ideal and Educational Fact in Communist China," in John Lindbeck, ed., *China: Management of a Revolutionary Society* (Seattle: University of Washington Press, 1971), especially pp. 264–69.

12. More than just in schools, Lin Biao and the PLA seem to have supported army involvement in the running of factories and other organs that were politically strategic, and for this the "area dictates" administrative schema was an almost perfect mechanism. The formula conveniently legitimized lateral shifts by military representatives into the Revolutionary Committees of civilian organs that were in the same geographic "area" as an army camp.

13. Quoted on Canton Radio, December 15, 1968, in *FBIS*, December 16, 1968, and *NCPRS*, December 16, 1968.

14. *Ibid.* Other interesting reports on the new factory-linked system are Canton Radio, in *FBIS*, April 21, 1969, p. D1, and in *FBIS* July 29, 1969, p. D3. Most informative of all is a piece in *Nanfang Ribao* of March 31, 1969 (also contained in *FBIS*, April 3, 1969, and *NCPRS*, March 31). This includes the following instructions:

There are four things to destroy and four to embrace, namely: Destroying the system of responsibility of the school principal pushed through by Liu Shaoqi and his agents, and embracing . . . the absolute leadership of the working class over the school; destroying the theory of the extinction of class struggle and embracing the viewpoint of never for a moment forgetting class struggle; destroying such absurd reactionary theories as "academic education first," "marks first," etc. and embracing the viewpoint of giving prominence to proletarian politics and taking the proletarian road of building the school politically; and destroying the theories of "studying for the sake of becoming officials" and "going to the countryside to acquire gold-plating," and embracing the idea of integrating with the workers and peasants.

15. E.g., the *Renmin Ribao* of March 24, 1969, ran a piece on such a worker-teacher in a Guangdong primary school who was heckled by the students until, according to the story's moral, she taught them why in the old society she and other workers had never attended school.

16. In 1974, for example, Shandong Radio (*FBIS*, March 25, 1974, p. C5) complained in a broadcast on the Worker Propaganda Teams that in recent years

an evil wind was whipped up to make the people think that the past was better than the present. Some regions, cities and counties have boldly cut their ties with school-run factories and farms and eliminated the system of tying schools to factories and production brigades. They did all this in the name of the consolidation of the educational order. As a result, some worker-teachers have been squeezed out of schools, schools have cut their ties with society, and other old educational systems calling for upholding the dignity of teachers and for giving first place to academic education have re-emerged, thus sidetracking the revolution in education.

17. *Guangzhou Zhongxue Hongdaihui* [Canton High School Red Guard Congress, a teachers' magazine], June 17, 1970, in *SCMP Suppl.* no. 276, p. 4.

18. E.g., see Canton Radio in *FBIS*, February 12, 1970, p. D1. Also *Guangming Ribao*, June 21, 1969 (in *SCMP* 4450, p. 7) and *Guangming Ribao*, November 11, 1970, p. 2.

19. This nomenclature and invitations to consider teachers suspect were common in the press and in statements by leaders up through the mid-1970s. The "Gang of Four" are now being pilloried in China as the villains responsible: "While making no specific analysis of intellectuals, the gang inserted the qualifier 'bourgeois' before intellectuals every time they were mentioned" (*Peking Review*, March 18, 1977, p. 19). But this phraseology was also Mao's, as in his famous May 7th statement that "The domination of our schools by bourgeois intellectuals can no longer continue."

20. E.g., an interviewee from the campus which had previously been the Guangdong Experimental School reports that almost a dozen of the former staff (out of perhaps 60–70 veteran teachers) remained locked up for some time in a couple of converted classrooms—including the former Experimental School's principal.

21. *Guangming Ribao*, April 23, 1969, in *SCMP* 4409, p. 6.

22. *Guangming Ribao*, October 14, 1969, in *SCMP* 4524, p. 1.

23. *Guangming Ribao*, December 12, 1971, p. 2.

24. *Guangzhou Zhongxue Hongdaihui*, no. 22, September 17, 1969; in *SCMP Suppl.* no. 260, p. 7.

25. *Ibid.*, p. 8. (This is a different essay in the same magazine.)

26. Political conditions in Fujian and Yunnan Provinces immediately after the Cultural Revolution obviously differed from Guangdong, since interviewees from those two prov-

inces report that the teachers and school leaders there had not felt it necessary to enact so strict a "class" policy. Consequently, even though their schools suffered from unruliness during 1968–70, there was not the same antagonism and tension as in Canton. Canton's strong class line clearly was making it all the more difficult to restore a semblance of order in its schools.

27. *Hong Qi* [Red Flag] (March 1969) reports: "These youngsters had a superiority complex before the great Cultural Revolution. Then after their parents got into trouble, they felt utterly disgraced and stayed aloof from the masses. Some even assumed a hostile attitude."

28. According not just to interviewees but also *Red Flag* magazine (April 1972), "some are blindly complacent, having a superiority complex and a lack of consciousness of [the need to] remold. Some are unwilling to lead a hard life, fearful of hardship and fatigue and particular about food and clothing, lacking in the courage to persist in tempering through practice" (*SCMM* no. 728). The article opined that the problems presented by the children of "a small number of cadres" could be summed up by two words: "arrogance" and "indulgence."

29. A different interviewee recalls, "On kids of good-class background the teachers used Thought work: reading together, persuasion, etc. For those of bad-class background, they just used scoldings, and if need be went to the kids' homes to tell the parents. No, they didn't go to protest at the homes of good-class kids: because they said such kids were 'easy to teach' [to be good], since they were *by nature* comparatively good." (My emphasis.)

30. E.g., in his widely circulated reading notes on a Soviet textbook, Mao had written: "The clever and bright often arise from people who occupy low position, are despised by others, have suffered indignities, and are young. There is no exception to this in a socialist society. According to the laws of the old society, the oppressed had a low culture, but they were more clever. There is some danger of this in the high-salaried stratum of socialist society. People in this stratum have more culture and wider knowledge, but compared with people in the low-salaried stratum they are more stupid. Precisely, the children of our cadres are different from those of non-cadres." (*Mao Zedong Sixiang Wansui*, in *JPRS* 61269, p. 306.)

31. This visit is described in Jonathan Unger, "Canton's No. 61 is a Very Red Schoolhouse," *Christian Science Monitor*, March 18, 1972.

32. Canton Radio, in *FBIS*, October 14, 1968, p. D2. By 1972 the total enrollment had risen to 800,000 (*FBIS*, March 9, 1972, p. D9). Most of the increased burdens fell upon the secondary schools, since the primary schools had withdrawn since 1968–69 from handling 6 grades of pupils and were now coping only with 5 grades.

Canton's population, including two suburban counties, was reported as 3 million in *China Reconstructs* (November 1972), p. 11. Seven years earlier, Chinese officials were providing almost identical figures—3.1 million—of which the suburban peasant population was put at 1,020,000 (*Hong Kong Standard*, October 18, 1965). From this and other evidence it seems the days of urban population expansion had been brought to an end, partly due to the rustication-of-youth program.

33. In 1966, on the Cultural Revolution's eve, Canton's high schools—junior and senior combined—had contained 108,000 students. By 1973–74 the high schools were enrolling 210,000 students. (Canton Radio, *FBIS*, January 18, 1974, p. D6).

34. It was officially estimated in 1968 that a fifth of Peking's school and university faculty members and administrators were to be denied their jobs in the new school system. (*Beijing Ribao*, reported by Agence France Presse, February 1, 1968.)

35. Canton Radio, in *FBIS*, September 12, 1972, p. D7. This seems to have been the policy nationally. *Renmin Ribao* (January 3, 1974, p. 1) was able to proclaim proudly that four times as many high school teachers and 2.6 times as many primary school teachers were Party members than before the Cultural Revolution. Since this was not due to large recent intakes of teachers into the elite Party, it meant instead that very large numbers of Party members had been brought in to *become* teachers.

36. Eg., *Guangming Ribao*, July 8, 1977, p. 2. This article is on a secondary school in one of Guangdong's smaller cities, where the younger teachers are said to be learning humbly from their seniors, in order to become "red and expert."

37. Canton proudly devoted a fair number of radio reports and news items to extolling the branch school system's virtues. Some of the more informative pieces are found in: *SCMP Suppl.* no. 268 (February 1970), pp. 33–38; *Guangming Ribao*, September 2, 1970, p. 3; *FBIS*, September 10, 1970, p. D5; *Zhongguo Xinwen*, September 18, 1970; *SCMP* no. 4758 (October 1970), pp. 227–29; Rewi Alley, "In and Around Canton in November 1970," *Eastern Horizon*, 1971, pp. 18–20; *FBIS*, January 31, 1974, p. C5 (on Fuzhou's efforts to emulate Canton's branch school system); *FBIS*, July 25, 1974, p. H6; *FBIS*, January 24, 1975, p. H5. At least some of Canton's schools had run into difficulties managing these schools, since the radio report of mid-1974 mentions a total of only 74 branch schools; five had apparently folded. See *Bei Dou* (Hong Kong), no. 8 (January 1978), pp. 32–36, for a former student's unhappy account of life at a branch school.

38. As an alternative to this rotation, some Canton schools also took over commune high school campuses in the districts surrounding Canton. Analogous to the ancient Greek cities that sent out their surplus population to settle new cities, an overcrowded Canton high school would establish a new school for its own young people in the rural commune premises. As one example, the No. 29 High School of Canton, which had become desperately overcrowded but had no room to expand at its urban base, founded Canton's No. 87 High School in one of these rural school buildings. No. 87 thereafter enrolled half of No. 29's graduating junior-high classes each year, providing them with two solid years of senior-high schooling at the rural facilities. The rural commune had been willing to give up its school buildings and grounds since the city in exchange assumed the financial burden of educating for free a hundred of the local peasant young people alongside the urban newcomers. But interestingly, the peasantry refused to permit the urban students even at these schools to go outside the school yard to interact with the local villages. The Maoist notion of having China's urban youths mingle with the "poor and lower-middle peasants" to imbibe their proletarian virtues was defeated by the peasantry's own distaste for the idea of having all those boistrous city teenagers around.

These new rural schools did, however, hold a signal advantage over their urban counterparts. Their students were in an environment continuously controlled by the school itself, uninfluenced by the social malaise or after-school street gangs of the city. Of all the secondary schools in my interview sample, by far the most orderly—and the one best able to shape its students' attitudes in the desired directions—was this boarding school in the countryside.

39. Canton Radio, July 29, 1978, in *BBC-SWB*, August 5, 1978 (FE/5883/B11/7).

40. *Renmin Ribao* [People's Daily] (March 7, 1969) carried a piece from Canton on a school which had devised its *own* textbook materials, despite the fears of some of its teachers that the academic coursework might be seen as a revisionist "restoration of the old." The school had prepared these sets of new teaching materials, the newspaper explained, due to complaints that its students were spending all their time doing labor, with

few lessons conducted even in the factories or fields. *Renmin Ribao* suggested to other schools that they follow the lead of the school in question, Canton's No. 61. But the newspaper neglected to inform readers that No. 61 was the new title for Attached High, formerly the most prestigious school in south China. Some of its teachers before the Cultural Revolution had helped prepare Guangdong's provincial texts. The teachers of most other schools would not possess the skills or courage to try similar compilations of materials, and the middle levels of the bureaucracy were still too cowed and disorganized to provide adequate materials for them.

41. *Guangzhou Zhongxue Hongdaihui*, September 17, 1969; in *SCMP Suppl.* no. 260, p. 17.

CHAPTER EIGHT. DOWN TO THE COUNTRYSIDE

1. Two secondary sources which discuss the problems faced by rusticating youths are Thomas Bernstein, "Urban Youths in the Countryside: Problems of Adaptation and Remedies," *China Quarterly*, no. 69 (March 1977); and Bernstein's *Up to the Mountains and Down to the Countryside* (New Haven: Yale University Press, 1977).

2. *Renmin Ribao* [People's Daily], December 23, 1968, p. 1.

3. Ironically, sending a superabundance of educated urban youths to the villages adversely affected the peasants' desires to see their own children educated. In a village portrayed in the national press, "after criticizing and repudiating the theory 'to study to become an official,' very few school-aged children, especially girls, were sent to school. . . . Some people said, 'Since even our university graduates have to work with picks, what can our children do after going to school?'" *Hong Qi* [Red Flag] (July 1970). In a second village, "the guardians of some students said: 'Even students in the cities have to come to the countryside, so it's useless to send our children to school.' Some also said: 'It'll do for our children to be able to read a few characters having something to do with the crops we're raising'. . . . Influenced by their families and society, some students also held this view: 'Since schooling offers us no future prospects, it's better for us to stay home and earn more work-points by laboring so that we can buy a new suit after the autumn harvest'." *People's Daily*, July 5, 1969, in *SCMP* 4457, p. 9.

4. By regulation, this settlement grant of Y230 was supposed to be spent in the following fashion: housing, Y100; 8 months' living expenses, Y80; farm tools, Y50. If a young person volunteered to settle in a village where he or she already had relatives the state's grant was lower—at Y180.

5. *China News Summary*, no. 594 (U.K. Govt.), December 10, 1975, p. 3.

6. Lin Biao, interestingly, already allegedly had plans to muster support in his sharpening conflict with Mao by proclaiming his own opposition to rustication. Lin reportedly intended to hoist the slogan "rustication is labor reform in disguise." His slogan had a twin appeal. It would play upon parents' concerns about the hardships of rural labor and upon the rusticated youths' resentments about the suspect status they had been given by Mao's injunction that they be "reeducated." (The slogan allegedly was proposed in a conspiratorial "571 Document," which the Party circulated widely in China after Lin Biao's death as proof of his treachery. The slogan was thereafter attributed to Lin in numerous broadcasts: e.g., Henan Radio, in *FBIS*, March 21, 1974, p. D1, and Hunan Radio, in *FBIS*, May 15, 1975, p. H2.)

7. This information comes from interviews; but see, e.g., Canton Radio, in *FBIS*, January 11, 1972, p. D5, for a Guangdong conference's summary of these nine new measures. A slightly different listing of the contents of this directive appears in *Zhonggong Yanjiu* (Taiwan) (November 1970), p. 25.

8. Wherever rusticated youths comprised a sixth or more of a production team's adult population, at least one sent-down youth was to sit on the team's leadership committee.

9. In 1978 a government spokesman announced that 900,000 (i.e., only 5 percent) of the 17 million rusticants have "married and settled permanently in the countryside" (*FBIS*, December 15, 1978, p. E5). This percentage is extremely low considering that all of the sent-down youths were of marriageable age and may have been in the countryside for up to a decade.

10. Canton Radio, in *FBIS*, August 8, 1975, pp. H4–H5. Hainan Radio reports a similar rate of return for the youngsters sent to work on Hainan Island (*FBIS*, August 21, 1975). In Jilin Province, fully a third of the youths who were rusticated after the Cultural Revolution had been able to leave one way or another by 1975. (Jilin Radio, in BBC-FE/4803/BII/11, January 14, 1975, p. 14.) Nationally, a third of the rusticants were legally back in the cities by mid-1977. (Suzanne Pepper, "An Interview on Changes in Chinese Education After the 'Gang of Four,'" *China Quarterly* [December 1977], p. 823.)

11. From an interview transcript by Edwin Lee, to whom I am thankful.

12. The information on this episode comes from several interviewees, including a university professor still in China. Similar reports appear in Joseph Lelyveld, "The Great Leap Farmward," *New York Times Magazine*, July 28, 1974; Thomas Bernstein, *Up to the Mountains and Down to the Countryside*, p. 82; and "Chairman Mao's Letter to Li," in B. Michael Frolic, *Mao's People* (Cambridge: Harvard University Press, 1980), pp. 43–48. The schoolteacher, named Li Qinglin, subsequently was promoted to become vice group leader of a county Revolutionary Committee Education Group and concurrently vice group leader of Fujian's provincial university recruitment program. In 1975 he was a representative to the Fourth National People's Congress and a member of the Congress' Standing Committee. In 1977 he was denounced in the Chinese press for connections with the "Gang of Four."

13. The actual settlement fees became Y480, with a Y20 travel bonus appended.

14. In late December 1978, 50,000 young people who had been assigned to state farms in Yunnan Province reportedly staged a general strike to protest what their leaflets called intolerable working conditions, "cheating and oppression." *New York Times,* January 14, 1979, p. 12. Also *Beijing Review*, no. 12, March 23, 1979, p. 4.

15. It is not clear how the schools determined which of its graduates on this urban list went to different particular urban postings. My interview data suggest that from 1971 onward neither the class line nor classroom behavior played any major part in this. E.g., poorly behaved non-red-class youngsters seem as often as other classmates to have been assigned to the desirable types of factories. The only major exception was that only good-class students could be assigned to factories which had anything to do with armaments.

16. Some impoverished parents of working-class background were even able to persuade schools to let their children secure an urban job directly after junior high, rather than continue with all of their classmates into a senior high school. In such cases, permission to drop out from school was seen as a class-line favor!

17. This information comes from interviews.

18. Interestingly, the pace of the rustication program seems to have been greatest in the most industrialized and richest provinces; Shanghai sent well in excess of a million. (*FBIS*, March 21, 1974, p. C8). A record kept of different provinces suggests that the poorer

inland provinces of the country sent a much smaller proportion of their urban populations. It seems industrialization was being pushed hardest by the government in the hinterlands. The coastal cities paid the cost in slower development and the loss of half of their younger generation; and the discontent and social unrest of the great cities in the 1970s—Shanghai, Peking, Tianjin, Canton—probably in consequence ran deeper than elsewhere.

19. A teacher at a factory-run secondary school in Yunnan Province recalls that parents tried therefore to gauge the upcoming year's local manpower needs. His own school had a policy of retaining youngsters a grade if they had been absent due to ill health, or skipped them a grade if the parents had sufficient influence at the factory. Parents played the game to the hilt, keeping their child "ill" at home or skipping the child forward a year in the hopes of getting the student graduated in a year when factory jobs were plentiful. The teachers joked that the school was being used as an employment agency.

20. E.g., Canton Radio, in *FBIS*, August 13, 1974, p. H3. By the end of 1974, 40,000 cadres in China had been sent to "work together" with and lead the rusticating youths. *FBIS*, January 21, 1975, pp. E1-E2.

21. About 100,000 from Guangdong had gone prior to the Cultural Revolution. They were joined in 1968–69 by an additional 300,000. (Canton Radio, December 10, 1969, cited in *China Topics* (U.K. Govt.), YB540, January 26, 1970, p. 7). Guangdong's policy of sending these urban youths back to the cities seems to have been applied with considerable rigidity. The sister of an interviewee had been trained before the Cultural Revolution to be a veterinarian, and she wished to continue in the countryside with her animal doctoring; but she was ordered back to the city in the summer of 1975 and assigned to work in Canton's construction industry. The only young people in the villages from the 1968–69 cohort who do not seem to have been sent home quickly were those who had misbehaved in the countryside (retained for a while as a punishment and warning to new rusticants, apparently), some of the barefoot doctors and village teachers, and some of those who had married.

22. As of mid-1979, 90,000 young people were growing rubber at ninety state farms on Hainan Island. In an indirect suggestion that they would be there for a long time to come, a radio report noted that "many" of them had decided to marry (*FBIS*, May 2, 1979, p. P4).

23. Information from interviews. In 1978 an American reporter was told by officials at a Guangdong commune that the young people came by rotation for about two years (*New York Times*, December 5, 1978, p. 2).

24. Canton Radio, in *FBIS*, January 8, 1975, p. H6. The figures for Guangdong province are 560,000 from 1968 through mid-1975 (Canton Radio, *FBIS*, May 9, 1975, p. H11), of whom 300,000 were pre-Cultural Revolution high school students who had gone down in 1968–69. By the end of 1975, the figures province-wide had jumped 140,000 to 700,000 (Canton Radio, December 25, 1975; in BBC-FE/5095/B11/8).

25. Canton Radio, in *FBIS*, June 12, 1975, p. H3; also Canton Radio, August 16, 1975, in BBC-FE/4996/B11/8.

26. An interviewee from an inland province where industrialization was rapid enough to absorb practically all of the new urban generation reports that his city's youths consistently felt when they went down to the countryside that they would be able to return to an urban life after three or four years. He attests that the rustication program there worked smoothly all along, and that high school graduates often went in high spirits.

27. *Zhongguo Qingnian Bao* [*China Youth News*], November 23, 1978, in *FBIS*, December 11, 1978, pp. E16–19.

28. *FBIS*, December 15, 1978, p. E4.

29. *Beijing Review,* November 23, 1979, p. 7. The figure cited is six million, but this apparently does not include the young people settled on state farms.

30. *Ibid.*

31. A government survey of Canton and nine other major cities showed that industrial employees as a percentage of the total urban employed had risen from 44 percent in 1957 to 56 percent in 1977, while employees in commerce and service trades (as a percentage of the urban employed) dropped by a third from 14.5 percent to 9.5 percent. *Beijing Review,* August 3, 1979, p. 3.

32. *Beijing Review,* October 19, 1979, p. 5; also see *China Reconstructs,* November 1979, pp. 21–23 and *Beijing Review,* February 11, 1980, pp. 13–21. In Guangdong, 400,000 urban jobs were opened up in 1979 and most were of these types. *Nanfang Ribao,* January 3, 1980, p. 1.

33. The effects of the declining birth rate should be felt in the job market by the mid-1980s. E.g., in Shanghai in mid-1979, the junior high school graduating class had 57 percent more pupils than Shanghai's graduating primary school class, composed of children three years younger. Continuing this demographic trend, in Canton 2,500 fewer 7-year-olds entered the first grade in 1980 than in the previous year, 1979. For Canton's figures, see *Nanfang Ribao,* Sept. 19, 1980, p. 1; for Shanghai, see Suzanne Pepper, "Chinese Education after Mao," *China Quarterly,* no. 81 (March 1980), p. 7.

CHAPTER NINE. TROUBLED SCHOOLS, 1970–76

1. As a second example, an interviewee who was the older brother of a student observes:

When my little brother graduated in 1973 he knew very little. When I scolded him for not having studied more, he retorted that studying was essentially useless, and so he hadn't. He kept saying that no matter what he did in his studies, his future was already determined. No, my brother didn't resent that fact, but just accepted it as the way the world is. [The boy was in line for an urban job.] When I used to tease him on his ignorance, he would tease me right back: 'You studied so much and know so much, and all you are today is a peasant tilling the soil!' [Laughs] I guess he got the best of the argument.

2. Russian schools in the 1920s ran into many similar problems in their links with factories. On this see Martin K. Whyte's illuminating "Educational Reform: China in the 1970s and Russia in the 1920s," *Comparative Education Review,* vol. 18, no. 1 (February 1974), pp. 112–28.

3. *Da Gong Bao,* November 15, 1970, p. 2.

4. *Guangming Ribao,* October 6, 1972; *Hong Qi,* no. 9, 1972. There had also been a debate three years earlier on whether science courses or the Industrial/Agricultural courses provided a better format, and both sides were represented in the *People's Daily* of September 22, 1969 (in *SCMP* 4510).

5. *Mao Zedong Sixiang Wansui;* p. 477 of the English-language *JPRS* translation. This was during a talk with Peking University Red Guard leaders. Mao observed, "It's good to know English. I studied foreign languages late in my life. I suffered. One has to learn foreign languages when one is young. . . . One cannot study geology without a foreign language. It's good to learn English. Foreign language study should be started in primary school."

6. Shanghai, home of the two Party leaders most influential in education (Yao Wenyuan and Zhang Chunqiao), had followed the logic of the post-Cultural Revolution reforms and had eliminated English from the city's schools. But with the Nixon visit, even Shanghai reestablished English as part of the core curriculum. A Shanghai high-school teacher recollects: "Up till then, many English teachers were down in the countryside working. When in 1971 it was decided to have English courses again, they had to be recalled."

7. On the reason for beginning the language instruction so young, see the comment by Mao Zedong in footnote 5.

8. A second high school English teacher, from a rural Guangdong senior high school, comments: "The kids didn't want to study English, because it's difficult. The real reason is that there's no use for it. One student said to me, 'I have no chance to meet foreigners, so why must I study English?' Another said to me sarcastically, 'Shall I use my English to discuss things with my mom and dad?' Such an outlook is part of the current thinking among students that you should only study for its utility, and for the present time, and not for the distant future."

9. An interviewee from Fujian reports, coincidentally, precisely the same phenomenon: a large hospital was near his school, and only the children of ranking doctors wanted to learn English—for pragmatic reasons. (Interestingly, though, learning English through radio courses became very popular as an after-work hobby among the *older* youths who had last been in school prior to the Cultural Revolution.)

10. E.g., this new turn of events can be seen clearly in a 1974 graduate's classroom where, to ameliorate the crush of students at the school, after junior high 2 the best 20 percent of the students in terms of behavior and academic work had been skipped a grade and placed together in a special senior high 1 class rather than going on to junior high 3 with the rest of their schoolmates. Three-quarters of this new special class were from revolutionary-cadre families! The interviewee himself had been one of the few middle-class students who had been sufficiently conscientious in his studies to be admitted to the class.

11. This information comes from interviews. But the official Chinese media more recently has reported the same earlier problems: ". . . the two different concepts of academic education on the one hand and 'giving first place to intellectual development' on the other were blurred, making it possible for them to label whomever they wanted as advocates of the latter concept. Consequently, all teachers who taught classes conscientiously, students who studied seriously, and people who frequented libraries were so labeled" (*Guangming Ribao*, December 12, 1976, p. 2). It should be noted that even in the above article it was considered morally/politically improper to advocate openly that "intellectual development" should be the primary purpose of a school system. The traditional/Maoist notions of education's rightful "moral" purpose still officially survived.

12. It should be observed that the various teachers quoted here on post Cultural Revolution education are not opponents of the government but legal emigrants who for the most part remained loyal to the principles of socialism. This particular citation is from a young man from Hong Kong whose parents prior to the Cultural Revolution had sent him to a university in China "for a socialist education." He had voluntarily remained in China after the Cultural Revolution and returned to Hong Kong in 1974 at his parents' request.

13. For this reason, secondary school teachers tried to get out of having to teach the Chinese language-and-literature (*yuwen*) course, since this was the discipline most closely related to "politics." A former teacher of English observes that "Teachers of Chinese language could easily become the targets of attack. You had to speak on political issues, and it was always possible to commit some error by differing slightly with the prevailing line

in what you said. Mature and educated people would be more understanding of such a situation and wouldn't criticize petty deviations. But students even by the fifth year of primary school were already sometimes becoming "active" and those in junior and senior high were the most dangerous, especially when they faced having to go imminently to the countryside. And that same poor group of Chinese language teachers also serve as the class masters and are the ones who have to mobilize them to go. If a teacher knows even a little English he'll want to teach that. It's safest, because the students know nothing of English, and that protects you from any sort of criticism."

14. In 1972, when rehabilitated leaders under Zhou Enlai were trying to start a drive to improve educational standards, Peking's *Guangming Ribao* (November 19, 1972, p. 2) carried the following report from an urban secondary school: "A Chinese language teacher [at the school] once selected two articles from the students' compositions for analysis. The first article was noted for its clarity in ideas, streamlined structure, and simple language, while the other had nothing but an empty argument presented in the form of a random collection of slogans without a central view. By bringing up these two articles, the teacher at first wanted the students to follow the good example of the first article. But in the classroom debate, some students acclaimed the second article. Fearful of committing the mistake of disparaging politics, the teacher abandoned his standard in judging compositions and concluded that "both articles are good."'

15. These appear in English in *SCMP* 5539. The Huang Shuai episode is described at length in *China Reconstructs* (August 1974), pp. 2–5.

16. *Renmin Ribao*, February 11, 1974, p. 1. Only short excerpts from the three cadres' letter were published.

17. A radio report from the following month suggests the disquiet among teachers aroused by the media campaign: "The idea of 'absolute authority of a teacher' having been criticized, a situation has evolved in which some teachers do not concern themselves with things emerging from among the students that are incompatible with Mao Zedong Thought. Taking an evasive attitude, they try to transfer from one unit to another. In doing the classroom work, some teachers are not resolute in supporting what is correct and in resisting and criticizing what is wrong. They just want to push responsibility onto student officers so that they themselves will not be held responsible. . . . Some teachers act according to the doctrine of the mean with regard to problems among students because they fear that students may rise up to rebel against them and criticize them for controlling, restricting, and repressing the students. They also fear that they may once again make mistakes involving the ideas of 'absolute authority of a teacher' and get themselves into trouble. They fear this and that. In a word, they fear that revolutionary action will be taken with regard to their bourgeois world outlook." (!) Henan Radio, March 10, 1974; in *FBIS*, March 14, 1974, p. D1.)

18. *Renmin Ribao* [Peoples' Daily], April 12, 1974, p. 1. The girl's initial letter of complaint also makes for interesting reading (*Liaoning Daily*, February 14, 1974, in *FBIS*, February 19, 1974, p. G2). A talk on Peking Radio by a Little Red Soldier pursued a similar militant stance: "Not long ago I realized that some teachers were not working according to Mao Zedong Thought, but were preaching 'teachers' dignity.' I bravely criticized them. I think we must use Mao Zedong Thought as a yardstick in measuring everything and should not follow our teachers blindly. When our teachers are wrong, we should dare to criticize them, because this is mutual help. As long as we [word indistinct], we will not fear other people's sarcastic remarks and attacks, or any bad marks our teachers give us when we graduate. We Little Red Soldiers must dare to fight. We must never let such revisionist ideas

as "intellectual education first" and "teachers' dignity" bind us. We will never be tame little lambs" (FBIS, March 8, 1974, p. B8). Other interesting broadsides appear in Renmin Ribao, October 19, 1973, p. 2; in FBIS, February 18, 1974, p. C4; and FBIS, January 18, 1974, p. D3.

19. Renmin Ribao, January 19, 1974, p. 2.

20. On this, see Peking Review, July 1, 1977, pp. 15–17; see also FBIS, March 7, 1977, pp. 14–17.

21. On this school, see chapter seven's footnote 38.

22. For example, Zhang Chunqiao was later accused of saying that Mao and the Party "had not solved the question of the changes in class relationships in the socialist period. . . . I've read through Chairman Mao's four volumes and I still don't understand the status of the different classes today" (China Reconstructs, November 1977, p. 3).

23. The dimensions of the problems and the difficulty of finding adequate solutions is admitted in a 1977 report on a conference of school teachers. A central passage reads: "These past several years . . . the regulations in school have become lax, and regardless of whether there has been any academic education, not a few students lack revolutionary idealism. Their concept of communist morality is weak, and the proportion of politically backward students has increased. Some students are influenced by the corruption of bourgeois thinking and have undesirable habits. The work of changing the political thought of these backward students will be an overriding problem for the classmasters these next several years" (Renmin Ribao, July 12, 1977, p. 1).

The radical faction similarly published acknowledgments of the problems. E.g., Shanghai's Liberation Daily (August 26, 1975) noted that the schools had "repeatedly issued notices and orders banning students from damaging public property," but this method "did not produce any results." A Shanghai broadcast of the previous day (quoted in Current Scene [October 1975], p. 16) had taken the position that such problems were unavoidable—that as long as class struggle exists, "quiet in the classroom and peace after school are impossible."

24. Peking Radio, April 7, 1979, in FBIS, April 19, 1979, p. R2.

25. Severe continued rowdiness was reported even in some of Peking's primary schools (Guangming Ribao, February 23, 1979).

26. Ming Bao, December 7, 1979, p. 1.

27. Fox Butterfield, "Peking is Troubled about Youth Crimes," New York Times, March 11, 1979.

CHAPTER TEN. THE FIGHT OVER HIGHER EDUCATION

1. H. H. Gerth and C. Wright Mills, eds., From Max Weber (New York: Oxford University Press, 1946), pp. 241–42.

2. Peking Radio, in FBIS, September 26, 1968, p. B5.

3. Alex Inkeles and Raymond Bauer, The Soviet Citizen (Cambridge, Mass.: Harvard University Press, 1961), p. 100; Nigel Grant, Soviet Education (Baltimore and London: Penguin Books, 1964), pp. 98–102.

4. The number of prior years of schooling remained the same. Under the pre-Cultural Revolution system, the junior high graduates who entered these vocational programs had had 9 years of education, and under the new system the senior high graduates had 9–10 years.

5. Nationwide, only a very small minority of China's 1,200 specialist and technical schools had reopened after the Cultural Revolution, according to *Guangming Ribao*, July 5, 1979, p. 4.

6. A campaign was mounted in mid-May 1975 to promote these "July 21st universities." Since factories simply had to alter the titles of their training courses, the campaign was able to report immediate and sweeping successes. Canton's July 21st universities jumped from twenty-one in May 1975 to over a hundred less than two months later (Canton Radio, in *FBIS*, May 27, 1975, p. H5; also Peking Radio, July 21, 1975). By December 1975 Canton claimed 155 (BBC-FE/5096/B11/8).

7. On this system in Guangdong see Alexander Casella: "Recent Developments in China's Recruitment System," *China Quarterly*, no. 62 (June 1975), pp. 300–1; also Canton Radio, in *FBIS*, July 10, 1974.

8. The enrollment team at the county capital allocated the quota among each of the county's communes: say, a large commune would get one university placement each year, a smaller commune once every two or three years. When offered an opening, the commune leadership selected a few applicants from among the candidates proposed by each brigade (that is, village) and passed its own choices up to the enrollment team at the county seat for the final decision. In Guangdong, for the first couple of years the commune level political leaders had largely determined the successful nominee, but some of the choices proved so obviously unfit for even the simplest university courses that this final process of vetting at the county seat soon became a point the universities insisted upon.

9. From the tour notes of Gordon White, in F. C. Teiwes: "Before and After the Cultural Revolution," *China Quarterly*, no. 54 (April 1974), p. 342. A new terminology soon arose to place such figures in a cosmetically favorable light; the enrollees were almost always labelled "worker-peasant-soldier students." For Wuhan University the published rural recruitment figures would simply have related that there were 38 percent "peasant students." This new tactic for categorizing university enrollments nicely disguised the elite origins of so many of the students. Most foreign writers on Chinese education were fooled by the trick.

10. In Canton, as of 1973, this quota of "young people who can be [politically] educated [to 'draw the line']" was set at 5 percent of university recruitments, so as to demonstrate to middle- and bad-background youths that it was possible to succeed if "activist." (A report from a Hungarian correspondent in China, translated into English in *JPRS* 58767, April 17, 1973.)

11. On this, see Appendix B.

12. This policy of recruiting technical and engineering students almost entirely from the factories elicited some published complaints that rusticated youths and peasants were being slighted. E.g., *People's Daily*, March 4, 1972, in *Chinese Education*, vol. 6, No. 2 (Summer 1973), pp. 20–21.

13. In Guangdong (unlike many other provinces) the universities did not make it a rule that the students who had been enrolled from factories would necessarily be returned to the units which sent them (Canton Radio, in *FBIS*, August 31, 1976, pp. H12, H14). Well over three-quarters of Guangdong's college graduates (including, of course, those from the countryside) found themselves assigned to entirely new postings by the national and provincial departments connected with their disciplines.

14. At Peking University the Revolutionary Committee was at first dominated by PLA men, and a majority of the first enrollments in 1970 had been composed of young soldiers. A minority of these were the children of high-level officers, but most apparently were army

recruits of peasant stock. With Lin Biao's fall, influence at the university shifted. In 1971 the intake was primarily of rusticated youths, and by far the greatest part of these were the children of Party officials. (Michael Sherington, "Which Door to Peking University?," *China Now* [January 1974]. Sherington was a teacher at Peking University.)

The means by which the Party officials in Peking could get their children into Peking University was as follows. The national universities sent out their own recruiting teams. Each selected a set of scattered counties and cities from which to enroll students; one national school might recruit from counties A, B, and C, while another national school concentrated on counties D, E, and F. These various teams went primarily to counties in Hebei, Inner Mongolia, and Heilongjiang, the very same provinces where most of Peking's rusticants had been sent. The universities in Shanghai similarly sent enrollment teams several thousands of miles to Xinjiang, so as to retrieve rusticated Shanghai youths.

In 1974–75, in the wake of an "anti-backdoor" campaign, the numbers of cadre children recruited through this means declined. But the 1971–75 figures for Peking's No. 1 Foreign Languages Institute suggest the overall results of the recruitment procedures:

Worker/poor-and-lower-middle peasant (including parents who are post-1949 Party officials or members)	63%
"Revolutionary cadres" (pre-1949 Party Officials)	25.5%
Middle-class	11.5%
Bad-class	0%
	(N = 2,024)

(David Crook, "Who Goes to College Now?," *Eastern Horizon* 15, no. 3 [1976], p. 12; the same article appears in *China Now* [July-August 1976]. Crook was a teacher there at the time.)

15. *Renmin Ribao*, January 28, 1974, p. 1. An interesting self-criticism was made by Zhong Zhimin's parents the following month, in which the father sounded peculiarly like an old-fashioned gentleman: "I thought that by making arrangements to get my children into universities I would give them a better chance in life to make a name for themselves and to enter into good marriages" (*FBIS*, February 27, 1974, p. C7).

16. The diverse reports on these young people reveal in some detail how informal channels operate among officials. Some of the most interesting of these "exposés" are contained in *FBIS*, February 11, 1974, pp. D2–4; *FBIS*, February 15, 1974, C11; *FBIS*, February 19, 1974, p. C7 and p. F3; *FBIS*, February 27, pp. H1–3; and *FBIS*, February 28, p. C1 and pp. C3–4. See also *Current Scene* 12, no. 3 (1974), pp. 22–23.

17. Peking Radio, November 16, 1976, in *FBIS*, November 22, 1976, p. E19. See also the *Peking Review* of April 15, 1977, p. 28, for a similar charge.

18. See footnote 47 below.

19. *Ming Bao*, January 14, 1976, citing *Guangming Ribao*.

20. A professor from the Foreign Ministry's No. 2 Foreign Language Institute (a majority of whose students those first several years were of urban-born "revolutionary cadre" origins) observed during an interview that "the way it was done in the first three years, the emphasis was put *only* on the political side and just about *nothing* was done to see if a student was intellectually capable or not. And that showed in the practical results. . . . When it came to writing Chinese, they were of course experts, because they had written posters. But when it came to arithmetic, geography, general knowledge, sometimes these students would be almost the level of primary school graduates."

21. Hainan Radio, August 15, 1972, in *FBIS*, August 23, 1972, p. D6.

22. *Ming Bao,* April 30, 1977. Also *Eastern Horizon* 16, no. 6 (June 1977). Note also *Da Gong Bao* (March 18, 1977), the Hong Kong Communist Party newspaper: "In 1973 the Party center, in the directive concerning the recruitment of university students, specified the necessity of exams. But the Gang of Four purposely created the Zhang Tiesheng incident to oppose this."

23. This charge of conspiracy was made in *Liaoning Daily,* November 30, 1976, cited in *Current Scene* (January 1977), p. 24.

24. After the fall of the "Gang of Four," China's national media published a photograph of a purported page of Zhang Tiesheng's exam paper, to show that he attempted the questions but could not answer any correctly. This photographed page of Liaoning's exam was rather easy, with problems that a primary-school graduate might have been expected to solve. One of the arithmetic problems:

> During military exercises a unit of the people's militia was directed by militia head-quarters to march 15 kilometers to a camping-site within two hours' time. What can be the militia unit's slowest speed (per hour) for it to arrive within this time? (*Ming Bao,* April 31, 1977, with a photo of the exam paper.)

25. This retreat frustrated secondary school teachers, many of whom had seen the renewed exams as an aid to restoring high-school educational standards and as a goal toward which their own teaching could be aimed. According to *Renmin Ribao:*

> In July last year the Tandong No. 6 High School [in Liaoning] first heard the news that exams were to be conducted for students enrolling for university. . . . Some teachers squeezed in time to help rusticated youths, who returned to the city to prepare, to catch up with their lessons. . . . Some teachers said delightedly: "If things go on in this way, there is some hope in teaching." It was at this juncture that the letter of Zhang Tiesheng was published. It immediately brought a strong response from the teachers. Some of them said: "This letter from Zhang Tiesheng is like a ladle of cold water. It has completely dampened our glowing enthusiasm for teaching." Some also said: "With the universities taking in such people as Zhang Tiesheng, what guarantee is there for quality? Can we still orbit a satellite in space?" . . . In the past few years, although very impressive achievements had been scored, there still lurked in the minds of the teachers the thought of "intellectual education comes first". . . . [A school leader] realized it was a fact that for 17 years after Liberation the bourgeoisie had exercised dictatorship over the proletariat on the educational front, and that the world view of the majority of the teachers was basically bourgeois. (!)

26. *Wen Hui Bao* (H.K.), November 19, 1973; this is an interview with one of the directors of Guangdong's college enrollment office.

27. *Guangming Ribao,* July 15, 1974, p. 3. The article, from a rural Guangdong county, notes:

> In 1973 we imposed a "general examination" on the candidates, which resulted in leading the young people astray. . . . This year, we abolished the "general examination," but a new form of struggle developed. Some said: "Let the masses of workers and peasants evaluate the political standards of the candidates. I am all for it. But the evaluation of their basic academic knowledge should still be done by persons with good education." To put it more plainly, what some persons were

saying was that the highest authority in admitting new students to institutes of higher learning should be held not by the great masses of workers and peasants, but by a small number of "educated" persons. To this, the workers and poor and lower-middle peasants sharply point out: "To evaluate the standards of college candidates separately is, in reality, to 'put intellectual education first' and to strangle the workers, peasants and soldiers with marks."

28. *Da Gong Bao,* November 16, 1973, p. 1; also *Wen Hui Bao* (H.K.), November 19, 1973. The Canton Medical School had quietly pioneered this approach the year before. See the visit to the school discussed in Robert McCormick, "Revolution in Education Committees," *China Quarterly,* no. 57 (January 1974), p. 136.

29. Some provinces alternatively adopted a three-month parole period, after which entrants who did "not meet enrollment stipulations" could be dropped from the rolls (e.g., Hubei Radio, in *FBIS,* June 29, 1973, p. D3).

30. *Peking Review,* November 11, 1977, p. 16.

31. *Ibid.*

32. *Peking Review,* September 3, 1971, p. 10; also told at Quinghua in 1975 to a foreign visitor whom I interviewed.

33. At Peking University, according to foreign students formerly there, during the three-year curriculum (later 3½ years) the labor included three months in the PLA, three on a factory production line, and three at the university farm.

34. As just one example, a visitor to Canton's universities in 1974 was told that classes had recently been suspended for ten days while students listened to broadcast denunciations of Lin Biao and Confucius. (William Shawcross, *Sunday Times of London,* April 21, 1974.) Similarly, at Shanghai's Foreign Language Institute the students in German studies "spent one week analyzing the counterrevolutionary two-faced tricks of swindlers like Liu Shaoqi [i.e., Chen Boda]. They afterwards realized that such swindlers have inherited the guise of old opportunists like Trotsky and conspired to stage a capitalist comeback" (Shanghai Radio, in *FBIS,* August 25, 1972, p. C3). With such crude ritualized political studies, such students probably left their university without much command of either German *or* politics.

35. *Guangming Ribao,* October 6, 1972, in *SCMP* 5238, p. 118. The author of this piece, Zhou Peiyuan, was one of China's foremost scientists, vice-chairman of Peking University's Revolutionary Committee and, perhaps most pertinently, well known to have been a close friend of Zhou Enlai. In this article, he pressed the case for students receiving a theoretical foundation in mathematics and the sciences. Within days he was obliquely attacked in Shanghai's *Wen Hui Bao,* the newspaper most closely associated with Zhang Chunqiao and Yao Wenyuan. *Wen Hui Bao* warned that anyone attempting to "reverse the verdicts" of the Cultural Revolution in education and science would inevitably pay for their efforts.

36. Canton Radio, in *FBIS,* February 9, 1976, p. H9. This complaint, shared by many in academics, had been voiced by Zhou Rongxin in October 1975.

37. *Guangming Ribao,* Dec. 6, 1972, pp. 1–2.

38. This was the strong impression of people I interviewed who had been factory personnel. More recently, as if to hammer home the point that university graduates were incompetent, in the autumn of 1977, after the "Gang of Four" had fallen, the Shanghai Scientific and Technical Group had all of the year's college graduates who already had been assigned to the city's technical and scientific departments take a special test. All the questions would relate to the "fundamental knowledge" contained in Shanghai's *high school* curriculum. The graduates were notified of the test in advance and given time off

from work to review their studies; 68 percent "failed" in math, 70 percent in physics, and 76 percent in chemistry. "Most astounding," according to *People's Daily* (October 23, 1977) "was that some people could not even answer one question on the basic knowledge of their own specialty. They could only hand in a blank script." Perhaps this is official hyperbole—but probably nearer the mark than the encomiums praising university education which had filled the Chinese press before Mao's death.

39. *Ming Bao,* September 1, 1977. A compilation of Zhou Rongxin's statements is contained in *Tel Quel* (Paris), no. 66 (1976), pp. 22–25.

40. Japanese reporters were told this officially at Qinghua in December 1975 (Kyodo Radio, in BBC-FE/5095/B11/1).

41. Roderick MacFarquhar was told this during a visit to Qinghua (*South China Morning Post,* Hong Kong, May 1, 1976).

42. *Ming Bao,* September 1, 1977.

43. *New China News Agency Weekly Release* (London), Issue 449, September 22, 1977, p. 11.

44. Two eyewitness reports by foreign university students studying in Peking are David Zweig, "The Peita Debate on Education and the Fall of Teng Hsiao-ping," *China Quarterly,* no. 73 (March 1978), pp. 140–45; and Alain Peyraube and Christine Sabean-Jouannet, "Boiter sur ses Deux Jambes: La Revolution de l'Enseignement en Chine," *Tel Quel,* no. 66 (1976), pp. 14–21. Two good secondary sources on these events are: D. I. Chambers, "The 1975- 76 Debate over Higher Education Policy in the People's Republic of China," *Comparative Education* 13, no. 1 (March 1977), pp. 3–12; and John Gardner, "Chou Jung-hsin and Chinese Education," *Current Scene* (November–December 1977).

45. *Hongweibing* (a Red Guard newspaper), December 22, 1966, p. 1; also *Dongfanghong Bao* [East is Red News], March 9, 1967, pp. 3–4, and *Dongfanghong Bao,* March 15, 1967, pp. 34. Also see Stanley Rosen, *The Origins and Development of the Red Guards* (Ph.D. diss., UCLA, 1979), chapter 3.

46. On January 6, 1976, little more than a day before Zhou Enlai's death, the front-page criticisms of the moderates' education proposals in *People's Daily* were by Zhang Tiesheng, the Liaoning youth who had handed in that famous "blank exam paper." Since then, Zhang had prospered politically from his examination score. A representative to the National People's Congress in 1975, he had been catapulted onto the Congress' Standing Committee. He now reportedly became a vocal participant in the campaign to overturn the new Education Minister. When Zhou Rongxin died in the campaign's aftermath, in April 1976, Zhang Tiesheng was alleged by Zhou's allies to have hounded the Minister to his death. In Hua Guofeng's first major address to the nation after the fall of the "Gang of Four," he denounced Zhang Tiesheng as the prime example of a "newly engendered counter-revolutionary." *Renmin Ribao,* December 28, 1976.

47. Deng Xiaoping was charged with having said, e.g., "Scientific and technical schools should be well run. You have to choose those students who are good in mathematics, physics, chemistry, and foreign languages. The children of cadres should not be given privileges. . . . We are in a crisis. The level of education is slowing down the realization of the four modernizations." Quoted in a report from Peking by Ross H. Munro, *The Christian Science Monitor,* March 30, 1976. The passage is from a talk by Deng of late September 1975, translated in full in Chi Hsing, *The Case of the Gang of Four* (Hong Kong: Cosmos Books, 1977), pp. 293–94.

48. The information on Yunnan comes from the reports of Western journalists who

visited the provincial capital, Kunming, in late April (*South China Morning Post*, Hong Kong, April 22, 1976, p. 1).

49. *People's Daily*, May 4, 1976, in *SPRCP*, no. 6096, p. 4. Also see *FBIS* May 6, 1976.

50. This was the impression obtained by several Hong Kong residents who visited relatives in Guangdong in 1975 and 1976 and who asked their relatives in my behalf about the education system.

51. Anita Chan, "Introduction," in Anita Chan and Jonathan Unger, editors, "The Case of Li Yizhe," *Chinese Law and Government* 10, no. 3 (Autumn 1977), pp. 1–112. Details of these intricate political maneuverings are described also in a serialized article, "Li Yizhe and I" (in Chinese), in *Bei Dou* (Hong Kong) in June, July, August, September, November, and December 1977 issues. For a more recent discussion, see *Dong Xiang* (Hong Kong), no. 5 (1979). Li Yizhe was the *nom de plume* of three former Rebels who put up a wall-poster in Canton in the autumn of 1974, largely condemning the Shanghai radicals but antagonistic as well to the more moderate Party bureaucrats. The poster became something of a *cause celebre* in south China. Readers of the Li Yizhe document will note with interest Li Yizhe's bitter comments on the 12-year-old Huang Shuai, on the exam-opponent Zhang Tiesheng, and on the cadre father of college drop-out Zhong Zhimin.

EPILOGUE: THE RETURN OF THE OLD ORDER, 1977–80

1. In Canton, for the 1978–79 school year, the following citywide entrance exams became mandatory:

Unified exams for entrance to junior high school	Unified exams for entrance to senior high school
Chinese	Chinese
Arithmetic	Mathematics
A foreign language	A foreign language
(Primary schools requested	Chemistry
to give own politics exam)	Physics
	Politics

(Canton Radio, June 22, 1978, in *FBIS*, June 27, 1978, p. H3.)

2. *Peking Review* (November 11, 1977, p. 17) noted that "an all-round appraisal will be made of the applicants morally, intellectually, and physically. Entrance examinations will be restored and admittance based on their results" (my italics).

3. *Nanfang Ribao* [Southern Daily], May 11, 1980, p. 3.

4. The Canton key-point high schools are listed in *Da Gong Bao* (Hong Kong), November 30, 1977, p. 1. See also Suzanne Pepper, "Chinese Education After Mao," *China Quarterly* no. 81 (March 1980), p. 35.

5. A letter published in *Guangming Ribao* (March 26, 1980) "revealed that the Party's central authorities want to expand education, but the provincial leaders do not see the point. . . . In a certain province the education department was told by the provincial authorities that 10 percent was to be deducted from the sum assigned to the administration of schools. In addition, the department was encouraged, as part of the present universal

saving campaign, to try to save another 25 percent" (*China News Analysis*, no. 1181, p. 3).

6. *Nanfang Ribao*, August 6, 1980, p. 1, and *Nanfang Ribao*, August 13, 1980, p. 2.

7. *Renmin Ribao*, [People's Daily], April 19, 1980, p. 3.

8. E.g., "The only way to narrow this gap . . . between rural and urban schools, a relic of history, is . . . to raise [rural] educational standards *on the basis of a growth in [local] production.* It cannot be done by changing the principle of selecting those with the best qualifications." (Peking Radio, May 11, 1978, in *FBIS*, May 17, 1978, p. E7.)

9. E.g., Canton Radio, January 17, 1979, in *FBIS*, January 19, 1979, p. H2; and *Guangming Ribao*, June 21, 1979. Throughout Canton's school system the qualifications of the teaching staffs had declined during the previous decade to such a degree that an initial survey of the newly revived key-point high schools revealed half the teachers there—mostly the younger ones—had received the equivalent only of a junior high school training. (*FBIS*, January 19, 1979, p. H2.)

10. This may have been particularly a necessity in the high school systems of Guangdong's smaller cities, which presumably had less influence than Canton and less access to provincial funds. (E.g., *Nanfang Ribao*, January 30, 1980, p. 2. and August 18, 1980, p. 2.) But even a provincial institute such as the South China Teachers College (among the least prestigious of the universities) had to turn to workshops and farming to supplement its regular funding. *Nanfang Ribao*, February 2, 1980, p. 1.

11. Guangming Ribao, December 6, 1979, p. 1. Also see "Reflections on Reforming the Structure of Secondary Education" (in Chinese), *The South China Teacher's College Journal (Philosophy and Social Science Edition)* [Canton], no. 1, (1980); also *Nanfang Ribao*, March 16, 1980, p. 2; *People's Daily*, April 19, 1980, in *FBIS*, April 21, 1980, p. L9; and a speech by one of China's Deputy Ministers of Education in *FBIS*, April 23, 1980, p. L3.

12. *Nanfang Ribao*, April 14, 1980, p. 2.

13. "Reflections. . . ," p. 79. On this revived vocational school program, also see *Nanfang Ribao*, May 11, 1980, p. 1, and March 21, 1980, p. 2, and *Beijing Review*, November 17, 1980, pp. 7–8.

14. Disappointments and tensions arising from this competition are broadly hinted at in several of the news articles from Canton. In Peking, only a ninth of the applicants to the technical-worker high schools could be admitted. (*Beijing Review*, September 1, 1980, p. 5.)

15. *Nanfang Ribao*, March 16, 1980, p. 2.

16. E.g., *Beijing Review*, January 7, 1980, p. 22; *China Reconstructs* (April 1979), p. 58; *Beijing Review*, May 18, 1979, p. 5.

17. New China News Agency, in *FBIS*, June 1, 1979, p. L18. See also Changsha Radio, in *FBIS*, January 2, 1979, p. H4.

18. *China Youth News* (December 5, 1978) cited in *China News Analysis*, no. 1181, p. 4.

19. Suzanne Pepper, p. 49, and personal reports from three travelers to China.

20. Information from a Cantonese who went abroad to study in 1980.

21. *Beijing Review*, August 11, 1980, p. 7.

22. *Nanfang Ribao*, April 2, 1980, p. 2; *Nanfang Ribao*, April 13, 1980, p. 2; *Beijing Review*, March 16, 1979, p. 7; *Guangming Ribao*, April 26, 1979 (two separate articles on p. 4); Hunan Radio, in *FBIS*, January 2, 1979, pp. H4–5. The Higher Education Department's deputy director lamented that "those secondary schools which had been putting too much

emphasis on getting their graduates into college . . . have been neglecting basics, [giving] too many reviews, too many mid-term exams, and have not been devoting enough time to the curriculum designed by the Ministry of Education." (*Notes from the National Committee [On U.S.-China Relations]*, vol. 10, no 3 [Fall 1980], p. 6.)

23. Suzanne Pepper, p. 39.

24. *Renmin Ribao*, February 18, 1978, p. 6. The Party subsequently moved to downplay "class" permanently by removing from the dossiers of most of the old landlords and rich peasants the legal "hats" (labels) that had stigmatized them as "enemies." They too became "citizens" and "people." See, e.g., *People's Daily*, January 30, 1979, in *FBIS*, February 1, 1979, pp. E17–20; "Zhongfa #4 (1979) of the Party Central Committee," in *Issues and Studies* (Taiwan) (September 1979), p. 111; and Canton Radio, May 12, 1980, in *FBIS*, May 16, 1980.

25. See, e.g., *Beijing Review*, February 16, 1979 (several essays).

26. *Peking Review*, July 28, 1978, p. 18.

27. *Ibid.*

28. *Ming Bao* (H.K.), October 23, 1977. Similarly, in order to tap the skills of the pre-Cultural Revolution university graduates, the maximum age limit for taking the newly reestablished graduate-school entrance examinations was hiked to 40 years of age, up five years from an initial announcement that the age limit would be 35 (*Renmin Ribao*, March 22, 1978).

29. E.g., *Renmin Ribao*, March 3, 1978, p. 4, and March 11, 1978, p. 4. Acquaintances with relatives in China report this also. For instance, one young woman from the senior-high graduating class of 1966, who had settled in the countryside, related in letters to Hong Kong that she was accepted into a teacher's college on the basis of her examination showing of December 1977, and that when she arrived at the college, she discovered a large majority of her new classmates were age 30–31, like herself.

These freshmen, who poured onto the campuses in early 1978, were far better prepared for college-level training than the students already there, the so-called "worker-peasant-soldier" students recruited under the radicals' policies. When one of the entering freshmen at Peking University pinned up a poem celebrating the triumph of the new order, which reads in part:

. . . They branded me behind my back as a "white expert,"
but now their rule has ended.
I have entered this forbidden zone of theirs,

angry polemics ensued. A responding wall-poster in behalf of the "worker-peasant-soldier" students declared:

. . . all kinds of snakes, monsters, and demons have been surging forward, shouting themselves hoarse against the worker-peasant-soldier students, saying they're all Zhang Tiesheng-type students. . . . They think they are the saviors of the world, whilst the worker-peasant-soldier students are all degenerate idiots. . . . Owing to the restoration of the Chinese bourgeoisie, China's history has been turned back ten years [i.e., back to the "revisionist" evils of pre-Cultural Revolution times].

Precisely because the pendulum had swung so sharply toward "expertise" in university admissions policies, the arguments and resentments over "class," rather than receding, had flared anew.

On these events in Peking, see Robin Munro, "Settling Accounts with the Cultural

Revolution at Beijing [Peking] University 1977–78," *China Quarterly* 82 (June 1980), especially pp. 308–21. (Munro was a student at Peking University at the time.)

30. Of these, 11 percent were from the senior-high graduating class and another 6 percent were high school underclassmen recruited under a special program for science and math "prodigies." (*Observations on the Relations Between Education and Work in the People's Republic of China: Report of a Study Group, 1978* [Berkeley: Carnegie Council on Policy Studies in Higher Education, 1978], p. 53.) The arguments for giving advanced university studies in the pure sciences and math to a group of teenagers not yet through high school was that, first, the high schools were not yet good enough to be of any value to such students and, second, that, as has been argued in the West, the mid and late teens are the ages when "receptivity [to new theoretical concepts] is stronger and thinking is more flexible." (*Xin Hua She* report in *Ming Bao*, October 23, 1977). On somewhat similar grounds, the age of 23 was recommended as the ceiling for foreign language majors; and almost all such students were soon being recruited directly from the graduating high school classes.

31. In addition, the institutes of higher education in a few specified fields—mining, petroleum engineering, and geology—were required by government directive to give priority to employees of the mining industries and to the young people of the mining districts. For these various directives, see the 1980 Guangdong higher education recruitment regulations in *Nanfang Ribao*, May 11, 1980, p. 3. For almost the same language in earlier years, see Canton Radio, in *FBIS*, March 10, 1978, p. H5; Peking Radio, in *FBIS*, June 13, 1978, p. E7; and *Xinhua She*, in *FBIS*, May 17, 1979, p. L17.

32. E.g., "back door deals [had left] no door at all . . . for the children of ordinary people wishing to attend colleges. . . . The new recruitment system [at least] provides children of workers and peasants with wide opportunity to take part in examinations for entering college." (*Peking Review*, July 28, 1978, p. 19.)

33. Susan Shirk, "Educational Reform and Political Backlash: Recent Changes in Chinese Educational Policy," *Comparative Education Review* (June 1979), p. 212.

34. Canton Radio, June 23, 1978, in *FBIS*, June 27, 1978, p. H1.

35. E.g., *Guangming Ribao*, January 20, 1978, p. 2, on violations by Party cadres in Shanxi province; also *Renmin Ribao*, February 20, 1978, on two dozen Party officials in one Hebei county who flagrantly abused the examination system in behalf of relatives; and *FBIS*, April 20, 1978, p. H6, on Guangdong abuses.

36. Another result, it was rumored, was that the sons and daughters of university professors were receiving unduly favorable treatment alongside the children of Party leaders.

37. From personal communications.

38. Robin Munro, p. 316; *New York Times*, September 14, 1979; *Beijing Review*, October 12, 1979, p. 6.

39. E.g., *Peking Review*, July 28, 1978, p. 18. As *Da Gong Bao Weekly* (February 16, 1978) put it: "in order to hasten the advent of real equality it is necessary to choose those most responsive to modern education to fill the limited number of college places so that modernization will develop as fast as possible." These very same arguments have been used in Russia to defend inequalities in educational access. See Murray Yanowitch and Norton Dodge, "Social Class and Education: Soviet Findings and Reactions," *Comparative Education Review* (October 1968), p. 266.

APPENDIX A: THE DEBATE OVER TALENT

1. The two essays discussed here appeared in *Yangcheng Wanbao*, July 27, 1961, p. 2. The debate was accorded serious attention in Canton. Two weeks after these essays had been published a conference of professors, teachers, and education administrators met in Canton to discuss the issues involved. A sizable minority of those present stuck to the first essay's view that the specific "process of teaching has no class nature at all." (*Yangcheng Wanbao*, Aug 10, 1961, p. 1.)

2. *NCNA*, April 9, 1960, in *CB* no. 623, p. 1.

3. Mao has reiterated this theme several times over the years, e.g. in 1961–62: "It is a law of the old society that the oppressed were of low cultural level but were more intelligent (*congming*), whereas the oppressors were of high cultural level but were always more stupid (*yunqun*)." Mao pursued the logic of this notion to an interesting conclusion: "There is also a certain danger of this amongst the high-paid strata of socialist society. Their educated knowledge is greater, but when a comparison is made with the low-paid strata they are seen to be more stupid. Thus the children of our cadres are not on a par with the children of non-cadres" (!). (*Mao Zedong Sixiang Wansui*, p. 391; a different translation appears in *JPRS* 61269, p. 306.)

4. A post-Cultural Revolution essay by the leadership of the Guangdong Teachers College puts the point clumsily but explicitly:

> From the standpoint of the landlords and bourgeoisie, . . . political swindlers like Liu Shaoqi and his ilk . . . advocated the theory of "educating the talented," saying "whether a person is intelligent or stupid is hereditary; we should cultivate those with talent". . . . According to the Marxist theory of cognition, a person's ability and knowledge are not hereditary but are acquired, . . . through taking part in class struggle, the struggle for production and scientific experiment. . . . Pupils [at the key-point schools] became increasingly stupid because they could not see how a worker works, how a peasant cultivates the land, or how goods are exchanged.

(Guangdong Teachers College Revolutionary Committee: "Refute the Reactionary Nature of 'Educating the Talented,'" broadcast by Canton Radio; in English in *FBIS*, Sept 3, 1971, p. D2.)

5. See, e.g. Donald Munro, "Man, State, and School," in Michel Oksenberg, ed., *China's Developmental Experience* (New York: Praeger, 1973).

6. "Running Key Schools Well," *Peking Review*, February 24, 1978, p. 16. (My italics.)

APPENDIX B: THE PRE-CULTURAL REVOLUTION UNIVERSITIES

1. Though not widely exercised, the national level of government did retain the right to override regional autonomy. In 1965, the graduating students at the South China Engineering Institute (a regional-level school located in Canton) were chagrinned to discover that most of them were to be assigned to Inner Mongolia, Xinjiang, and northern Manchuria, in line with China's crash program to populate and industrialize the frigid borderlands facing Russia.

2. The exact number varied from year to year.

3. This entire application procedure was strikingly similar to both Taiwan and the Soviet Union, and the roots most likely can be traced both to pre-Liberation and Russian practices.

4. These exams, averaging two hours apiece, were spread over a 3-day exam period. The enrollment procedures, exam requirements, and testing-center timetables are contained in *Guizhou Ribao* (Guizhou Province), June 26, 1960; translated in *SCMP Suppl.* no. 25, pp. 10–14. Also e.g., see *SCMP* no. 2764 for 1962 and *Renmin Ribao,* May 31, 1963. In the 1960 exams, all of the Set B candidates had to take the math section but this was "for the reference" of the schools and departments concerned, and was not to be counted in the cumulative exam totals. In the 1964 and 1965 exams, candidates in philosophy, finance, and economics also were to take the math exam, but similarly for "reference only."

5. These Examination Outlines were found in Macau in a second-hand book store: *1957 Gaodeng xuexiao zhaosheng kaushi dagang* [Outline of the 1957 Entrance Examinations for Higher-level Schools] (Peking: The People's Educational Publishers). *Ibid.* for 1960.

6. A Communist Youth League branch of a senior high school classroom in Hunan wrote to Peking at the very beginning of the Cultural Revolution complaining, somewhat justly, that "These examinations in the subject of 'politics' are divorced from 'proletarian politics'. . . . The outcome of the examination depends on how many of the points listed in the outline the students can remember. Is this really an examination in politics?" (Peking Radio, June 18, 1966, in *FBIS,* June 23, 1966, p. CCC13.)

7. The 1964 enrollment regulations can be found in *SCMP* 3234.

8. The 1965 regulations are in *SCMP* 3492.

9. See *SCMP* 3234 and *SCMP* 3492. A good description of some of these changes is presented in K. Hsu: *Chinese Communist Education: The Cultural Revolution* (Ph.D. diss., George Peabody College for Teachers, 1972, [UM No. 72-25389]), p. 234.

10. This schema did not hold for China's less prestigious schools of higher education, since they came under the control and financing of the different individual provincial governments, which recruited students from within their own borders. However, each province's Higher Education Bureau did save at least some places at each provincial university for applicants from each of the various districts, to assure at least a given minimum of rural and small-town representation in higher education. (Most of my information on the selection process derives from interviews with a former professor and half a dozen former university students. On this system of quotas, see also Marianne Bastid's discussion in Centre d'étude du Sud-est Asiatique et de L'Extreme Orient, *Education in Communist China* [Brussels, 1969], p. 78.)

11. In 1960, Guangdong's Committee for Student Enrollments, using a rare tone of apology, helped pinpoint which disciplines these were:

Specialized institutes of agriculture, forestry, mining, metalurgy, geology, geography, water conservancy, etc., have increased their enrollment targets this year, but relatively few students have volunteered to enroll in these institutes. As a result, some students are assigned to schools or specialized classes they did not choose. We believe these students will understand.

(*Yangcheng Wanbao,* August 20, 1960, in *SCMP* 2347.) Almost precisely these same disciplines were the least popular twenty years later (*FBIS,* May 13, 1980, p. L4).

12. The applicant who wished to avoid such a Hobson's Choice did have the opportunity to take preventive measures. For one thing, if you were not accepted at the departments to which you actually were applying, you at least held a likely chance of avoiding being assigned to an undesired discipline in a different branch of subjects. The applicant in Physics had far fewer chances of unwanted acceptance at an Agricultural Institute than did a candidate in Medicine, which like Agriculture was in the Natural Science exam-set.

13. *Nanfang Ribao,* September 7, 1961, p. 1. The "great majority" of that year's 2,300 graduates of the secondary-level medical specialist schools were, according to this report, likewise being dispatched to rural areas.

14. *Da Gong Bao* (Hong Kong), October 7, 1965.

15. During the Leap, such makeshift "institutions of higher education" sprouted in great abundance. In 1957 Guangdong had contained only 7 colleges. By August of 1959, there were 115. (*Yangcheng Wanbao,* August 15, 1959, p. 1.) Almost all of these soon collapsed. By 1963, only 11 full-time campuses remained. (*Ming Bao,* Hong Kong, December 30, 1963, p. 6).

16. *People's Daily,* June 4, 1960, in *SCMP* 2285.

17. *Zhongguo Qingnian Bao* [China Youth News], August 16, 1966, p. 3.

18. This information derives from two Cultural Revolution sources: an article by a writing group in the Ministry of Higher Education, which appeared in *Jiaoxue Pipan* [Pedagogical Critique], August 20, 1967, translated in *Chinese Sociology & Anthropology* (Fall/Winter 1969–70), p. 59; and a journal called *Jiaoyu Geming* [Education Revolution], translated in Peter Seybolt, ed., *Revolutionary Education in China: Documents and Commentary* (White Plains: International Arts and Sciences Press, 1973), p. 49.

19. Interview by Anita Chan.

20. *Zhongguo Qingnian Bao,* August 16, 1966, p. 3. This essay from the early Cultural Revolution seems quite deliberately to have left out of its tabulations any of the other figures for 1963. These omissions were probably intended to conceal a trend evident that year at other institutes of higher education, where the numbers of bad-class entrants were beginning to be curtailed, to the benefit of the "revolutionary cadre" offspring and, temporarily, those of the "middle classes."

Data on enrollments at Canton's Sun Yatsen University are available for some years. The figures, from a Cultural Revolution speech by the university's Party Secretary, seem weighted too far in favor of red-class enrollments to be entirely believable. But the same trend as Peking University in bad-class enrollments is evident.

Admissions to Sun Yatsen University, Canton

Inherited "class" category of entrants	1960	1961	1962
Red-class	69%	73%	40%
Middle-class	23%	19%	30%
Bad-class	8%	8%	30%

(John and Elsie Collier: *China's Socialist Revolution* [London: Stage 1, 1973], p. 130. The Colliers were teaching at Sun Yatsen University when the Cultural Revolution erupted.)

21. Numbers of Students at Sun Yatsen University:

1963	4,800	(*Zhongguo Xinwen*, March 16, 1963)
1965	4,500	(*Xing Dao Ribao*, Hong Kong, February 16, 1965)
1966	4,000	(*Zhongguo Xinwen*, March 11, 1966)

22. It must be noted, though, that the Chinese tend to define "national security" in the very broadest of terms, so that in a whole range of disciplines political credentials and class background did come into consideration for a prominent share of the postings. A former professor at a Peking language institute recalls that "political" factors, in particular class origins, largely determined which tenth of the graduates were recommended to the Foreign Ministry, which graduates would instead become translators in industry and the military, and which ones would become ordinary schoolteachers.

23. Numbers of students entering graduate studies in Guangdong Province and China:

	Guangdong	China
1962–63	50+ (*Yangcheng Wanbao*, September 3, 1962)	1,000 (*NCNA*, August 29, 1962, in *SCMP* 2813, p. 18)
1963–64	20+ (*Nanfang Ribao*, October 24, 1963, p. 3)	800 (*Guangming Ribao*, October 14, 1963, p. 1)
1964–65	65 (*Yangcheng Wanbao*, October 27, 1964, p. 1)	1,280 (*Renmin Ribao*, October 22, 1964)

24. In all of China in 1963, only 800 of the more than 10,000 candidates who were allowed to take the exams were accepted (*NCNA*, October 15, 1963). In 1964, the 1,280 entrants were selected from more than 12,000 such preselected applicants (*Zhongguo Xinwen*, October 23, 1964, in *JPRS* 27,935). In Guangdong the competition seems to have been even fiercer; in 1963, more than 700 were allowed to apply for the 20+ places, an acceptance rate of less than 3 percent (*Nanfang Ribao*, October 24, 1963, p. 3).

The sheer size of China's graduate programs in the late 1970s stood in striking contrast to the 1960s, though this is still a far smaller figure than would be expected of a country China's size. Chinese universities and institutes enrolled 10,500 postgraduate students in 1978 (*FBIS*, January 11, 1979, p. E15), and by 1980 China had a total of more than 22,000 postgraduate students. (*Beijing Review*, January 5, 1981, p. 8.) This exceeded the combined totals for the decade and a half from Liberation up to the Cultural Revolution.

25. See for example *People's Daily*, January 17, 1966, in *JPRS* 36,453, and *Guangming Ribao* of the same date, p. 1, in *URS*, vol. 42, no. 13.

For Further Reading

An enormous number of books and papers on Chinese education have been published. The following bibliographies contain nearly complete listings of those written during the 1950s and 1960s.

Bibliography of Asian Studies (published annually by the *Journal of Asian Studies*).
Stewart Fraser, compiler. *Chinese Communist Education: Records of the First Decade.* Nashville: Vanderbilt University Press, 1965; pp. 422–96.
Steward Fraser, compiler. *Chinese Education and Society: A Bibliography.* White Plains, N.Y.: International Arts and Sciences Press, 1973.
G. William Skinner. *Modern Chinese Society: An Analytical Bibliography, Vol. I.* Stanford: Stanford University Press, 1973; pp. 197–208, 322–24.

The following short list, each section relevant to a chapter of this book, contains papers that I think are good choices as university course assignments. These tend to be relatively concise, informative, and readable.

1. UP THE SCHOOL LADDER
   R. F. Price. *Education in Communist China.* London: Routledge & Kegan Paul, 1970; chapter 4.

2. THE SENIOR HIGH BULGE AND DWINDLING CAREER OPPORTUNITIES
   John Gardner. "Educated Youth and Urban-Rural Inequalities," in John W. Lewis, ed., *The City in Communist China.* Stanford: Stanford University Press, 1971.
   Gordon White. "The Politics of *Hsia-hsiang* Youth." *China Quarterly* no. 59 (July/September 1974).

3. FLAWED REFORMS: RURAL AND URBAN ALTERNATIVES TO THE REG-
ULAR LADDER
Robert Barendsen. "The Agricultural Middle School in Communist China," in
Roderick MacFarquhar, ed., *China Under Mao*. Cambridge, Mass.: MIT
Press, 1966.
Julia Kwong. "The Educational Experiment of the Great Leap Forward,
1958–59: Its Inherent Contradictions." *Comparative Education Review* 23,
no. 3 (October 1979).

4. MEMORIZATION AND TESTS
William Kessen, ed. *Childhood in China*. New Haven: Yale University Press,
1975; chapters 3 and 4 (on educating small children).
Jonathan Unger. "Primary School Reading Texts and Teaching Methods in the
Wake of the Cultural Revolution." *Chinese Education* 10, no. 2 (Summer
1977).

5. STUDENT IDEALS AND COMPETITION: THE GATHERING STORM
Anita Chan. *The Children of Mao: A Study of Politically Active Chinese
Youths* (forthcoming book), chapter 3.
Michel Oksenberg. "The Institutionalization of the Chinese Communist Rev-
olution: The Ladder of Success on the Eve of the Cultural Revolution." *China
Quarterly* no. 36 (October/December 1968). Also appears in John W.
Lewis, ed., *Party, Leadership and Revolutionary Power in China*. Cam-
bridge University Press, 1970.
Susan Shirk. *Competitive Comrades: Career Incentives and Student Strategies in
China*. Berkeley: University of California Press (forthcoming); *passim*.
Martin K. Whyte. *Small Groups and Political Rituals in China*. Berkeley:
University of California Press, 1974; chapter 6.

6. THE CULTURAL REVOLUTION
Gordon Bennett and Ronald Montaperto. *Red Guard: The Political Bio-
graphy of Dai Hsiao-ao*. Garden City, N.Y.: Doubleday, 1971.
Anita Chan. *The Children of Mao: A Study of Politically Active Chinese
Youths* (forthcoming book), chapter 4.
Hong Yung Lee. "The Radical Students in Kwangtung During the Cultural
Revolution." *China Quarterly* no. 64 (December 1975), pp. 645–83.
Hong Yung Lee. "Conclusion," in *The Politics of the Chinese Cultural
Revolution*. Berkeley: University of California Press, 1978; pp. 323–48.
Richard Kraus. "Class Conflict and the Vocabulary of Social Analysis in China."
China Quarterly no. 69 (March 1977).
Ronald Montaperto. "From Revolutionary Successors to Cultural Revolution-
aries: Chinese Youths in the Early Stages of the Cultural Revolution," in
Robert Scalapino, ed., *Elites in the People's Republic of China*. Seattle,
University of Washington Press, 1972.

Gordon White. *The Politics of Class and Class Origin: The Case of the Cultural Revolution.* Canberra: Australian National University, Contemporary China Center Paper no. 9, 1976.

7. BACK TO SCHOOL, 1968–70
   Donald Munro. "Egalitarian Ideal and Educational Fact in Communist China," in John Lindbeck, ed., *China: Management of a Revolutionary Society.* Seattle: University of Washington Press, 1971.
   Donald Munro. "Man, State and School," in Michel Oksenberg, ed., *China's Developmental Experience.* New York: Praeger, 1973.

8. DOWN TO THE COUNTRYSIDE
   Thomas Bernstein. "Urban Youths in the Countryside: Problems of Adaptation and Remedies." *China Quarterly* no. 69 (March 1977).
   Anita Chan, Richard Madsen, and Jonathan Unger. *Chen Village: The Recent History of a Peasant Community in Mao's China* (in press), chapter 4.
   B. Michael Frolic. "Chairman Mao's Letter to Li," in *Mao's People.* Cambridge: Harvard University Press, 1980; pp. 42–57.

9. THE TROUBLED SCHOOLS, 1970–76
   Martin K. Whyte. "Educational Reform: China in the 1970s and Russia in the 1920s." *Comparative Education Review* 18, no. 1 (February 1974).

10. THE FIGHT OVER HIGHER EDUCATION
    Dale Bratton. "University Admissions Policies in China, 1970–1978." *Asian Survey* 19, no. 10 (October 1979).
    Gordon White. "Higher Education and Social Redistribution in a Socialist Society: The Chinese Case." *World Development* 9, no. 2 (February 1981).

11. THE RETURN OF THE OLD ORDER, 1977–80
    "Letter from a Chinese College," *New York Review of Books,* September 25, 1980.
    Suzanne Pepper. "Chinese Education after Mao," *China Quarterly* no. 81 (March 1980).
    Suzanne Pepper. "Education and Revolution: The 'Chinese Model' Revised." *Asian Survey* 18, no. 9 (September 1978).
    Susan Shirk. "Educational Reform and Political Backlash: Recent Changes in Chinese Educational Policy." *Comparative Education Review* 23, no. 2 (June 1979).

Index

Studies of the East Asian Institute

THE LADDER OF SUCCESS IN IMPERIAL CHINA, by Ping-ti Ho. New York: Columbia University Press, 1962.

THE CHINESE INFLATION, 1937–1949, by Shun-hsin Chou. New York: Columbia University Press, 1963.

REFORMER IN MODERN CHINA: CHANG CHIEN, 1853–1926, by Samuel Chu. New York: Columbia University Press, 1965.

RESEARCH IN JAPANESE SOURCES: A GUIDE, by Herschel Webb with the assistance of Marleigh Ryan. New York: Columbia University Press, 1965.

SOCIETY AND EDUCATION IN JAPAN, by Herbert Passin. New York: Teachers College Press, Columbia University, 1965.

AGRICULTURAL PRODUCTION AND ECONOMIC DEVELOPMENT IN JAPAN, 1873–1922, by James I. Nakamura. Princeton: Princeton University Press, 1966.

JAPAN'S FIRST MODERN NOVEL: UKIGUMO OF FUTABATEI SHIMEI, by Marleigh Ryan. New York: Columbia University Press, 1967. Also in paperback.

THE KOREAN COMMUNIST MOVEMENT, 1918–1948, by Dae-Sook Suh. Princeton: Princeton University Press, 1967.

THE FIRST VIETNAM CRISIS, by Melvin Gurtov. New York: Columbia University Press, 1967. Also in paperback.

CADRES, BUREAUCRACY, AND POLITICAL POWER IN COMMUNIST CHINA, by A. Doak Barnett. New York: Columbia University Press, 1967.

THE JAPANESE IMPERIAL INSTITUTION IN THE TOKUGAWA PERIOD, by Herschel Webb. New York, Columbia University Press, 1968.

HIGHER EDUCATION AND BUSINESS RECRUITMENT IN JAPAN, by Koya Azumi. New York: Teachers College Press, Columbia University, 1969.

THE COMMUNISTS AND CHINESE PEASANT REBELLIONS: A STUDY IN THE REWRITING OF CHINESE HISTORY, by James P. Harrison, Jr. New York: Atheneum, 1969.

HOW THE CONSERVATIVES RULE JAPAN, by Nathaniel B. Thayer. Princeton: Princeton University Press, 1969.

ASPECTS OF CHINESE EDUCATION, edited by C. T. Hu. New York: Teachers College Press, Columbia University, 1969.

DOCUMENTS OF KOREAN COMMUNISM, 1918–1948, by Dae-Sook Suh. Princeton: Princeton University Press, 1970.

JAPANESE EDUCATION: A BIBLIOGRAPHY OF MATERIALS IN THE ENGLISH LANGUAGE, by Herbert Passin. New York: Teachers College Press, Columbia University, 1970.

ECONOMIC DEVELOPMENT AND THE LABOR MARKET IN JAPAN, by Kōji Taira. New York: Columbia University Press, 1970.

THE JAPANESE OLIGARCHY AND THE RUSSO-JAPANESE WAR, by Shumpei Okamoto. New York: Columbia University Press, 1970.

IMPERIAL RESTORATION IN MEDIEVAL JAPAN, by H. Paul Varley. New York: Columbia University Press, 1971.

JAPAN'S POSTWAR DEFENSE POLICY, 1947–1968, by Martin E. Weinsten. New York: Columbia University Press, 1971.

ELECTION CAMPAIGNING JAPANESE STYLE, by Gerald L. Curtis. New York: Columbia University Press, 1971.

CHINA AND RUSSIA: THE "GREAT GAME," by O. Edmund Clubb. New York: Columbia University Press, 1971. Also in paperback.

MONEY AND MONETARY POLICY IN COMMUNIST CHINA, by Katherine Huang Hsiao. New York: Columbia University Press, 1971.

THE DISTRICT MAGISTRATE IN LATE IMPERIAL CHINA, by John R. Watt. New York: Columbia University Press, 1972.

LAW AND POLICY IN CHINA'S FOREIGN RELATIONS: A STUDY OF ATTITUDES AND PRACTICE, by James C. Hsiung. New York: Columbia University Press, 1972.

PEARL HARBOR AS HISTORY: JAPANESE-AMERICAN RELATIONS: 1931–1941, edited by Dorothy Borg and Shumpei Okamoto, with the assistance of Dale K. A. Finlayson. New York: Columbia University Press, 1973.

JAPANESE CULTURE: A SHORT HISTORY, by H. Paul Varley. New York: Praeger, 1973.

DOCTORS IN POLITICS: THE POLITICAL LIFE OF THE JAPAN MEDICAL ASSOCIATION, by William E. Steslicke. New York: Praeger, 1973.

JAPAN'S FOREIGN POLICY, 1868–1941: A RESEARCH GUIDE, edited by James William Morley. New York: Columbia University Press, 1973.

THE JAPAN TEACHERS UNION: A RADICAL INTEREST GROUP IN JAPANESE POLITICS, by Donald Ray Thurston. Princeton University Press, 1973.

PALACE AND POLITICS IN PREWAR JAPAN, by David Anson Titus. New York: Columbia University Press, 1974.

THE IDEA OF CHINA: ESSAYS IN GEOGRAPHIC MYTH AND THEORY, by Andrew March. Devon, England: David and Charles, 1974.

ORIGINS OF THE CULTURE REVOLUTION, by Roderick MacFarquhar. New York: Columbia University Press, 1974.

SHIBA KŌKAN: ARTIST, INNOVATOR, AND PIONEER IN THE WESTERNIZATION OF JAPAN, by Calvin L. French. Tokyo: Weatherhill, 1974.

EMBASSY AT WAR, by Harold Joyce Noble. Edited with an introduction by Frank Baldwin, Jr. Seattle: University of Washington Press, 1975.

REBELS AND BUREAUCRATS: CHINA'S DECEMBER 9ERS, by John Israel and Donald W. Klein. Berkeley: University of California Press, 1975.

HOUSE UNITED, HOUSE DIVIDED: THE CHINESE FAMILY IN TAIWAN, by Myron L. Cohen. New York: Columbia University Press, 1976.

INSEI: ABDICATED SOVEREIGNS IN THE POLITICS OF LATE HEIAN JAPAN, by G. Cameron Hurst. New York: Columbia University Press, 1976.

DETERRENT DIPLOMACY, edited by James William Morley. New York: Columbia University Press, 1976.

CADRES, COMMANDERS AND COMMISSARS: THE TRAINING OF THE CHINESE COMMUNIST LEADERSHIP, 1920–45, by Jane L. Price. Boulder, Colo.: Westview Press, 1976.

SUN YAT-SEN: FRUSTRATED PATRIOT, by C. Martin Wilbur. New York: Columbia University Press, 1976.

JAPANESE INTERNATIONAL NEGOTIATING STYLE, by Michael Blaker. New York: Columbia University Press, 1977.

CONTEMPORARY JAPANESE BUDGET POLITICS, by John Creighton Campbell. Berkeley: University of California Press, 1977.

THE MEDIEVAL CHINESE OLIGARCHY, by David Johnson. Boulder, Colo.: Westview Press, 1977.

ESCAPE FROM PREDICAMENT: NEO-CONFUCIANISM AND CHINA'S EVOLVING POLITICAL CULTURE, by Thomas A. Metzger. New York: Columbia University Press, 1977.

THE ARMS OF KIANGNAN: MODERNIZATION IN THE CHINESE ORDNANCE INDUSTRY, 1860–1895, by Thomas L. Kennedy. Boulder, Colo.: Westview Press, 1978.

PATTERNS OF JAPANESE POLICYMAKING: EXPERIENCES FROM HIGHER EDUCATION, by T. J. Pempel. Boulder, Colo.: Westview Press, 1978.

THE CHINESE CONNECTION, by Warren Cohen. New York: Columbia University Press, 1978.

MILITARISM IN MODERN CHINA: THE CAREER OF WU P'EIFU, 1916–1939, by Odoric Y. K. Wou. Folkestone, England: Wm. Dawson & Sons, 1978.

A CHINESE PIONEER FAMILY, by Johanna Meskill. Princeton: Princeton University Press, 1979.

PERSPECTIVES ON A CHANGING CHINA: ESSAYS IN HONOR OF PROFESSOR C. MARTIN WILBUR, edited by Joshua A. Fogel and William T. Rowe. Boulder, Colo.: Westview Press, 1979.

THE MEMOIRS OF LI TSUNG-JEN, by T. K. Tong and Li Tsungjen. Boulder, Colo.: Westview Press, 1979.

UNWELCOME MUSE: CHINESE LITERATURE IN SHANGHAI AND PEKING, 1937–1945, by Edward Gunn. New York: Columbia University Press, 1979.

YENAN AND THE GREAT POWERS: THE ORIGINS OF CHINESE COMMUNIST FOREIGN POLICY, 1944–1946, by James Reardon-Anderson. New York: Columbia University Press, 1980.

UNCERTAIN YEARS: CHINESE-AMERICAN RELATIONS, 1947–1950, edited by Dorothy Borg and Waldo Heinrichs. New York: Columbia University Press, 1980.

THE FATEFUL CHOICE: JAPAN'S ADVANCE INTO SOUTHEAST ASIA, 1939–1941, edited by James W. Morley. New York: Columbia University Press, 1980.

CLASS CONFLICT IN CHINESE SOCIALISM, by Richard Kurt Kraus. New York: Columbia University Press, 1981.
EDUCATION UNDER MAO: CLASS AND COMPETITION IN CANTON SCHOOLS, 1960–1980, by Jonathan Unger. New York, Columbia University Press, 1982.